T0376636

Evolutionary Psychology and Terrorism

This book explores the evolutionary context of terrorism and political violence. While evolutionary thinking has come to permeate both biological and social-science theorizing, it has not yet been applied systematically to the areas of terrorism and political violence. This volume seeks to do this for the first time. It presents a collection of essays on evolutionary psychology and terrorism, which encourage the reader to approach terrorism from a non-traditional perspective, by developing new approaches to understanding it and those who commit such acts of violence.

The book identifies evolutionary thought as heuristically important in the understanding of terrorism, explores the key conceptual themes and provides an evolutionary (and cross-species) understanding of the community-wide effects of terrorist attacks. The contributors bring forwards innovative ideas and concepts to assist the practitioner, analyst and academic to better understand and respond to the threat of terrorism. In doing so this book challenges existing assumptions about terrorism and those who carry out such acts, in order to move the debate into new areas characterized by an emphasis on intellectual quality and rigour, an interdisciplinary approach, and a drawing together of theory and practice. The intention is to provide a sufficient discussion to enable the reader to both understand the relevance of evolutionary thinking to terrorism and political violence, and to appreciate the practical implications of conceptualizing problems in this way.

This book will be of much interest to students of terrorism and political violence, psychology, criminology and security studies.

Max Taylor was until retirement Professor in International Relations at the University of St Andrews and Director of CSTPV (Centre for the Study of Terrorism and Political Violence). He is currently Visiting Professor at the Department of Security and Crime Sciences, UCL, London, and is Editor of the journal *Terrorism and Political Violence*.

Jason Roach is Reader in Crime and Policing, and the Director of the Crime and Policing Group at the University of Huddersfield.

Ken Pease is a forensic psychologist, former Professor of Criminology at Manchester University and Acting Head of the Home Office Police Research Group.

Evolutionary Psychology and Terrorism

Edited by Max Taylor, Jason Roach and Ken Pease

Routledge
Taylor & Francis Group
LONDON AND NEW YORK

First published 2016
by Routledge
2 Park Square, Milton Park, Abingdon, Oxon OX14 4RN

and by Routledge
711 Third Avenue, New York, NY 10017

Routledge is an imprint of the Taylor & Francis Group, an informa business

© 2016 selection and editorial material, Max Taylor, Jason Roach and Ken Pease; individual chapters, the contributors

The right of the editor to be identified as the author of the editorial material, and of the authors for their individual chapters, has been asserted in accordance with sections 77 and 78 of the Copyright, Designs and Patents Act 1988.

All rights reserved. No part of this book may be reprinted or reproduced or utilized in any form or by any electronic, mechanical, or other means, now known or hereafter invented, including photocopying and recording, or in any information storage or retrieval system, without permission in writing from the publishers.

Trademark notice: Product or corporate names may be trademarks or registered trademarks, and are used only for identification and explanation without intent to infringe.

British Library Cataloguing-in-Publication Data
A catalogue record for this book is available from the British Library

Library of Congress Cataloging-in-Publication Data
Evolutionary psychology and terrorism / edited by Max Taylor, Jason Roach and Ken Pease.
pages cm. -- (Political violence)
Includes bibliographical references and index.
1. Terrorism--Psychological aspects. 2. Evolutionary psychology. I. Taylor, Maxwell, 1945- II. Roach, Jason, 1969- III. Pease, K. (Kenneth)
HV6431.E9344 2016
363.32501'9--dc23
2015006599

ISBN: 978-1-138-77458-2 (hbk)
ISBN: 978-1-138-92876-3 (pbk)
ISBN: 978-1-315-77242-4 (ebk)

Typeset in Times New Roman
by GreenGate Publishing Services, Tonbridge, Kent

Printed and bound in the United States of America by Edwards Brothers Malloy on sustainably sourced paper.

Contents

Illustrations

Figures

Tables

Author biographies

Matthew R. Donati, BS, is a graduate student at Georgia State University. His primary research and clinical interests include the mechanisms of mindfulness- and acceptance-based behavioural therapies, technology-enhanced third-wave behavioural treatments for obesity and addiction, and the analysis of verbal behaviour.

Paul Ekblom is Visiting Professor in the Department of Security and Crime Science at University College London, and the Applied Criminology Centre, University of Huddersfield; also Professor of Design Against Crime at Central Saint Martins, University of the Arts London. His research interests cover design, evolution, conceptual development and knowledge management in the prevention of crime and terrorism.

Mary L. Hill, MA, is a doctoral student at Georgia State University. Her research and clinical interests include mindfulness- and acceptance-based therapies, eating disorders, body image, anxiety and mental health stigma.

Jordan Kiper is a PhD candidate in the department of anthropology and member of the Evolution, Cognition, and Culture Lab at the University of Connecticut. His research centres on the naturalistic study of religion and morality, the social construction of reality, and the politics of human rights and traumatic memory in post-conflict settings. His dissertation examines the religious violence, role of nationalism and propaganda in conflict, and politics of traumatic memory among perpetrators and survivors of the Yugoslav Wars in Serbia.

Akihiko Masuda, PhD, is an associate professor of psychology at Georgia State University. His primary areas of interest are acceptance- and mindfulness-based behavioural therapies, sociocultural diversity and Zen Buddhism. He is the author of over 80 peer-reviewed papers and book chapters, and the editor of Mindfulness and Acceptance in Multicultural Competency.

Rick O'Gorman has conducted research and published on a wide range of topics, including leadership, attitudes, social norms, altruism, social policing, non-verbal behaviour and animal behaviour. Having obtained his PhD from the State University of New York at Binghamton, he has worked at the University of Kent, Sheffield Hallam University and the University of Essex. His current interests revolve around evolutionary approaches to a variety of topics, including altruism and prosociality, relatedness and friendships, morality, social policing, social norms, disgust and conformity, culture, the interplay of social behaviour and neurohormones, and the impact of the female ovulatory cycle on mate preferences for intelligence. His research has been funded by the British Academy, the European Office for Aerospace Research and Development, the Economic and Social Research Council, and the Templeton Foundation.

Ken Pease OBE is a chartered forensic psychologist and currently Visiting Professor and Fellow of University College London and Visiting Professor at the University of Loughborough. He has held chairs at the Universities of Manchester and Saskatchewan.

Jason Roach is a chartered psychologist, a Reader in Crime and Policing, and the Director of the Crime and Policing Research Group at the University of Huddersfield. He has published work in areas including criminal psychology, police decision-making, homicide, criminal investigative practice, terrorism and cold case investigation. His current research includes patterns of child homicide, developing street psychology for police officers and self-selection policing. Jason continues to work with police forces with regard to reducing and investigating serious crime.

Charlotte Sanson is currently a PhD student at the University of Huddersfield, exploring the relationship between distance from crime and feelings of safety.

L. Ward Schaefer is a graduate student in clinical psychology at Georgia State University. His primary research interest is the mechanisms of change in mindfulness- and acceptance-based interventions.

Aiden Sidebottom is a lecturer in the Department of Security and Crime Science at University College London. His main research interests are crime prevention evaluation and evidence-based policing.

Andrew Silke is the Head of Criminology and the Director for Terrorism Studies at the University of East London. He has a background in forensic psychology and criminology and has worked both in academia and for government. He has written extensively on terrorism and counterterrorism, and recent books include *Terrorism: All That Matters* (Hodder and Stoughton) and *Prisons, Terrorism and Extremism* (Routledge). He serves by invitation on the United Nations Roster of Terrorism Experts and the European Commission's European Network of Experts on Radicalization and formerly on the European Commission's Expert Group on Violent Radicalization. He has provided invited briefings on terrorism-related issues to select committees of the House of Commons and was appointed in 2009 as a Specialist Advisor to the House of Commons Communities and Local Government Committee for its inquiry into the government's programme for preventing violent extremism. In 2010 he gave invited oral testimony before the Canadian Special Senate Committee on Anti-terrorism. He is a member of the Cabinet Office National Risk Assessment Behavioural Science Expert Group.

Richard Sosis is James Barnett Professor of Humanistic Anthropology and Director of the Evolution, Cognition, and Culture Program at the University of Connecticut. His work has focused on the evolution of religion and cooperation, with particular interests in ritual, magic, religious cognition and the dynamics of religious systems. To explore these issues, he has conducted fieldwork with remote cooperative fishers in the Federated States of Micronesia and with various communities throughout Israel. He is co-founder and co-editor of the journal *Religion, Brain and Behavior*, which publishes research on the biological study of religion.

Max Taylor was until retirement Professor in International Relations at the University of St Andrews and Director of CSTPV; prior to that, he was Professor and Head of the Department of Applied Psychology at University College Cork, Ireland. He is a legal and forensic psychologist with wide international experience of research and consultancy in the area of terrorism, terrorist behaviour and Internet crime. He is editor of the journal *Terrorism and Political Violence*.

Richard Wortley is Director of the UCL Jill Dando Institute of Security and Crime Science. He is a psychologist and began his career working in that capacity in the prison system for ten years. His main research interests centre on the role that immediate environments play in criminal behaviour, and the implications this has for crime prevention. He has published widely in this field, including eight books.

Abbreviations

ACC	anterior cingulate cortex
AQAP	Al Qaeda in the Arabian Peninsula
CBS	contextual behavioral science
CCO	conjunction of criminal opportunity
CTO	conjunction of terrorist opportunity
EEA	environment of evolutionary adaptedness
EP	evolutionary psychology
EVIL DONE	exposed, vital, iconic, legitimate, destructible, occupied, near and easy
MAOA	(neurotransmitter) monoamine oxidase inhibitor A
MLS	multilevel selection framework
MS	mortality salience
PDE	perceived distance effect
PTSD	post-traumatic stress disorder
RFT	relational frame theory
SHC	septo-hippocampal circuit
TMT	terror management theory

1 Introduction

What has evolution got to do with terrorism?

Max Taylor, Jason Roach and Ken Pease

The origins of this volume of collected papers lie in a series of concerns, perhaps not of great moment in themselves, but sufficient to suggest a general sense of unease about progress towards the understanding of terrorism and the terrorist. The first issue is recognition of how meagre is the contribution of psychology to that enterprise. Before the events of 9/11, terrorism was certainly recognized as a problem, but the academic response to it was limited and the topic attracted relatively few researchers from a narrow range of disciplines; there were even fewer researchers with a discipline base in psychology. Since 9/11 there has been an enormous outpouring of generously funded research, spawning papers and comment by scholars from a much wider range of disciplines. Arguably little of substance has emerged. Sageman (2014) critically commenting on the state of terrorism research, asserted that 'we are no closer to answering the simple question of "What leads a person to turn to political violence?"' We concur. The factors that may be associated with engagement in terrorism are doubtless complex. They may be idiosyncratic, socially and/or politically determined, or religiously motivated. Personally expressed reasons may be fundamental or incidental. The mosaic of reasons will vary over time. While we wallow in our ignorance, rates of recruitment into terrorism provide a striking metric suggesting that Sageman was indeed correct in his diagnosis.

Part of the problem may lie in the assumptions Sageman implicitly makes. He seems to imply that terrorism research is something that intrinsically supports government-determined approaches to terrorism problems and interventions, rather than an academic area of inquiry in its own right, where knowledge rather than politics and administrative convenience is preeminent. The rationale seems to be that scholarship on terrorism is primarily to provide a toolkit for the state. Howard Becker (1967) wrote a classic criminological paper entitled 'Whose side are we on?' that captures some of the qualities of debate on this issue. Calling something terrorism implies one is on the side of the victimized state or its population. It would take a brave (and certainly unfunded) scholar to write an appreciative account of terrorism. Attempts at objectivity are never popular in politically febrile times; yet perhaps to lose this objectivity diminishes the agenda we should follow.

Sageman challenges us with the provocative statement that 'intelligence analysts know everything but understand nothing, while academics understand everything but know nothing'. He rightly attributes this to the fact that access to data is the fundamental quality on which understanding and knowledge is based, and in this area such access tends to be controlled by government, which tends either not to make it available for academic analysis, or to selectively release data for a specific purpose to scholars who are deemed 'sound'. This is incontestable. However, the claim that academics understand is arrogant and in the circumstances set out above untestable. In short, we concur with Sageman's diagnosis; intellectual progress in this area is modest, mediated through state processes, with the inevitable corollary that those processes will attempt to direct understanding.

The state seems effectively to have asserted a monopoly over attempts to control and understand terrorism, and even community-based efforts seem largely to follow from state intervention, rather than arising out of a sense of civil concern, thereby discounting in advance the possibility that political grievances absent a remedy could conceivably justify an action labelled terrorist. An alternative reading is that the pejorative terms in which the matter is couched precludes alternative approaches. Terrorism is rarely a label which the terrorist claims for her actions.

The absence of a coherent victim voice sets terrorism apart from other kinds of predation, such as child abuse. There, victim issues have led directly to innovation in understanding and change in investigative practice and resource deployment, perhaps resulting in criticism of official practice and intervention but to the benefit of child victims. In part, such influence might be a function of scale (there are very many more victims of, for instance, child abuse than victims of acts labelled terrorist, at least in the Western world), but it might also be because the state has effectively excluded similar civil involvement in terrorism, perhaps through fear of compromising information and security, but also because there has been seen to be political capital in excluding the involvement of non- state partners in the attempted management of terrorism.

A particularly pernicious quality of terrorism research is the way funding is effectively routed as a one-sided relationship in the service of state, rather than as an open partnership between researchers and potential funders. Such research often more closely resembles consultancy activity rather than inquiry, with restrictions on publication limiting critical peer review. Sheltering beneath the need for security, access for researchers to information is selective, and the allegation of 'aiding terrorism' can be liberally used to control access and investigation. The notion of the independent researcher seems far removed from this area. A further indicator of this is the lack of any professional or learned society that encourages terrorism-badged research and critical analysis.

We are convinced that this is counterproductive, not simply in terms of acquisition of knowledge, but also in terms of the development of effective intervention. There is little evidence that enhanced security-based intervention research addresses the issues that give rise to terrorist behaviour (and indeed might arguably on occasions have a causal role), and we are firmly of the belief that the development of evidence-based knowledge will not come from state influenced or directed research.

Sageman's critical analysis also implies that immediacy and access to knowledge of events is all that is needed to move the field forward, and that states acting effectively as rate-limiting agents could remedy this by being more open in sharing information. But knowledge of events without the appropriate theoretical underpinning is of limited use. Are enormous volumes of material from state-generated intercepts, surveillance and descriptions really the route to understanding, or do we need to employ more robust conceptual apparatus and methodologies?

Accessibility to data, and its nature, leads us to our next issue of concern – an overdependence on limited knowledge of one-off events, which for most researchers in practice is mediated less by government (largely due to the limitations placed on access), and more by the news media (although clearly there is a symbiotic relationship between media output and state intervention). Terrorism is dramatic – indeed it might be argued that this is a necessary quality of terrorism. Drama, while it may attract attention, is rarely conducive to systematic analysis. The legal maxim 'hard cases make bad law' reflects this, and it is equally relevant to our understanding of terrorism. Journalists, as people with access and often with physical presence, have largely become the medium through which knowledge of terrorism is disseminated. Talk of 'open source' material is often a euphemism for a journalistic report, where in the distributed and compromised news environment in which we now live, accuracy, completeness and veracity cannot be taken for granted. News and current affairs programmes have become the principal public arena in which 'experts', whose expertise is often of doubtful provenance, explore the subject where live events and subjective, unsystematic and personal experience replace systematically gathered evidence. As the Sage has it, the plural of anecdote is not data.

If we look at terrorism from a narrower psychological perspective, the situation is even more dire. Psychological analyses in the world of journalistic coverage rarely progress from the naive and unsystematic, and with occasional (and notable) exceptions, psychological theorizing in this area is either non-existent, or trivial, and seems to operate at the level of common sense rather than evidence-based analysis. In part this may be because the concepts of terrorist and terrorism are unclear and contradictory, and make little psychological as opposed to political sense. It may also be that anything short of demonizing the terrorist is beyond the pale. In our view, this is also in part the result of an approach to understanding premised more on a Kühnian notion of scientific progress and paradigms, a top-down way of looking at the world, rather than the incremental growth model of knowledge acquisition associated with Popper. The notion that knowledge might incrementally progress, where hypotheses are systematically tested out with a core grounding using empirical evidence as opposed to ideological or political assertion, does not characterize the area.

In our view, an implication of this in terms of introducing new ideas through a sense of incremental growth in knowledge, is that efforts need to be made to access as wide a range of evidentially based views as possible. A collection of papers, rather than a monograph, seems to be the sensible way of approaching this, where disparate views are expressed, not all of which may take root, but which in aggregate should maximize the range of new ideas introduced. We hope that we have attained at least this objective in this volume.

These issues, therefore, influenced the origins and structure of this volume. The principal aspiration in proposing the volume was to initiate a discussion of how we might conceptualize terrorism and the terrorist from a different yet legitimate and robust perspective. It is associated with another volume of collected papers (Taylor and Currie 2012) that explores the idea of affordance in understanding terrorism and terrorist behaviour.

Why psychology? Why evolutionary psychology?

Terrorism does not seem to have captured the attention of many psychologists. For example, a rapid perusal of papers published in the premier journal in the area, *Terrorism and Political Violence*, shows very few substantive psychology papers, and almost all reference to psychology where it occurs seems to be, put bluntly, superficial. There is no academic journal of which we are aware which is devoted primarily to behavioural or psychological aspects of terrorism, and few psychologists seem to be professionally engaged in the study of the broader issues associated with terrorism, preferring to explore more limited issues like risk assessment and management, interrogation, surveillance techniques or other forensic topics. There is sometimes even a seductive sense of 'Minority Report' aspiration that distorts analysis even further![1] An area where there might have been an expectation to see a substantive contribution of psychology is in terms of understanding terrorist motivation, especially in the radicalization of young people. Yet, while deradicalization programmes have been established, there seems to be little if any analysis of what might be underpinning processes, and surprisingly little use in either programme delivery or evaluation of what we already know about behaviour change. For example, assumptions about the closeness of the relationship between attitude and behaviour change seem to be unquestioned, despite evidence to the contrary. Even more conspicuous is the lack of substantive psychological evaluation of outcome. This latter omission is however an attribute of many terrorism-related policy initiatives. For example, the disruption we all face when travelling by air is usually justified in terms of counterterrorism measures, yet there is little or no systematic evaluation of their value or efficacy (Linos *et al.* 2007) despite the fact that methodologies are available, drawing for example on public health experience of the effectiveness of mass interventions of the kind we experience at airports. Indeed, it appears even less relevant to those charged with combating terrorism on the ground, as one of us recently experienced when conducting a 'what works?' type project for a UK Security Service. Outcome evaluation means 'sort of works' or 'is seen to be doing something', rather than intervention efficacy and outcomes being properly evidenced, say by randomized control trials.

One reason for weaknesses in psychological endeavours in this area undoubtedly relates to problems in defining terrorism. But regardless of definitional nuance, a critical quality of terrorism that attracts broad acceptance is that it is manifest in violence. Despite definitional uncertainties, such violence presumably has as much psychological meaning and legitimacy as any other form of violence; its incidence, however, is much lower than many other forms of socially troubling violence (Mueller 2009). All violence (like all behaviour) is situated in a particular environment, and has a history and context. What seems problematic about the way in which we have approached terrorism is the attempt to place it outside of this broadly understood framework, into political contexts for which there seems to be no meaningful distinctive psychological base. If we reshape this question in motivational terms, and ask what motivates the terrorist, we do not think there would be any dispute about identifying a wide array of factors; where problems arise is privileging one kind of explanation (based on political ideology) over other kinds of explanations in the absence of evidential verification. This is not to say that ideology as a political concept, for example, is not a factor as a form of rule governance or scripting (see Taylor and Horgan (2001) for example), but we also know that for many people ideology or political intention does not seem to be an essential (as opposed to perhaps a necessary) quality of terrorist behaviour (McCauley and Moskalenko 2011). Sometimes 'revenge' is all you need (Silke 2003) not love.

It would be presumptuous to seek a redefining of terrorism to meet the needs of psychological analysis, and certainly it would be inappropriate simply to dismiss such substantive work as exists. Yet there is a case to be made for resetting our approach to psychological understanding of terrorism, moving away from assumptions about particular approaches (Taylor 2010) and establishing the ground work for a broad-based evidence-led analysis. Allied to this, in our view it is important to re-establish the grounding of our understanding of terrorism and the terrorist within the major frameworks of psychological understanding. This book of collected papers seeks to do this by focusing on evolutionary psychology (EP) as a basis for developing ideas and understanding.

Resetting and viewing our approach to terrorism and the terrorist through a psychological lens may have other benefits. Contemporary understanding of terrorism seems to largely place it out of our normal understanding of aberrant behaviour. Seeing terrorism as part of the continuum of problematic behaviour (of which there are many kinds) helps us to draw on what we already know about challenging, violent and predatory behaviours, both in terms of intervention with offenders, and the development of preventative strategies of control. In this sense whether or not a terrorist has a political agenda, or is motivated by some political imperative, is largely irrelevant as a core factor. It may well be very important in determining the direction violence might take, but it is not in itself a sufficient explanation. In simple terms, many people are exposed to violent political ideologies, but few become terrorists. The answer to this conundrum seems likely to lie not in the particular qualities of ideology, but in the complex set of factors influencing individual behaviour.

Why EP? In our view perhaps of all the approaches to psychology it offers the best potential for an integrative approach, embracing biological, behavioural and social perspectives operating within a sense of a complex and dynamic system. Understanding the terrorist calls on a wide range of knowledge. As with all kinds of violence, there is a biological substrate that can be identified, and as with all behaviour systems the violence we are concerned with is in some sense instrumental, drawing on and being influenced by environmental, biological and social systems. We have no doubt that other approaches to psychology also enable integrative understanding, and do not claim that an EP approach necessarily is a better or more productive way of thinking about the terrorist and terrorism. Nor are we seeking to privilege a *psychological* approach above other ways of understanding. But we do feel the need to assert a strong confident argument for locating our understanding of terrorism within a broad biological and environmental psychological framework.

Our sense of understanding the role that EP might play in understanding terrorism and the terrorist acknowledges a debt to the broader framework of understanding proposed by Tinbergen (1963), who suggested that there are multiple levels at which behaviour can be explained. From his essentially biological perspective, Tinbergen identified four types of explanation of behaviour, two of which relate to proximal explanations,[2] and two of which relate to evolutionary explanations (McDougall-Shackleton 2011). In simple terms, these can be reduced to: What is it for? How did it develop during the lifetime of an individual? How did it evolve over the history of a species? How does it work? (after Bateson and Laland 2011).

- Factors that operate within the lifetime of an organism not related to development are in these terms *proximate explanations* of behaviour; these embrace what Bateson and Laland (2011) describe as 'current utility' – the immediate mechanisms that precipitate or maintain a particular behaviour, which might include hormonal changes, nutrition and neural changes. Morphology, and the functional constraints of for example the visual system on behaviour, also fit into this category.
- *Developmental explanations* describe how a behaviour came about and is sustained over the course of the organism's lifetime. These might include learning, and changing capacity through maturation. These necessarily

interact with proximate explanations as can be seen, for example, in how myelination describes a physical process that enables fine muscular control of physiological structures (like limbs), which in turn facilitates and enables complex reciprocal engagement with the environment reflected in learned responses, and increased adaptive capacity.

- *Evolutionary, functional or natural selection explanations* describe how natural selection and other evolutionary processes interact to shape behaviour. The concept of 'niche' seems appropriate here, as might the concept of affordance, and the sense in which the organism fits into its environment.
- *Phylogenetic explanations* look at a species' evolutionary history and explain where the behaviour in question first appeared. Explanations in these terms seem very distant from proximate explanations, but it is of course on the substrate of phylogenetic, evolutionary and developmental changes that proximate factors depend.

A noteworthy quality of Tinbergen's framework is his emphasis on bringing explanations together, and the need for analysis to proceed at multiple levels to provide a complete explanation of behaviour. Different levels do not, however, imply a ranking of importance, nor a hierarchy. But while Tinbergen offers a framework for the analysis of behaviour as a whole (and with a very broad perspective), quite clearly when we look at specific behaviour there are circumstances when a more micro-level framework is also appropriate. Terrorist behaviour is one such, and a useful complementary micro-level analysis is offered by Peters (1958) drawing on an essentially philosophical perspective. Peters explored the levels at which behaviour can be explained but more narrowly focusing on the sense of 'why' questions about motivation (which largely address the proximate and developmental elements in Tinbergen's framework). Like Tinbergen, Peters suggested that answers to 'why' questions about behaviour may be answered in a variety of ways, and that any explanation must acknowledge this, and draw from it. Peters identifies four answers to 'why' questions.

1 *'His' or 'her' reason explanations.* We might ask why did someone do that, in the sense of to bring about or achieve some end through action or decision not to act. Such explanations generally assume some sort of specific directive disposition with often implicit or concealed assumptions about rationality and efficiency; for example an individual chooses some means which leads to an end *if* she has the information *and* she wants the end (both are necessary). Such explanations are often associated with notions of rule-governed behaviour (rules in terms of behavioural rules, or broader cultural/social rules/norms, or even notions like ideology). The presence of rules may even be described as 'traits' but the achievement of an end or goal enables pursuit in particular ways (which we might describe as the expression of traits). This kind of explanation represents

a simple purposive model, but it is often complicated by norms entering into and maybe defining ends and means. For example, passing an exam may be described as an end, but it is wholly defined by particular social conventions (the concept of passing an exam, for example, is an entirely arbitrary end). Furthermore, ends in this sense generally aren't the terminating points of behaviour – for ends don't terminate activity, but are ends because previous activity varies concomitantly with changes necessary to define it as an end. End explanation, therefore, seem to have strong social-convention qualities.

2 *'The' reason explanations.* 'His' or 'her' reason may in some senses be seen to be delusional or artificially invented because they are invariably contingent; their dependence on social convention, for example, placing them in a relativist framework, rather than reflecting some kind of absolute or underlying state, thus making absolute comments about 'why' questions difficult. In contrast, some explanations of why might be framed in terms of 'the real' reason, as opposed to following a convention. And 'real' reasons may not be conscious, because we may not be aware of why we 'really' do things. Freudian explanations of behaviour, for example, with their emphasis on unconscious motivation, might be thought to fall into this category, as might explanations in terms of neurophysiology or other physiological processes. In a slightly different sense, 'the' reason explanations may also reflect a privileging of third-party observer's reasons, rather than those of the individual. The expert psychological testimony used in court often assumes this kind of explanation, where the accused, for example, has to have his or her behaviour explained because a first-person account may be unreliable.

3 *Causal explanations.* Peters suggests that these are accounts that generally are related to deviations of behaviours from some norm or other. Most explanations in terms of pathology probably fit this category, and they relate often to some kind of actual physical or conceptual underlying state – of biology, evolution or pathogenic activity. Pathology as an intervening variable may of course reflect reality, but in this sense might not be 'causal', but rather predisposing. Given this, psychopathology as a hypothetical construct probably becomes more to do with the observer rather than the individual.

4 *End state explanations.* These are often used in relation to physiologically determined states, such as needs for nutrients or reproduction, and often draw on concepts like homeostasis with associated assumptions of functionality. These explanations are often framed in terms of need reduction, and are often in origin specific accounts that are then used in very general contexts. The notion of homeostasis is quite pervasive in these kind of explanations, and we can see this in political accounts that emphasize deprivation as a motivating factor which essentially draw on homeostatic assumptions (Stagner 1977).

From both Tinbergen's and Peters's perspectives, to give a causal explanation of an event involves at least showing that given other conditions being presumed unchanged, a change in one variable is a sufficient condition for a change in another. Of particular relevance to our understanding of terrorism and the terrorist, for any given piece of behaviour, all of the above accounts may provide explanations, and may in some circumstances even describe 'necessary' conditions. But as Tinbergen noted, none in isolation offers a 'sufficient' account; to achieve this, we need to proceed at multiple levels.

An added complication is that in the absence of a firm empirical base, choice of account may be more to do with the observer rather than that which is observed. In many ways, this seems to characterize a lot of the theorizing around terrorism. If you start off with an ideological position from which to view the world, that perspective, rather than evidence, orders what you give weight to. The significance of both Tinbergen's framework and that of Peters is that they very effectively complement each other, providing an evidential framework for generating from an EP research perspective complex integrative questions particularly appropriate for our understanding of terrorist behaviour, and also terrorism. The idea of level of analysis expressed in the above terms is significant because in understanding the processes that determine our behaviour, knowledge of one level can guide research and understanding at other levels. A complete explanation of terrorist behaviour will require an explanation of both cause and function and is a feat nobly attempted in this volume by Ekblom, Sidebottom and Wortley, who use the Conjunction of Terrorist Opportunity, a framework developed for analysing individual terrorist events (Roach *et al.* 2005).

Is an assertion of an EP approach merely a substitution of one kind of ideology with another? Ideologies are generally taken to be abstracted normalized beliefs. There is a sense therefore that an assertion of any particular way of looking at the world, an evolutionary perspective or otherwise, amounts to that. In the context of terrorism, however, ideology tends to relate to political perspectives, which privilege some views over others. The agenda proposed here, however, is not concerned with justification or privileged perspectives, but with the identification of factors that might control and limit the expression of terrorist behaviour – and therein lies it strength.

This book, therefore, at its core argues for an opening out of explanation from the narrow confines of disciplines, to embrace the processes and complex contingencies that characterize terrorism and the terrorist. It offers a perspective from EP to do this, because that approach seems to offer an integrative framework and the possibility for recognizing and working out the implications of the different levels of analysis proposed by both Tinbergen and Peters. It locates explanation within a broad framework, recognizing the contextual qualities of behaviour, helping we hope to move understanding away from notions of extreme, or aberrant, towards explanations that recognize utility and adaptation for the individual in the ecological niche they occupy.

Explanations drawn from evolutionary perspectives may be very challenging. The kind of short-term priorities that characterize much social thinking retreat into irrelevance when viewed from the complex but broad perspective of evolutionary thinking, particularly when seen through a psychological lens. We can illustrate this by reference to a concept that pervades many of the contemporary political responses to terrorism – that of national interest.

Reference to national interest is frequently used to justify interventions designed to limit the incidence of terrorist behaviour as a means of preserving important national and international values. Incursions into Iraq and Afghanistan, for example, have been justified by the British government through reference to defending British national interest. Rice (2008) presents a detailed analysis of what is essentially a case for a benevolent (in US terms) national interest driving policy towards responding to an array of threats including terrorism. Yet in the scheme of things, reliance on concepts like this offer little by way of enduring psychological substance. Taylor (2014) has discussed at some length an evolutionary and ecological context to understanding national interest, and explored some of the inconsistencies and weaknesses of the concept.

A particular difficulty with a concept like national interest is that it is often presented as an absolute that drives behavioural choices, but is in practice a very transient and limited concept. We can illustrate this rather graphically with the following example given in Taylor (2014). In the grounds of Jervaulx Abbey, North Yorkshire in the UK, there is a commemorative bench. Like others there that identify and commemorate loved ones, this carries a plaque but of a rather different character from others there. It says 'It is upon the Navy under the providence of God that the safety and welfare of this Empire depend'. This phrase is a variant of the preamble to the original Articles of War of the British Navy produced in Charles II's reign (1630–1685). Variants on this quotation are frequently used, but unlike the original quotation which makes reference to 'realm', or the similar reference in the Navy Discipline Act 1866 which makes reference to 'Kingdom', this particular commemorative plaque refers to 'Empire'. Judging from other benches nearby that have date attributions, this one is not particularly old, but shows some weathering – perhaps it is 80 or 90 years old.

Eighty or 90 years constitutes two or three generations, the lifetimes of perhaps our grandparents. When the bench was made, reference to Empire would not have been especially out of place; now such reference is inconceivable, which of course reflects how times have changed. Within our grandparents' lives, the British Navy was a major world force celebrated as the guardian of an Empire that was real and tangible; now the British Navy has been emasculated to the point of near irrelevance (Blackham and Prins 2010), and the Empire no longer exists. The significance of this is not a cry to return to the past, but simply to emphasize how in a relatively short period of time what might have seemed like a fundamental quality and order of life has simply disappeared. The decline of the British Empire was extraordinarily rapid; as Ferguson (2010) notes 'the United Kingdom's age of hegemony was effectively over less than a dozen years after its victories over Germany and Japan' in the Second World War.

Reference to national interest provides at best a very transient base for the development of security policy, albeit relevant to our purpose. We can understand these changes in the UK from an ecological and evolutionary perspective. Ferguson suggests this kind of rapid decline is not unusual, and reflects the tendency for complex adaptive systems suddenly to move from stability to instability. British society has gone through a process of change which lived through seems to be moving in unpredictable directions. The challenge for policymakers trying to optimize possible ecological choices is to recognize the potential of unpredictability, and to understand that self-corrective and feedback systems have utility in a complex unstable world. Policy makers need to better understand self-organizing, interactive, adaptive and affordance opportunities as policy tools in a world that thrives on variance and redundancy. For a nation, such as the UK, that has lost economic and military power, this might be the best mechanism for the expression of national interest that we can achieve. Such an understanding derives, however, not from a political sense of national interest, but from the working out of the inexorable forces of adaptation, change and environment. National interest deceptively offers one sense of a 'big' explanation of behaviour, but all too often it is grounded in the local and the immediate, relating more to short-term political need. Because of that, it cannot be the substance around which explanations of behaviour can be grounded (Taylor 2014).

Analyses of responses to terrorism that draw on a sense of national interest therefore are flawed if they do not recognize the complex reciprocity of the adaptive evolutionary context in which violence is expressed. And a part of that equation necessarily relates not just to the use of violence by terrorists, but the use of violence by the state as a response to terrorist violence. Just as we noted from Peters (1958) above 'ends don't terminate activity, but are ends because previous activity varies concomitantly with changes necessary to define it as an end', so interventions against presumed terrorists, however benevolent in intent, themselves have reciprocal consequences, resulting in adaptation, change and development. Johnson (2009) for example uses the notion of adaptation in the sense used here to explain why in asymmetric warfare, stronger sides paradoxically experience disadvantage. Whatever else it might be therefore, national interest is not a fixed unchanging endpoint of policy choice, and a failure to recognize its transient qualities can mislead and distort understanding.

So why terrorism?

Although the influence of evolutionary thinking has been slowly permeating academic criminology for several decades now (and for our purposes, terrorism is predominantly a subset of crime), it has tended to take the less recognizable guise of 'sociobiology', with the most notable text being Tony Walsh and Kevin Beaver's *Biosocial Criminology* (2009). Indeed most of the applications of evolutionary thinking to aspects of crime and criminality have not come from criminologists (Roach and Pease 2013). To say that the take-up of evolutionary thinking by British criminologists has been slowly hesitant would be a gross understatement, especially when compared with criminological thinking in other parts of the world (e.g. the US) where, although undoubtedly present, reticence to this kind of thinking about crime has been markedly less prominent (see Roach and Pease 2013 for a discussion of why this might have been the case).

Recently there has been a little more room for optimism with regards the incorporation of an evolutionary-based thinking into British criminology, mainly under the Crime Science umbrella where a number of recent publications have explored our understanding of areas such as 'fear of crime' (Sidebottom and Tilley 2008), 'preventing violent crime' (Roach and Pease 2011), and 'rational decision-making and situational crime prevention' (Ekblom 2015 in press) through an evolutionary lens.

Jason Roach and Ken Pease's *Evolution and Crime* (2013) constitutes a modest attempt to sketch out the what, why and how evolutionary approaches can bring fresh thinking and perspectives to the wider understanding of criminal (i.e. rule-breaking) behaviour. Although the writers readily acknowledge that the aim of this book was nothing more than to provide a guide for criminologists not familiar with the evolutionary approach, their hope was that it would help others in some small way to have the courage to begin thinking about crime differently – from the traditional study of the proximal influencers of criminal behaviour, through to more ultimate (evolutionary) functional explanations way back upstream. Explanations, for example, for the likely functional origins of violent behaviour (such as child homicide) are viewed using an evolutionary perspective, along with long-established criminological conundrums like why it is young men who commit most of the crime, and why indeed crime itself is essentially a 'man-thing'. Moreover, briefly, evolutionary psychological explanations for why it is ubiquitous that young males commit most of the crime in any area of the planet rest upon the idea that male brains are actually hardwired for risk -taking (or time discounting) in adolescents to optimize the chances of attracting sexual partners (Daly and Wilson, 2005). After all, impulsivity, as most criminologists would agree, is a major correlate in offending by young males (e.g. Farrington, 1998; Jolliffe and Farrington, 2004). Of obvious significance here is the question why it is that most suicide bombers in recent times have been (and are likely to be in the future) young males (Kanazawa, 2007).

This volume

The contributions to this volume are presented in a rough evolutionary order from the wider focus of why and how an evolutionary framework can and should be applied to terrorism (and those that carry out such acts) through to more specific examples of how adopting an evolutionary approach would enhance understanding of specific aspects of terrorism such as underlying motivations, the role of empathy, and the generation of fear and terror.

In Chapter 2, Max Taylor explores the misperception that EP might not be seen as a natural bedfellow with terrorists, terrorism or political violence as they all describe different categories of concepts in relation to both qualities and timescales. However, Taylor points out that there are commonalities and points of overlap sufficient to, at the least, encourage further exploration and argues that as part of that exploration, there is at least the potential for rethinking the way we look at the terrorist and terrorism, by distinguishing between terrorism and terrorist behaviour.

In Chapter 3, Paul Ekblom, Aiden Sidebottom and Richard Wortley, begin by setting out some prevalent misconceptions about EP which they argue account for the lack of interest in the approach among terrorist researchers, and that need to be dispelled before they can proceed with their proposed analysis. Next, they set out the parameters of their analysis, and describe terrorism in a manner that is amenable to an evolutionary perspective. Given the difficulties in defining terrorism, they select the concept of tribalism as a significant exemplar of a terrorism-supporting mechanism and as a focus for analysis. They then move to the main goal of their chapter: integrating the proposed causes of terrorist behaviour, from ultimate causes rooted in our evolutionary past to proximal causes and goals in the immediate environment. This analysis is conducted within the framework of the 'conjunction of terrorist opportunity' (CTO) (Roach *et al.* 2005), a conceptual model that seeks to link a range of situational and offender-based, proximal causes of terrorist events. They conclude by reflecting on the implications of our exercise for research and prevention.

In Chapter 4, Paul Ekblom begins by summarizing the key features of the process of biological evolution, and co-evolution, before moving to show how closely related evolutionary processes apply to cultural (including technological) change, opening the knowledge-transfer process up to a range of natural, and human, co-evolutionary struggles, to show how such a widened perspective can apply to terrorism and counterterrorism. The chapter concludes with discussion of a range of lessons for how to run terrorist arms races, drawing heavily on those most human of culturally evolved adaptive processes, design, research, theory and evaluation.

In Chapter 5, Jordan Kiper and Richard Sosis look at 'why terrorism terrifies us?' They begin with a review of the spectrum of psychological and behavioural responses to terrorist attacks, before moving to consider the evolutionary significance of such responses and connect them to an anxiety module that underlies threat-compensation strategies. They locate the module that responds to terrorism among several other anxiety modules in the brain's precaution system. To end they propose a synthesis of material and a proposed module that has not been previously discussed in EP.

In Chapter 6, Akihiko Masuda, Matthew Donati, L. Ward Schaefer, and Mary Hill, provide a highly innovative contextual behavioral science (CBS) account of terrorism. They begin with a brief overview of contemporary evolutionary perspectives that view evolution as ongoing processes of behaviour interacting in and with a situational and historical context, before presenting key philosophical assumptions of CBS, followed by its bottom-up conceptual account of complex human behaviour, called relational frame theory (RFT), highlighting the impact of symbolic behaviour on an individual's overall behavioural repertoire. Finally, the chapter proposes a CBS account of issues related to terrorism, such as terrorist acts for perpetrators and negative reactions to terrorist acts among the targets of terrorism, and potential solutions for these issues.

In Chapter 7, Rick O'Gorman and Andrew Silke, explore how EP offers a new approach to understanding one potentially critical factor for engaging in terrorism: the human propensity for altruism and punishment. An emerging evolutionary framework for understanding altruistic behaviour in humans is introduced which identifies its impact on prosocial behaviour, punishment, morality, and how recent developments have revealed human inclinations to police the behaviour of others. This framework is then used to explore the existing terrorism literature for relevance.

In Chapter 8, Jason Roach, Ken Pease and Charlotte Sanson look at how different distances from acts of terrorism produce varying levels of fear/terror. The chapter examines fluctuations in fear of crime and notions of personal risk alongside national and international terrorist events, and regional variations in these variables alongside terrorist events within the UK. The hypothesis tested is that there is a relationship between feelings of fear and personal vulnerability within a relatively small range of the terror events, which they call the 'perceived distance effect' (PDE). This is linked to the notions of very restricted personal geographic ranges suggested in the work of Robin Dunbar, Jared Diamond and Mark Pagel. The findings of a small empirical study presented suggest that distance from a terror event should be considered the most significant factor in the levels of fear generated, with obvious implications for those trying to reduce its 'footprint of fear'.

Looking backwards looking forwards

As noted at the beginning of this chapter, the origins of this volume draw on a sense of scepticism and unease with contemporary research on terrorists and terrorism, allied to a concern about how research is related to public policy development. Recent attacks in Boston, London and Paris have attracted immense media attention and condemnation, and as ever in the aftermath of terrible events like these, the public are assured that lessons have been learned, and that they will never happen again – yet they do.

It is of course wholly unrealistic to imagine that all determined murderers can be deterred or intercepted, and knee-jerk responses by political leaders to be seen to be doing something inevitably fail. Indeed, in dealing with IRA terrorism pre 9/11 the British government seemed tacitly to accept this limitation on policy outcomes. It can be argued that this resulted in a slower and more thoughtful working out of consequences of policy initiatives (Taylor 2011), at least in terms of the extensive process of negotiation that preceded the emergence of peace in Northern Ireland, which contrasts with the at times frenetic legislative initiatives that have characterized post 9/11 thinking. This volume offers a different lens through which to see terrorism and the terrorist, and while it is certainly not presented in terms of a panacea that will redress all our problems in understanding terrorism, it is argued that the ability of an evolutionary framework to draw together multiple strands of inquiry is a helpful way of addressing the weaknesses of narrower approaches.

In a way, the evolutionary approach outlined in this volume enables the drawing together of past and future: the past by recognizing the multiplicity of influences that shape and determine our behaviour (biological, environmental and contextual), and the future by emphasizing the notion of process and adaptation as critical qualities that determine behaviour change. We believe this lays the groundwork for the emergence of empirically based multifactorial explorations of the processes that both underpin the emergence of terrorism and determine its expression. We also recognize that robust empirically based research is sparse and difficult to do, and we also recognize that this volume might be characterized as one of exhortation, rather than being based on empirical evidence. We hope that through this volume we can at least encourage researchers to move beyond the confines of their disciplines to embrace and fill the lacunae we have identified.

We do not necessarily feel that this will lead to a step change in responding to terrorism, and do not present the approach adopted here in those terms. But we would argue that policy choices informed by systematic knowledge are more likely to succeed than choices driven by media coverage and perceived immediate political necessity. In this spirit we hope we can contribute.

Notes

1 We should here acknowledge our own shortcomings here. While the first-named editor is a terrorism specialist of long standing, the second has terrorism as a secondary publication focus, and the third has made no contribution at all to research on terrorism as distinct from criminology.

2 An explanation that accounts for immediate causality.

References

Bateson, P. and Land, K.N. (2011) Tinbergen's four questions: An appreciation and an update. *Trends in Ecology and Evolution*, xx, 1–7.

Becker, H.S. (1967) Whose side are we on? *Social Problems*, 14, 239–247.

Blackham, J. and Prins, G. (2010) Why things don't happen: Silent principles of National Security. *RUSI Journal*, 155, 123–158.

Daly, M. and Wilson, M. (2005) Carpe diem: Adaptation and devaluing the future. *Quarterly Review of Biology*, 80, 55–60.

Ekblom, P. (2015) Evolutionary approaches to rational choice. In W. Bernasco, H. Elffers and J.-L. Van Gelder (eds), *The Oxford Handbook on Offender Decision Making*. Oxford: Oxford University Press.

Farrington, D. (1998) Individual differences and offending. In M. Tonry (ed.), *The Handbook of Crime and Punishment*, pp. 241–68. New York: Oxford University Press.

Ferguson, N. (2010) Complexity and collapse: Empires on the edge of chaos. *Foreign Affairs*, 89.

Johnson, D. (2009) Darwinian selection in asymmetric warfare: The natural advantage of insurgents and terrorists. *Washington Academy of Science*, Fall, 89–112.

Jolliffe, D. and Farrington, D. (2004) Empathy and offending: A systematic review and meta-analysis. *Aggression and Violent Behaviour*, 9 (5), 441–476.

Kanazawa, S. (2007) The Evolutionary Psychological Imagination: Why you can't get a date on a saturday night and why most suicide bombers are Muslim. *Journal of Social, Evolutionary, and Cultural Psychology*, 1 (2), 7–17.

Linos, E., Linos, E. and Colditz (2007) Screening programme evaluation applied to airport security. *British Medical Journal*, 335, 1290.

McCauley, C. and Moskalenko, S. (2011) *Friction: How Radicalization Happens to Them and Us*. Oxford: Oxford University Press.

McDougall-Shackleton, S.A. (2011) The level of analysis revisited. Philosophical transactions of the Royal Society. *Biological Sciences*, 366, 2076–2085.

Mueller, J. (2009) *Overblown: How Politicians and the Terrorism Industry Inflate National Security Threats, and Why We Believe Them*. New York: Free Press.

Peters, R.S. (1958) *The Concept of Motivation*. London: Routledge Kegan Paul.

Rice, C. (2008) Rethinking the national interest: American realism in a new world. *Foreign Affairs*, July/August, www.foreignaffairs.com/articles/64445/condoleezza-rice/rethinking-the-national-interest.

Roach, J. and Pease, K. (2011) Evolution and the prevention of violent crime. *Psychology*, 2 (4), 393–404.

Roach, J. and Pease, K. (2013) *Evolution and Crime*. London: Routledge.

Roach, J., Ekblom, P. and Flynn, R. (2005) The conjunction of terrorist opportunity: A framework for diagnosing and preventing acts of terrorism. *Security Journal*, 18 (3), 7–25.

Sageman, M. (2014) The stagnation in terrorism research. *Terrorism and Political Violence*, 26, 565–580.

Sidebotton, A. and Tilley, N. (2008) Evolutionary psychology and fear of crime. *Policing*, 2 (2), 167–174.

Silke, A. (ed.) (2003) *Terrorists, Victims and Society: Psychological Perspectives on Terrorism and its Consequences*. West Sussex: Wiley.

Stagner, R. (1977) Homeostasis, discrepancy, dissonance. *Motivation and Emotion*, 1, 103–138.

Taylor, M. (2010) Is terrorism a group phenomenon? *Aggression and Violent Behavior*, 15, 121–129.

Taylor, M. (2011) New Labour, defence and the war on terror. In O. Daddow and J. Gaskarth (eds), *British Foreign Policy: The New Labour Years*. Basingstoke: Palgrave Macmillan.

Taylor, M. (2014) National interest and strategy: An ecologically grounded analysis. In T. Edmunds, J. Gaskarth and R. Porter (eds), *British Foreign Policy and National Interest: Identity, Strategy and Security.* Basingstoke: Palgrave Macmillan.

Taylor, M. and Currie, P.M. (2012) *Terrorism and Affordance*. London: Continuum Press.

Taylor, M. and Horgan, J. (2001) The psychological and behavioural bases of Islamic fundamentalism. *Terrorism and Political Violence*, 13, 37–71.

Tinbergen, N. (1963) On aims and methods of ethology. *Zeitschrift für Tierpsychologie*, 20, 410–433.

Walsh, A. and Beaver, K.M. (2009) *Biosocial Criminology: New Directions in Theory and Research.* New York: Routledge.

2 Evolutionary psychology, terrorism and terrorist behaviour

Max Taylor

At first sight, evolutionary psychology (EP) does not seem to belong in the same context as terrorists, terrorism or political violence. At the very least, they seem to be describing different categories of concepts in relation to both qualities and timescales, and indeed the former does not seem to offer obvious insights in to the latter. However, as we will explore in this chapter, there are commonalities and points of overlap sufficient to, at the least, encourage further exploration. It will also be argued that as part of that exploration, there is the potential for rethinking the way we look at the terrorist and terrorism and in so doing offer some new approaches to how we understand the relationship between the concept of terrorism and terrorist behaviour. In order to explore this relationship further, this paper will particularly focus on terrorist behaviour.

At the outset and by way of introduction we will briefly explore some issues around what we might mean by evolution and EP, and terrorism and the terrorist, and then discuss how, given this, an evolutionary perspective might further our understanding of what these terms refer to.

Evolution and evolutionary psychology

An immediate and rather obvious difficulty in applying evolutionary perspectives to the cut and thrust of day-to-day behaviour (terrorist or otherwise) relates to a sense of potential timescales. The idea of evolution at least as it might apply to species embraces long timescales; the millennia that passed as organisms evolved for example from water to land, or the aeons during which the dinosaurs thrived and eventually became extinct. Evolutionary timescales for our early ancestors are typically counted in million year units; we might for example estimate that primates diverged from other mammals around 85 million years ago, with perhaps the precursors of humans diverging from primates around 2.3 million years ago, with our own direct ancestors evolving some 400,000 to 250,000 years ago. From the perspective of an individual life, these timescales are unimaginable.

We mean by evolution the inherited biological changes that occur as a result of adaptation to the environment through what Darwin referred to as 'natural selection'. The minimal timescale of inherited biological change for individuals (as opposed to species) in this sense seems to be several lifetimes, as the genetic biological consequences of adaptation are passed on to succeeding generations. This is a more manageable temporal horizon perhaps, but still seemingly unrelated to our everyday concerns.

On the other hand, understanding day-to-day concerns do relate to the capacities that we inherit, the building blocks from which our behaviour emerges, as it were. While evolutionary change, therefore, relates to generational factors, the effects of the *consequences* of evolutionary change (that might be thought of as our capacity to do things) are of course evident now. As understood here, EP extends the general notion of biological adaptation into the realms of psychology, by locating explanations of behaviour and psychological phenomena as *functional products* of adaptation and natural selection within their environments. This in a sense sidesteps the problem of timescales noted above. Genovese (2003) captures this sense in his comment that 'brains evolve to solve proximal environmental and social challenges'.

Darwin recognized the need to locate the expression of evolutionary processes in the individual, by suggesting that organisms, rather than societies or cultures are the agents of selection. It is the individual, not the species or some generic group of organisms, which must struggle for survival in the circumstances in which it finds itself, or the circumstances it can create for itself. Focusing on the process of adaptation in this functional sense for the individual is important because it not only greatly reduces the timescales we might focus on, but it also places both the process and consequences of evolution within the framework of everyday life. Thus the expression but not necessarily the acquisition of adaptive behaviour lies in the here and now, rather than millennia away. The mechanisms that underlie what we currently see and experience, therefore, may well have their origins in the very distant past, but these mechanisms have functional utility now and are evident in what we experience, what we do and what we see in the behaviour of others. This, then, is the agenda that EP addresses.

Four key insights (after Tybur and Griskevicius 2012) derived from an EP approach can be identified that may be helpful in exploring this further.

1 *Behaviours have evolutionary qualities even when people are not aware of them.* Conventionally, behavioural psychologists have focused on explanations of behaviour that emphasize immediacy of consequence; at its simplest, we repeat behaviour that is reinforced or rewarded. Such a focus has both a common-sense and a strong empirical base, and through it we see, for example, how what we experience changes what we do, or in a more technical sense how perhaps reinforcement can affect the probability of responding, through processes like shaping for example or discriminative learning. To place this into the broader context of this chapter, our current anxieties in relation to terrorism frequently place

emphasis on the role of immediacy in the action of ideology as a critical factor that turns people to political violence, and generally some kind of incremental process (analogous to shaping) is drawn on by way of explanation. Ideology in this sense is used as a proximal[1] factor influencing behaviour. So, we worry about the circulation of extreme ideological material because, presumably, we assume it may influence what people will do.

But we know that behaviour exists within a much broader context, and in particular that both the morphology and topography of behaviour have origins beyond and largely unaffected by the proximate events that might shape immediate behaviour; these precursor conditions constitute the framework from which behaviour might flow and be influenced by immediate factors. As a proximate influence (or an immediate influence), therefore, ideology may or may not be a critical factor in the development of terrorism; but its expression (as with all behaviour) requires a biological and behavioural substrate that reflects our evolutionary past.

Perhaps one of the most distinctive contributions of EP is that it seeks to understand the relationship between such proximate and precursor causal accounts. But critically, understanding behaviour in these terms becomes understanding a multifactorial process rather than a 'state'. The idea of process extends beyond the individual, and this is also critical to our understanding. Adaptation of one organism necessarily changes the environment in which other organisms exist, and they in turn adapt (or not) to changed circumstances. We may or may not be aware of these processes, but they do not require a cognitive basis to be significant. This has been termed 'escalation' by Vermeij (1987), and it describes the changes in the capacities of for example both 'enemies' and 'victims', predators and the predated upon, as they adapt to changing circumstances. Echoes of this process can be seen in the concept of an 'escalation trap' in terrorism: Neuman and Smith (2005) describe this driver of increased engagement with violence as effectively a form of reciprocal feedback. Bruckner and Rubin (1985) identify similar processes in their analysis of the conditions that lead to increased and persistent engagement in conflict.

2 Our psychology has its roots in our biological past, and is in consequence fundamentally organized to solve distinct evolutionary problems. One way of looking at evolutionary problems is to think of them in big global terms as survival and reproduction, but those problems extend from those generalities in a much more specific and mundane immediate sense to include food acquisition, evading predators, attaining status, caring for offspring, sexual attraction, social interaction, etc. Each of these problems are different, and what we see in behaviour, even though it might appear instrumentally grounded in the present, is the interplay between proximate consequences and a complex of evolutionary factors that set

the grounding for certain behaviours that themselves change and adapt to circumstances. The concept of affordance is relevant here (Gibson 1979). Thus, developmental factors and the processes of learning are the major agents for that grounding, which enable adaptation, change and adjustment to take place.

3 *Our behaviour has essentially evolved to serve the individual, not the species or bigger notions like ecologies.* This might be one of the more controversial qualities of an EP approach, because it challenges many of our presuppositions about social motivation and the causes of behaviour. We can illustrate this as follows: Dawkins (1976) suggests that altruistic behaviour is often taken as indicative of a collective quality to human behaviour and is also frequently described as being a motivating condition. But from an evolutionary perspective, it might be argued that this is essentially the expression of a mechanism for individual benefit that has in passing collective qualities. This means that cooperation and perhaps collective behaviour more generally might be essentially and primarily for our own benefit, and only incidentally might benefit the collective as well (although there is also a sense of course of individual benefit from collective action). That social factors may be important determinants of our environment doesn't invalidate this simple point.

There are many examples of the primacy of an individual rather than collective substrate to behaviour in animal behaviour, and perhaps the most obvious is described by Hamilton (1971) in the selfish herd theory. Individuals belonging to species that are subject to predation generally seek, when threatened, to put others between themselves and the predator, which inevitably results in the formation of aggregations that offer greater safety when flight is not possible. At first sight, this might be described as a form of social behaviour and cooperation, and might even be described in motivational terms. However, there is an alternative view. As predation risk is greatest at the periphery and least at the centre, an alternative account might suggest that the strongest or most dominant animals move to lower risk central positions, leaving less strong animals at greater predation risk at the periphery. In this sense therefore the aggregations are the expression of individual safety driven by the needs of the individual and its physical strength. We can of course think about this behaviour in motivational terms, but if this is the right term, the motivation is individual survival based on protection against predation, not social contact per se. Human behaviour may well be more complex than this, but the strength of the fundamental argument seems clear. An important consequence of this is that it challenges, if not inverts, many of the assumptions that we bring to our understanding of collective behaviour.

There is, of course, a paradox here. As Vermeij (1987) points out, adaptive escalation arising from natural selection seems to be the dominant driver of adjustment to the environment, but it cannot be sustained without circumstances that create selection among populations and species. In a sense, therefore, extinction of some elements of a species through selection may be necessary for further evolution of the individual member. 'The fate of individuals is perhaps dictated by adaptations for coping with hazards, but the fate of populations and species to which these individuals belong depends on the imposition of agencies to which the individuals are not adapted.' (Vermeij 1987, p. 419).

4 Our psychology is designed to fit an ancestral environment in which our biological structures evolved, which differs from the present environment. The conditions in which behavioural capacity has evolved tend to lag behind the changes that we experience and have adapted to, and it might be argued that this tension is a critical factor in determining our immediate behaviour. Our capacity to learn and make short-term adjustment to behaviour ameliorates this tension, but at a fundamental level we remain rooted in our biological past.

In a simple way this can be illustrated by how we respond to food tastes. As a general rule, we have an evolved preference for sweet as opposed to sour tastes; left to their own devices children, for example, show taste preferences for sweet rather than sour (Ventura and Mennalla 2011) across a wide range of cultures and circumstances. Carbohydrates, high in caloric value, tend to be equated with sweetness, and therefore in environments where access to food might be challenging, preference for sweetness had clear survival value indicating higher caloric value. In our current Western environments, however, where we are not nutritionally challenged, the consequences of such preferences are maladaptive, potentially dangerous and illness inducing, causing obesity, diabetes and contributing to a whole range of life-threatening illnesses. What follows from this is that paradoxically the consequences of biological adaptation may not always be positive in the short term when proximate circumstances change.

Behaviour may well be the functional product of biological adaptation, but it can also be argued that we have acquired mechanisms to temper the narrowness and maladaptive qualities of reflexive responding that seem to be implied by emphasizing a biological substrate to behaviour. We do adjust to our environment in the short term, and furthermore we show considerable variation in the way that adjustment is expressed, through biological processes of both maturation and through learning. From the perspective outlined here, the challenge is to understand the extent to which the biological substrate to behaviour interacts with these more proximal causes.

In summary, as used in this paper, EP focuses on the role of evolution and biological adaptation on the functional development of human behaviour. A central premise is that evolutionary processes such as adaptation have shaped our biological and genetic makeup, which in turn shape our behavioural responses to the environment. In these terms, EP is perhaps best seen as a way of thinking about the cause and explanation of behaviour. Tinbergen (1963) argued that there are multiple levels at which behaviour can be explained, rather in the same way that Peters (1958) argued that there are complementary but different way of explaining motivation (these issues are considered in more detail below). EP offers a way of thinking about behaviour that grounds it firmly within our evolutionary past and biological present.

There is in many quarters some reluctance to thinking about explanations of behaviour in these terms. Rejection of ideas as a matter of principle that seem to imply eugenics and racial stereotyping, which for some may be associated with biological approaches to behaviour, represent one thread of concern; another thread relates to the rise in popularity of environmental accounts of behaviour focusing on learning and social development, although the force of this kind of objection has been diminished as we have gained knowledge of cognitive science and neuropsychology. More generally, evolutionary thinking seems challenging for approaches to understanding human behaviour based on assumptions of equality and 'sameness' (and even notions of free will). A further objection to evolutionary thinking arises from what is known as the 'naturalistic fallacy', the belief that if something can be demonstrated to be the result of biology, then this provides a moral justification for that behaviour. Similarly, explanations of behaviour in terms of genetic disposition seem to offer little opportunity to effect change through proximal intervention.

These are real enough objections and concerns, but excluding scientific inquiry because it results in uncomfortable knowledge, or conflicts with what are essentially ideological positions on the nature of behaviour or the human condition, doesn't seem a sufficient reason for rejecting that knowledge. In fact, the objections noted above to EP seem to miss the central fact that understanding behaviour is about understanding the process of interaction between environment and its influences, and the genetic and biological bases of our behaviour. Neither represent a sufficient explanation; but to achieve progress we need to acknowledge the complexity of the causes of behaviour, and the processes that support behaviour.

Terrorism and the terrorist

In contrast to the apparently millennial timescales associated with evolutionary change, terrorism seems to be essentially a transient and above all a modern phenomenon, with its origins in human choice driven by local immediate concerns rather than the inexorable response of adaptation to long-term environmental events, mutation or genetic drift. However, as we noted earlier, from the perspective of EP, explanations of behaviour and psychological phenomena can be seen as *functional products* of adaptation and natural selection. It is that sense of adaptive functionality that we will draw on to better understand the terrorist.

Although there is no agreed universal definition of what constitutes terrorism, it is used most frequently to refer to the use of violence in some way to influence social or political change or debate largely (but not exclusively) through the use or threat of use of gratuitous violence to intimidate individuals, a population, or group. This can be clearly seen in the FBI definition of terrorism, which refers to two central characteristics:

1 violent acts or acts dangerous to human life that violate federal or state law:
2 acts that appear to be intended (i) to intimidate or coerce a civilian population; (ii) to influence the policy of a government by intimidation or coercion; or (iii) to affect the conduct of a government by mass destruction, assassination, or kidnapping.

Similar themes are apparent in UK legal provision, where the Prevention of Terrorism Act 2000 defines terrorism as the use or threat of action where:

> 1.1 (b) the use or threat is designed to influence the government or an international governmental organisation or to intimidate the public or a section of the public, and
> 1.1 (c) the use or threat is made for the purpose of advancing a political, religious, racial or ideological cause.
> 1.2 Action falls within this subsection if it…
> 1.2 (a) involves serious violence against a person,
> 1.2 (b) involves serious damage to property,
> 1.2 (c) endangers a person's life, other than that of the person committing the action,
> 1.2 (d) creates a serious risk to the health or safety of the public or a section of the public, or
> 1.2 (e) is designed seriously to interfere with or seriously to disrupt an electronic system.

Terrorists are generally regarded as the people who do these things, and typically are not identified in any other way, such as being a criminal (which of course by definition they are as their identification involves criminality in some form) or people experiencing mental illness (although there may well be at times a difficult line to be drawn between problematic challenging behaviours, psychopathic behaviour and terrorist behaviour). Although use of the term 'terrorism' is pretty well universal in political discourse, there is generally a lack of agreement outside of 'The West' on how to legally define terrorism (as evidenced by the failure of the United Nations to develop an agreed definition of terrorism). The lack of agreement tends to hinge around notions of legitimacy or appropriateness (as in resistance to an oppressive regime or anti-colonialism). However the above are broadly characteristic of the accepted usage of the term, regardless of how local jurisdictions express them.

From a historical perspective, the first use of the term is most commonly associated with the 'terrorisme' of the reign of terror before and during the French Revolution, and the use of irregular warfare against Napoleonic armies, although the use of instrumental violence to intimidate at an individual or collective level of course hugely predates those events. Rapoport (1984) for example describes the use of what seems to be a modern sense of terror by religious traditions such as the Thuggee, the Zealots-Sicarii and the Assassins, but as Sandler *et al.* (1983) notes 'Terrorism is an activity that has probably characterized modern civilization from its inception.' Indeed, Girard (2010) suggests that the fears we experience as a result of terrorist acts have roots in our very distant past and contain profound symbolic qualities: 'Ancient archaic fears resurface today with new faces' (p. 24).

Contemporary usage of terrorism tends to focus on the use of violence in a political context, but its historical antecedents seem to be well expressed in the medieval song 'L'homme armée',[2] which also captures a sense of the contemporary meaning of terrorism:

> *L'homme, l'homme, l'homme armé, l'homme armé,*
> *L'homme armé doibt on doubter.*
> *On a fait par tout crier,*
> *Que chascun se viegne armer, d'un haubregon de fer.*
> *L'homme, l'homme, l'homme armé, l'homme armé,*
> *L'homme armé doibt on doubter.*

This translates as:[3]

> The man, the man, the armed man, the armed man,
> one must beware the armed man.
> The word is that everyone
> must arm himself with a hauberk.[4]
> The man, the man, the armed man, the armed man,
> one must beware the armed man.

Although the origins of this song are unclear, it probably dates from the fifteenth century. Some traditions suggest it relates to the fall of Constantinople to the Ottoman Turks in 1453, an event that sent shock waves throughout Europe. If this is so, it emphasizes the sense of violent change associated with the aspirations, if not necessarily the reality, of contemporary terrorism. In any event, 'Beware the armed man' seems an appropriate epithet to apply to terrorists.

But not all 'armed men' are terrorists of course, which itself presents some inconsistencies and difficulties in interpretation and in knowing who to include or exclude (as in, for example, the case of state agents such as the police or an army engaging in acts of terrorism as opposed to non-state sanctioned civilians, as opposed to armed criminals); this helps to account for the difficulties in coming to a general legal agreement about definitions of terrorism. To add to the complexity, in everyday language our use of terms like 'terrorist' and 'terrorism' are confused and complex. Sometimes both terms are used as adjectival and/or noun description of kinds of behaviour, sometimes both are used as a judgment on an event, and sometimes they are terms of abuse, used to describe the activities of opponents (but generally speaking not the activities of 'our' side). Academic definitions of terrorism tend to emphasize a political context and motivation or intention, but in everyday language both terrorism and terrorist may be used without political contexts perhaps as much as within, drawing inconsistently on most or all of these usages and so loosing uniformity and consistency of meaning.

To add further to the complexity, sometimes both terms are used to refer to individuals, sometimes to large aggregations that even call themselves 'armies'. The Provisional IRA for example, widely accepted to have been a terrorist organization, modelled itself in its organizational structure on a military template, thereby affirming its legitimacy. Sometimes the terms are used to refer to small clandestine groups or even individuals, but sometimes we use both terms to refer to large entities (like Islamic State for example) that control areas of land greater than many nation states, and who are far from clandestine in their operation. In contemporary usage we also see terms like ideology drawn on to provide or account for not just a necessary sense of direction or motivation, but as an essential quality – assumed intention as well as behaviour then becomes part of its definition.

This has reached the point in the UK when even alleged intention and access to ideological material alone becomes a crime. For example, possession of the Al Qaeda in the Arabian Peninsula (AQAP) magazine 'Inspire' is in the UK an offence under section 58 of the Terrorism Act 2000. Mohamed Hasnath, a 19-year-old East Londoner, was found guilty of possession of 6 editions of the magazine on a memory stick, and a further edition on a laptop, and was sentenced in May 2012 to 14 months imprisonment. Presumably the purpose of such a law is to deter the distribution of material on the grounds that it contributes to the sense of intention, or even more strongly, that it might 'cause' intention and therefore behaviour – very dubious assumptions.

Therefore, even though 'terrorist' and 'terrorism' may be redolent with technical and legal meaning, neither are special technical terms with a limited accepted usage, but rather have, in everyday-usage terms, multiple meanings. In summary, it's a mess! We might be able to identify a terrorist when we see one, but we seem to have difficulty in precisely defining one. Sonorous statements and political posturing for news coverage by political leaders drawing on these terms generally add to confusion.

Perhaps in its most fundamental meaning, a terrorist is a person who does or proposes to do an action of or related to terror however identified. We are used to news reports referring to terrorist killings, 'terrorist plots' or 'terrorist networks' related to use of instrumental violence: they are almost commonplace elements of our news coverage. But if the core meaning of the term relates to the creation of terror in some sense, this extends beyond jihadi or politically extreme groups engaging in acts of terror to embrace other scenarios, including if we are consistent even mundane settings such as domestic disputes; bizarrely, at least in journalistic usage it seems to even extend to animals. For example, a recent report in the UK made reference to police acting against dogs 'terrorising' families;[5] and a bold swan 'becomes the second generation of feathered friends to terrorise punters' in Cambridge.[6] In everyday language, it seems that swans and dogs might engage in terrorist acts as well as politically motivated individuals.

Usage of this kind is of course ridiculous and seems to reduce the argument to the absurd, but it does suggest one thing – underneath all the complexity of meanings and usage, a critical element of what we mean by terrorist and terrorism is 'terrorizing' in some way, a sense of the performance or threat of instrumental violent actions that generate fear in an audience. Thornton (1964) in an early analysis of terrorism identified three central qualities of terrorism: violence, the nature of that violence and its symbolic qualities. If we strip out connotations and implications of some higher purpose, then that common thread of violence as experienced by the audience that threatens, or produces, a sense of fear in some form (actual or symbolic) seems to be a central and necessary quality.

To follow through on the above rather silly example, swans on the River Cam are not seeking to establish a 'Swan State', or destabilize the current UK government, or even the Cambridge Local River Authority. They are perhaps acting in defense of territory, or perhaps they have had previous negative experience of punters and are seeking to defend themselves from what they see as aggression; it is not difficult to imagine some sense of functional outcome for the swan, whatever the interpretation might be we put on it, and in any event through their actions they cause fear. In current usage it seems that we can quite properly label their actions as 'terrorist' because of what they do, not what they aspire towards, and it only seems an odd usage if 'political intention' is seen as a necessary requirement. That sometimes usage has additional connotations doesn't invalidate this simple point.

Without engaging in a rather sterile survey of the multitude of definitions of terrorism, perhaps the simplest sense we can make of this is to recognize the complex and at times inconsistent usage, and to see both terrorism and terrorist (and indeed the broader concept of political violence) as essentially 'fuzzy' concepts, concepts where meaning can vary according to conditions and context, with vague, imprecise, uncertain, ambiguous, inexact, or probabilistic qualities.

Fuzzy concepts are commonplace notions in many areas of application, where uncertainty characterizes membership of a category. The concept of fuzzy sets has emerged from set theory (Gottwald 2010) to accommodate complexity. In what is termed classical set theory (which in many ways parallels a rational and in societal terms a legal way of approaching problems), an element may either belong to a set or not – you are guilty or not; belonging to a category therefore is a binary choice. In fuzzy set theory in contrast, an element has a degree of membership of a category, and membership may be probabilistic and contingent. A consequence of such fuzziness or uncertainty about conceptual terms is that inferences may be approximate, rather than clear cut and precise. Given the complex but fuzzy hinterland of meanings to terrorism and the terrorist, and given the weakness and fragmentation of the area, this seems a useful starting point for exploring what the conceptual issues might be. Perhaps our most effective starting point that follows from this, therefore, is to establish boundaries around the concepts we use, rather than seek to generate spuriously precise all-embracing definitions, whether legal or otherwise.

One important boundary area was identified (if perhaps inadvertently) by Sageman (2014) in the assumptions made by him in his recent critical paper on terrorism research. In that paper Sageman implicitly assumed that our role (i.e. that of the researcher) was to help the various government and commercial agencies concerned with the management of terrorism and the terrorist, rather than progress knowledge acquisition. A central element of his argument was that we have little idea of what 'turns a person to terrorism', which may indeed largely be true, but experience suggests the answer is unlikely to lie with buying into the assumptions of government agencies, nor setting the intellectual and conceptual agenda from theirs. Governments may of course have their own parochial agendas to identify people as terrorists, but in a much broader sense, the requirements of government-determined legislative and legal needs are essentially premised on binary categories, rather than fuzzy category membership. The struggles of the British government to criminalize contact with ideological material (with the flawed assumption that this somehow determines, rather than at best correlates with, behaviour) as in the example given above illustrates the weakness of this kind of approach, as well as illustrating a failure to recognize the rather obvious and elementary difference between correlation and causation. (Possession of ideological material may well be correlated with terrorist activity; many if not all terrorists are found to have in their possession ideological material. But, of course so do large numbers of people who are not engaged in terrorist activity; correlative relationships are not the same as causal relationships.) If we accept that terrorism is a meaningful concept, governments, it seems, are unlikely to be the sources of our conceptual understanding and that may constitute one very important boundary area.

A further boundary we might usefully identify relates to recognizing that there is a fundamental, if fuzzy, difference between the concept of 'the terrorist' and 'terrorism'. These concepts clearly address related areas and undoubtedly overlap in the fuzzy sense identified above, but from the perspective developed here it might be suggested that they are different and represent different categories of analysis, perhaps analogous to the distinction that might be made between the criminal and criminality. The concept of 'terrorist' refers to an *individual* behaving in a particular way in a particular context, who does something violent, challenging or inappropriate that is perceived as threatening, aggressive or in other ways intimidating and causing fear to an audience. A critical conceptual boundary, therefore, is that what the terrorist does is what identifies him as a terrorist, not the views he holds, or the nature of any influencing ideology. Behaviour in this sense therefore becomes the principle quality through which we identify the terrorist, and that behaviour is generally illegal.

As we will broadly understand and use the concept of the terrorist here, therefore, it concerns behaviour involving fear-inducing violence (against people or property). It is not, however, random or purposeless, and is essentially instrumental (in an actual or symbolic sense) and purposive for the perpetrator (which may not be apparent to or shared by the observer or the victim). That instrumentality and purposiveness which characterizes terrorist behaviour is frequently assumed to be political in character, but what recent research has revealed is that what we might discern as 'terrorist motivations' (that is to say the motivations that underpin engagement in a particular example of terrorist behaviour) don't necessarily involve complex political ideology and don't necessarily even involve any political purpose, but do draw from things like broad political context, personal affronts or injury, risk taking and status seeking, and a need for affiliation or affection and peer pressure (see for example McCauley and Moskalenko 2011).

In contrast, the use of what the terrorist does in a collective political context, driven or coordinated by ideology or religious or political purpose (often expressed by a leader 'speaking' and interpreting on his or her behalf) is what we might argue terrorism is concerned with. Terrorism therefore seems to be best regarded as essentially a second-order activity, essentially a strategy (Neumann and Smith 2005) that is used to generate an outcome for a group, movement, network or organization which may be partially premised and dependent on the actions of terrorists in the sense of fuzzy categorical relationships, but conducted in a public arena, and perhaps involving other people as well, and always constructed around an array of explicitly political or religious agendas.

From this perspective, terrorism may be a strategic construction of a political leader or activist or an ideology, but it might also just as well be a construction of media coverage. It certainly has a reality in the sense that terrorism is concerned with terrorizing and fear induction through violence, although the sense of fuzzy boundary means that what we might refer to as terrorism also leaks into insurgency, guerilla warfare, civil war, actual war and criminality (and indeed, might be accurately so described). But, as such it is always a process rather than an event, in which critically the underlying motivations of those engaged in propagating terrorism might well diverge from those factors involved in controlling, coordinating and facilitating individual terrorist behaviour. As in any process, it might be expected that pressures to adapt and change will be evident depending on the terrorism environment; these pressures, however, and the nature of adaptation may well be different from the pressures experienced by individual terrorists. We need to further explore these issues. Furthermore, it might also be assumed that the pressures affecting terrorism dynamically interact with the pressures affecting the terrorist – a testable hypothesis that might also merit further exploration.

Because of our failure to recognize these simple points, we confuse for example what in times past we would clearly term wars operated by insurgent groups that have more in common in terms of structure, logistics and capacity with armies than with clandestine terrorists. Thus, we fight 'wars on terror' and look for global conspiracies that confuse categories, and of course in consequence fail. We similarly confuse aetiological influences by failing to recognize the relationship between complex dynamic factors.

Terrorism in this sense outlined above therefore seems to be a broadly collective strategic activity of some form, at times indistinguishable or overlapping with forms of irregular warfare (or even conventional warfare), where actions of terrorists among others might be used for some further essentially political as opposed to acquisitive or personal end, along with other things (like media engagement, political activism, etc.), by an organization, a collective or some kind of structured network. Terrorism, therefore, is not simply an aggregate of terrorist behaviour nor simply a tactic, but is something rather different and rather more. What follows from this, therefore, is that understanding *terrorism* in the sense used here as a form of strategy and warfare (conducted by many or few) may well necessarily lie within political domains; understanding the *terrorist* for our purposes only tangentially so. A reworking of a rather hackneyed adage may help explain this and the consequences of thinking in this way: one man's terrorist is always a terrorist – one man's terrorism may well be another man's war of liberation.

Taylor and Horgan (2006) explored the idea of terrorism as process in some detail, and located that debate within an ecological framework. In that paper they drew attention to a distinction made by Clarke and Felson (1993) drawn from the criminological literature between 'involvement' and 'event' decisions. Involvement refers to processes through which individuals choose to become involved (in their example) in criminal activities in general, in contrast to event decisions that relate to the commission of a particular crime. What is critical in this distinction is that the factors that might determine event criminal decisions may be different from those that concern involvement decisions; and furthermore, such relationships that there may be are in the sense used above fuzzy. In many respects this distinction parallels the distinction made above between terrorist behaviour and terrorism. To summarize, therefore, terrorism is not simply an aggregate of terrorist behaviour, and may be influenced by different factors from those that influence terrorism.

In what follows we will be primarily concerned with terrorist behaviour, and we can probably best conceptualize the various causal factors involved in the sense we are using here in terms of complex processes, characterized as adaptive interactions between the individual, the environment, such organization or group as may be accessible (real, virtual or imagined), and the responding authorities. And of course, a critical necessary element of that complex process is the biological substrate that behaviour necessarily draws on. Elements of the discussion about terrorist behaviour may also inform our thinking about terrorism, but presumably other and perhaps different factors (such as cultural or social) may well also be involved.

For an individual terrorist an important element is the audience identified by the terrorist (which may or may not be the audience addressed by terrorism) for whom fear (among other things) is an important sought-for effect that follows from violence. But because we are looking at a complex and dynamic process, what we see at any time is essentially a snapshot of the progress of an essentially idiosyncratic adaptive process, an element of which may involve escalation. Early European terrorists such as members of the Brigate Rosse or Red Army Faction recognized this when they spoke about the effects on themselves of committing a crime and thereby becoming illegal (Taylor 1991). Committing a crime crossed a barrier which placed them at risk, but also confirmed their trajectory towards further violence, further confirmed by the public consequences of their acts in terms of news coverage, political response, police activity, etc. This emphasizes the sense in which actions interact with an individual's social and psychological environment, changing the context for behaviour.

Recognizing the distinction between terrorism and the terrorist, and focusing on terrorist behaviour has a further value. It enables us to categorize terrorist behaviour as a form of a more general category of aggressive and violent behaviour, rather than something separate and different. The swan terrorizing punters on the River Cam is showing species and context appropriate aggressive behaviour, just as does the jihadi from his perspective executing a Western hostage or the IRA volunteer placing a bomb. Recognizing the centrality of aggression, as opposed to any form of 'special' account drawing on political or ideological legitimacy for the terrorist, is critical in that it also enables us to draw on the rich knowledge base of causes (both proximal and fundamental) of aggression and violence (see for example Shakelford and Hansen 2013); the distinction between terrorist behaviour and terrorism enables this. Furthermore, the strength of approaching this from an EP perspective now becomes clearer – what EP offers is an understanding of these complex aggressive behavioural processes that will lie in part in our evolutionary past, and in the adaptive and functional history that characterizes the emergence of aggressive behaviour, as well as in the immediate proximate context and consequences that control and influence that behaviour. Evolutionary approaches to the problem of terrorism sets the scene for this more complex dynamic analysis.

The above discussion has emphasized the need to focus on the role of behaviour in the identification of someone as a terrorist, because it is this focus that will then allow us to begin to systematically understand what causes or motivates a terrorist. It also suggests that the concept of terrorism, as a secondary quality, might for our immediate purposes be relegated to the sidelines. By dissecting out the notion of the political purpose as a necessary primary factor from our understanding of the terrorist, and focusing on the instrumentality and expression of the behaviour for the individual as aggression, intimidation and fear-inducing caused by a range of factors we can begin to take away motivational confusion. However, clearly when dealing with something so complex as terrorist behaviour, we need to draw on a variety of perspectives.

'Dissecting out the notion of the political' is neither to dismiss politics or the organizational context in which a terrorist operates, as potential causal elements of terrorist behaviour; clearly political and organizational context enables us to make another fuzzy distinction between criminal violence and intimidation and terrorist behaviour for example, or engagement in irregular from conventional warfare. But it is to relegate it to one of a number of potential causes and correlates of terrorist behaviour in individual circumstances, rather than a central causal quality. Furthermore, as an individual adjusts to and adapts to the environment (including that created by the individual's own actions and the organization that he or she becomes involved with), we are essentially dealing with a process of incremental reciprocal change, and it may well be that at the level of the individual as behaviour develops, so the relative influence of factors change, including that of political or organizational context. Indeed, a process similar to this is described by Taylor and Horgan (2006). A similar thread of argument is also offered by Taylor (2010) questioning whether terrorism is necessarily a group phenomenon. He refers to situations where PIRA activity, an organization that claimed control over its members through its alleged 'army' structure, nevertheless was from time to time driven by individual actions, rather than planned group activity, but which were then absorbed into the broader narrative. The issue here, of course, is not one perspective or the other: it is recognizing and trying to understand the complex reciprocity inherent in terrorist action.

Of some relevance to this, and what might help to place the issue into perspective, Lopez and McDermott (2012) draw attention to an important distinction that might be made between evolutionary factors involved in individual behaviour, and species-typical adaptations shared by a species as a consequence of natural selection; this distinction parallels the distinction made above between terrorist behaviour and terrorism: 'those (behaviours) that were designed by natural selection and that tend to be universal or those that were not designed by natural selection and that tend to be found in some individuals but not in others' (Lopez and McDermott 2012). An echo here can be heard of the comments noted above by Vermeij (1987, p. 419): 'The fate of individuals is perhaps dictated by adaptations for coping with hazards, but the fate of populations and species to which these individuals belong depends on the imposition of agencies to which the individuals are not adapted.' This might be one way in which we might embrace the political from an evolutionary perspective, and similarly further clarify the distinction between terrorist behaviour and terrorism. We really need to explore these issues further.

Although there have been notable contributions to thinking about politics and international relations in general from an evolutionary context (e.g. Alford and Hibbing 2004; Thayer 2000; Thompson 2001), the full exploration and appreciation of this approach to political thinking remains limited. There has however been much more success in using evolutionary thinking to understand the more limited issue of national security (Sagarin and Taylor 2008). An application of this approach can be seen in Johnson (2009), who explores the notion of adaptation in asymmetric warfare, as an extension of natural selection applying to competing entities. Counter-intuitively, he concludes that stronger sides may suffer a disadvantage in asymmetric warfare, of which terrorism is one example. He notes that three conditions are necessary for this to take place: variation, where weaker sides have greater diversity of combatants and higher rates of innovation; selection, where stronger states apply greater pressure on weaker states resulting in faster adaptation; and replication, where weaker sides are exposed to longer periods of combat, and therefore gain experience and as a result show greater adjustment to conditions. This helps to explain perhaps why, despite overwhelming superiority of force, since 1945 stronger sides at war are less likely to win than weaker sides (Arreguín-Toft 2001). As Johnson notes, these are suggestive ideas, which merit further exploration as to how best to model asymmetric warfare in terms of predator-prey systems, host-parasite systems or some other approach (Drapeau *et al.* 2008; Johnson and Madin 2008; Lafferty *et al.* 2008).

Evolutionary psychology and terrorist behaviour

The behaviour that we regard as 'terrorist' is undoubtedly complicated. Its identification is made more complex, however, by the 'ideological, social, cultural and psychological detritus' (Bloom 2003) that we have inherited in the way we think about and use the term 'terrorist'. By firmly locating our understanding within an evolutionary-psychology perspective we can begin to untangle that complexity, by recognizing and focusing on levels of analysis, and recognizing synergies and dynamic complexities that follow from that. In a general sense, terrorist behaviour may be a construction or a summary, but it does embrace contextually appropriate actual behaviours associated with aggression, intimidation and threat. Our genetic and biological endowment creates a context that facilitates understanding of those processes that influence the proximate determinants of those behaviours. However, neither the genetic or biological endowment to behaviour nor its proximate causes in themselves offer an explanation of the form of problematic behaviour which we refer to as terrorist.

Substantive investigations exploring EP and terrorism are sparse and limited. Given the lack of evidential depth, one approach to at least identify potential avenues for further exploration may be to explore research related to analogous areas, such as antisocial behaviour. In a sense what the terrorist does is a form of antisocial behaviour, but it is of course something more than that as well; however exploring this further may allow instructive commonalities and synergies to emerge. Fergussen (2010) for example has identified the role of evolutionary understanding with respect to antisocial behaviour. He suggests that over 50 per cent of the variance in antisocial behaviour can be explained through genetic influences. The extent to which we want to locate terrorist behaviour within the category of antisocial is perhaps a matter to explore further, but the significance and more general applicability of his point remains as a challenging starting point to explore further.

Reflecting on the relationship between terrorist behaviour and antisocial behaviour suggests a need to explore in greater detail what actually constitutes terrorist behaviour. EP has a rich set of functional descriptors of behaviour that falls within the framework of terrorist behaviour – aggression, threat, escape – that relate both to proximate events and our evolutionary substrate. More general terms such as extreme behaviour fail to capture the functionality of an evolutionary approach, and even though Taylor (1991) sought to locate a term like fanatic in a behavioural context (as a way of embracing terrorist behaviour), it too lacks the sense of the functionality that an EP perspective can give. Peters (1958) helps us to understand how we might explore the context associated with these problems, and Tinbergen (1963) gives a framework for understanding them within a broader framework (see Chapter 1).

Extending this analysis further, perhaps the most significant quality an EP perspective can bring to understanding the terrorist is a focus on explanations of both cause and function, associated with a functional analysis of the behaviour of the terrorist, recognizing the interplay between these factors in the emergence of specific individual behaviour. However, despite the enormous resources devoted to the study of the terrorist, we have hardly begun to even address these problems. Taylor and Currie (2014) have begun in some measure to approach this problem from an evolutionary and functional perspective, as have McCauley and Moskalenko (2011) from slightly different perspectives, but the area still lacks a determined and coherent research investment.

An exploration of the role of affordance (as defined below and in Norman 1988; Gibson 1979; Taylor and Currie 2014) in the emergence of terrorist behaviour offers an example of how function and cause might be integrated. Affordances have a foot, as it were, in both evolutionary and proximate causal explanations; an affordance exists relative to action capabilities of a particular actor, the existence of an affordance is independent of the actor's ability to perceive it, and an affordance does not change as the needs and goals of the actor change. An affordance, therefore, is a quality of the environment that enables, facilitates or makes possible an action. The central point is 'the essential complementarity between organism and environment' (Scarantino 2003) either acquired by proximate influences or being part of how the world is, which describes the niche, or functional space, in which the organism lives (Taylor 2014), which in turns describes *how* an organism lives in its environment as opposed the narrow sense of where it lives. As a tool for further exploring terrorist behaviour, this seems to offer many advantages.

Whether or not you agree with them, the arguments presented here would not be particularly challenging within a biological or behavioural psychology framework, but they probably are from the perspective of international relations and political science. The study of terrorism is bedeviled by assumptions about motivation and cause, which frequently confuses post hoc ideological proscription with scientific analysis. Perhaps this is most evident in what had become known as critical terrorism studies. Jones and Smith (2009) critically review this approach, and highlight the way in which from this perspective a sense of relativism permeates much academic analysis of terrorism, and terrorist behaviour. Booth (2008) illustrates this in the following: 'terrorist actions are always – without exception – wrong, they nevertheless might be contingently excusable" (p. 66). This is often associated with the assertion that 'grievances or the social conditions … breed terrorism' (Stohl 2008, p. 7).

A problem of this way of thinking is that it fails to recognize the distinction between terrorist behaviour and terrorism. By recognizing that simple distinction, we can avoid contaminating our analysis of behaviour from the relativism implied by both Booth and Stohl above. In contrast, by adopting a scientific and evolutionary-based approach we can attempt to explore and understand the origins, causes and facilitating process associated with terrorist behaviour. The appropriateness in moral terms of engaging in terrorist behaviour, or the use to which that behaviour is put in the process of terrorism may well have great merit in broad social terms, but as we have explored here, if our task is to understand the complex of circumstances that determine terrorist behaviour, and the development of evidence-based intervention, it has little relevance. The implementation and implications of such intervention may well be a matter for moral debate, but the development of preventative or remedial understanding is surely not.

What also follows from this, however, is that understanding terrorist behaviour is not something that is necessarily confined to contextually appropriate non-state actors. The instrumental intimidation, aggression and threat that seem to be the central qualities of terrorist behaviour can be displayed by many different actors, including the security structures of a state, and our understanding of this as an element of an evolutionary process cannot be confined to one social or occupational group. Terrorists behave in certain ways, which generate responses from a range of people, including the general public, the police and security services. Likewise what we have described here as terrorist behaviour might be displayed by a wide range of actors, state associated or otherwise. Understanding evolutionary change draws on a sense of reciprocal process; as Girard (2010) notes in his discussion of the escalation of violence within an evolutionary context 'we have to think of reciprocal action both of what provokes the trend to extremes and as that which suspends it … which makes adversaries more and more alike' (p. 10).

Although Girard approaches this from his own particular perspective (of the mimetic principle) he recognizes the significance of Clausewitz's sense of 'the primacy of defense over attack' (p. 10) that is always used as a justification for further aggression: a driver for the reciprocity of escalation of violence by both state and non-state actors with a very clear evolutionary substrate.

The distinction between terrorist behaviour and terrorism is also useful in developing our understanding of the process of radicalization. It is often assumed that one of the challenges of contemporary analysis is the identification of the factors that lead people into engagement with a terrorist lifestyle and/or violence. Much of the literature on radicalization focuses on the role of social qualities and ideology as potential factors leading people towards engagement with violence; yet a commonplace observation is that many people are exposed to the alleged precipitators of violence, but relatively few ever become violent.

While the concepts used are undoubtedly fuzzy in the sense used earlier, this chapter argues that the nature of the problem is that it is a categorical error to confuse explanations of terrorism with explanations of the aetiology of terrorist behaviour, which is what radicalization refers to. McCauley and Moskalenko (2011) note that we can identify a 'concatenation of mechanisms' (p. 214) associated with individual and group-level factors that seem to be linked with eventual radicalization and perhaps engagement with violence, but which seem to be associated with nested rather than separate qualities. What is challenging is that while these nested qualities in themselves may offer necessary conditions for the emergence of radical activity and perhaps violence, none either individually or in combination seem to offer a sufficient explanation. The missing element in the explanation may be the individual expression of evolutionary functionality and adaptation for the person involved. It might be challenging for contemporary views to explore this kind of approach, but it remains as viable an explanation as others.

In fact there are some indications of progress. The uncertainty we see when thinking about the causes of radicalization is mirrored in other areas of social concern, such as studies of the relationship between child maltreatment and antisocial behaviour, where commonalities of experience do not seem to predict subsequent negative outcomes. For example, Caspi *et al.* (2002) explored the relationship between child maltreatment and antisocial behaviour by conducting a longitudinal study of 1,037 male children from birth to adulthood. They found that a functional polymorphism in the gene encoding the neurotransmitter monoamine oxidase inhibitor A (MAOA) moderated the effect of child maltreatment. 'Maltreated children with a genotype conferring high levels of MAOA expression were less likely to develop antisocial problems'; conversely '85% of cohort males having a low-activity MAOA genotype who were severely maltreated developed some form of antisocial behaviour' (p. 853). More recently, Tiihonen *et al.* (2015) looked at the genetic background of 895 Finnish offenders and found links between MAOA, with the strongest associations with offenders who have committed repeat acts of violence. They also similarly identified an association with a gene variant called CDH13, which has previously been linked to psychiatric disorders.

There has been a proliferation of studies exploring the relationship between genotypes and behaviour, many of which seem to offer extraordinary and challenging insights that on close examination reveal methodological flaws and conceptual weaknesses (Manuck and McCaffery 2014). However, Caspi's early study (referred to above) has been broadly confirmed, and a meta-analysis of 27 independent studies found that childhood maltreatment predicted antisocial outcomes for boys of low-activity MAOA genotype (Byrd and Manuck 2013). Closer analysis suggests however that this relates for the boys with low-activity MAOA to early experience of abuse, neglect and ill treatment, and does not extend to girls, nor to other early-life adversarial experience. The limitation of generalization in this specific case may indicate an important qualification to such research which may well equally apply to the more recent research reported by Tiihonen (2015); it is often highly specific, and for experimental study it requires such a degree of variable control (of environment, of experiences) as to be largely unattainable given current technology. There is also insufficient evidence on the prevalence of these various genetic disorders in the general population. On the other hand, such analyses will lead to a much more discriminating sense of aetiological influences on problematic behaviour; the moral to draw from this in the study of terrorist behaviour is obvious.

However it seems likely that knowledge in this area will grow, and that these early suggestive studies of genotypic influence on broad categories of behaviour will increase in significance. But as Manuck and McCaffery (2014) note, as

> a practical matter … genetic variance in environmental exposures does not preclude environmental interventions to alleviate their ill consequences. And recognizing that, for instance, adversities of early rearing may have a heritable component is no more an argument against interventions to redress such circumstances than is the observation that, by genotype, some children may be protected from adversity.
>
> (p. 63)

More generally, the use of evolutionary thinking in understanding social problems related to violence and criminality is growing (see for example Roach and Pease 2013), and Durrant and Ward (2011) have usefully reviewed criminological areas where evolutionary thinking has advanced our understanding. This approach has offered for example insights into the peaking of offending during adolescence, why male to male violence is more common than female to female violence, cross-national variation in offending and factors related to consumption and addiction to psychoactive drugs. Terrorist behaviour is a form of criminal activity, and it may be reasonable therefore to assume that parallels may be drawn in these terms, although the low incidence of terrorist activity limits generalizations.

It should be clear from the above that thinking about terrorist behaviour and terrorism from an EP context does not decontextualize the complex problems associated with terrorism and terrorist behaviour, nor does it offer a relativist approach. In contrast it locates our understanding within a broader biological framework. And as Johnson (2009) notes with respect to war, but which might as readily be applied to terrorism and terrorist behaviour: 'War may be complex but so is nature. If they share common underlying principles then we should at least explore them in case they offer novel ways to win the conflicts we are currently losing'.

Final comments

This chapter has sought to present a rationale for understanding terrorist behaviour from the perspective of EP, as a framework for conceptual and scientific analysis. It takes as a fundamental assumption the need for, as Darwin (1872) describes, 'the struggle for life' to be conceptualized as the individual coping with their biological and environmental surroundings in order to survive, and it places our understanding of terrorist behaviour within a clear sense of process, reflecting proximal, ecological and evolutionary pressures. In order to achieve this, a critical distinction is made between terrorist behaviour and terrorism. I would argue the value of this approach is that it frees the researcher from the assumptions about cause and context that have bedeviled the analysis of terrorists and terrorism, and allows a conceptually clear functional basis for analysis to emerge.

It may be of course that the proposed EP perspective outlined above is little more than yet another metaphor to understand complex social processes; the definitional and conceptual complexity of terrorism may indeed suggest metaphorical rather than evidence-based analysis. But by grounding the analysis in a biological and evolutionary framework, there is at least an evidence base on which to draw. Indeed, a case might be made that the concept of terrorism is in effect an epiphenomenon of the primary phenomenon of strategy in warfare, which if we follow Clausewitz injunction is itself the mere continuation of politics by other means. The same may not, however, be claimed for terrorist behaviour. Whatever construction we might place on terrorism as a process, the terrorist behaviour we are concerned about (of violence, intimidation, threat) is real, does kill and injure people, and has parallels in arenas other than the political. The EP perspective suggested here encourages a focus on both process and form, and may even offer a more evidence-based approach to understanding prevention.

Notes

1 An event that is closest to, or immediately responsible for, causing some result in terms of physiological or biological factors (after Tinbergen (1963)). See further discussion below.

2 See Currie and Taylor (2011)
3 Jenkins, K. (2000) *The Armed Man: A Mass for Peace*. Complete Vocal Score. Boosey and Hawks. London.
4 Iron chain-mail vest.
5 *Birmingham Mail*, No. 18 2013 www.birminghammail.co.uk/news/local-news/stourbridge-police-act-against-dogs-6314182.
6 www.express.co.uk/news/uk/498935/Asbo-swan-becomes-second-generation-to-terrorise-Cambridge-punters.

References

Alford, J.R. and Hibbing, J.J. (2004) The origin of politics: An evolutionary theory of political behaviour. *Perspectives on Politics*, 2, 707–723.

Arreguín-Toft, I. (2001) How the weak win wars. *International Security*, 26 (3), 93–128.

Bloom, R.W. (2003) The evolution of scientific psychology and public policy. In R.W. Bloom and K. Dess (eds), *Evolutionary Psychology and Violence: A Primer for Policy Makers and Public Policy Advocates*. Westport, CT: Prager Publishers.

Booth, K. (2008) The human faces of terror: Reflections in a cracked looking-glass. *Critical Studies on Terrorism*, 1, 65–79.

Brockner, J. and Rubin, J.Z. (1985) *Entrapment in Escalating Conflicts*. New York: Springer.

Byrd, A.L. and Manuck, S.B. (2013) MAOA, childhood maltreatment and antisocial behavior: Meta-analysis of a gene-environment interaction. *Biol. Psychiatry*, 75, 9–17.

Caspi, A., Mcclay, J., Moffitt, T., Mill, J., Martin, J., Craig, I., Taylor, A. and Poulton, R. (2002) Role of genotype in the cycle of violence in maltreated children. *Science*, 297, 851–854.

Clarke, R.V. and Felson, M. (1993) Introduction: Criminology, routine activity, and rational choice. In R.V. Clarke and M. Felson (eds), *Routine Activity and Rational Choice: Advances in Criminological Theory*, vol. 5, pp. 1–14. New Piscataway, NJ: Transaction.

Currie P.M. and Taylor M. (2011). *Dissident Irish Republicanism*. London: Continuum Press.

Darwin, C. (1872) *The Origin of Species by Natural Selection or the Preservation of Favoured Races in the Struggle for Life*, 6th edn, reprinted. New York: Colliers.

Dawkins, R. (1976) *The Selfish Gene*. Oxford: Oxford University Press.

Drapeau, M.D., Hurley, P.C. and Armstrong, R.E. (2008). So many zebras, so little Time: Ecological models and counterinsurgency operations. *Defense Horizons*, 62, 1–8.

Durrant, R. and Ward, T. (2011) Evolutionary explanations in the social and behavioural sciences: Introduction and overview. *Aggression and Violent Behavior*, 16, 361–370.

Fergussen, C.J. (2010) Genetic contributions to antisocial personality and behavior: A meta-analytic review from an evolutionary perspective. *Journal of Social Psychology*, 150, 160–180.

Genovese, J.E.C. (2003) Piaget, pedagogy and evolutionary psychology. *Evolutionary Psychology*, 1, 127–137.

Gibson, J.J. (1979) *The Ecological Approach to Visual Perception*. Boston, MA: Houghton-Mifflin.

Girard, R. (2010) *Battling to the End: Conversations with Benoît Chantre*. East Lansing: Michigan State University Press.

Gottwald, S. (2010) An early approach toward graded identity and graded membership in set theory. *Journal of Fuzzy Sets and Systems*, 161, 2369–2379.

Hamilton, W.D. (1971) Geometry of the selfish herd. *Journal of Theoretical Biology*, 31, 295–311.

Johnson, D. (2009) Darwinian selection in asymmetric warfare: The natural advantage of insurgents and terrorists. *Washington Academy of Science*, Fall, 89–112.

Johnson, D.D.P. and Madin, J. S. (2008) Population models and counterinsurgency strategies. In R. Sagarin and T. Taylor (eds), *Darwinian Security: Perspectives from Ecology and Evolution*, pp. 159–185. Berkeley and Los Angeles: University of California Press.

Jones, D.M. and Smith, M.L.R. (2009) We're all terrorists now: Critical—or hypocritical—studies 'on' terrorism? *Studies in Conflict and Terrorism*, 32, 292–302.

Lafferty, K.D., Smith, K.F. and Madin, E.M.P. (2008) The infectiousness of terrorist ideology: Insights from ecology and epidemiology. In R. Sagarin and T. Taylor (eds), *Darwinian Security: Perspectives from Ecology and Evolution*, pp. 159–185. Berkeley and Los Angeles: University of California Press.

Lopez, A.C. and McDermott, R. (2012) Adaptation, heritability and the emergence of evolutionary political science. *Political Psychology*, 33, 343–362.

Manuck, S. and McCaffery, J.M. (2014) Gene environment interaction. *Annual Review of Psychology*, 65, 41–70.

McCauley, C. and Moskalenko, S. (2011) *Friction. How Radicalization Happens to Them and Us*. Oxford: Oxford University Press.

Neuman, P.R. and Smith, M.L.R. (2005) Strategic terrorism: The framework and its fallacies. *Journal of Strategic Studies*, 28, 571—595.

Norman, D. (1988) *The Design of Everyday Things*. New York: Basic Books.

Peters, R.S. (1958) *The Concept of Motivation*. London: Routledge Kegan Paul.

Rapoport, D. (1984) Fear and trembling: Terrorism in three religious traditions. *American Political Science Review*, 78, 658–677.

Roach, J. and Pease, K. (2013) *Evolution and Crime*. London: Routledge.

Sagarin, R. and Taylor, T. (eds) (2008) *Natural Security: A Darwinian Approach to a Dangerous World*. Berkeley: University of California Press.

Sageman, M. (2014) The stagnation in terrorism research. *Terrorism and Political Violence*, 26, 565–580.

Sandler, T., Tshirhart, J.T. and Cauley, J. (1983) A theoretical analysis of transnational terrorism. *American Political Science Review*, 77, 36–54.

Scarantino, A. (2003) Affordances explained. *Philosophy of Science*, 70, 949–961.

Shakelford, T.K. and Hansen, E.D. (eds) (2013) *The Evolution of Violence*. New York: Springer.

Stohl, M. (2008) Old myths, new fantasies and the enduring realities of terrorism. *Critical Studies on Terrorism*, 1, 5–16.

Taylor, M. (1991) *The Fanatics. A Behavioural Approach to Political Violence*. London: Brasseys Defence Publishers.

Taylor, M. (2010) Is terrorism a group phenomenon? *Aggression and Violent Behavior*, 15, 121–129.

Taylor, M. (2014) Introduction. In M. Taylor and M. Currie (eds), *Terrorism and Affordance*. New York: Bloomsbury Academic.

Taylor, M. and Currie, M. (eds) (2014) *Terrorism and Affordance*, paperback edn. New York: Bloomsbury Academic.

Taylor, M. and Horgan, J. (2006) A conceptual framework for addressing psychological process in the development of the terrorist. *Terrorism and Political Violence*, 18, 585–601.

Thayer, B.A. (2000) Bringing in Darwin: Evolutionary theory, realism and international politics. *International Security*, 25, 124–151.

Thompson, W.R. (ed.) (2001) *Evolutionary Interpretations of World Politics*. New York: Routledge.

Thornton, T.P. (1964) Terror as a weapon of political agitation. In H. Eckstein (ed.), *Internal War: Problems and Approaches*, pp. 71–99. New York: Free Press.

Tiihonen, J., Rautianinen, M.-J., Ollila, H.M., Repo-Tiihonen, E., Virkkunen, M., Palotie, A., Pietiläinen, O., Kristiansson, K., Joukamaa, M., Lauerma, H., Saarela, S., Tyni, S., Vartiainen, H., Paananen, J., Goldman, D. and Paunio, T. (2015) Genetic background of extreme violent behavior. *Molecular Psychiatry*, 20, 786–792.

Tinbergen, N. (1963) On aims and methods of ethology. *Zeitschrift für Tierpsychologie*, 20, 410–433.

Tybur, J.M. and Griskevicius, V. (2013) Evolutionary Psychology: A fresh perspective for understanding and changing problematic behavior. *Public Administration Review*, 73, 12–22.

Ventura, A.K. and Mennalla, J.A. (2011) Innate and learned preferences for sweet taste during childhood. *Current Opinion in Clinical Nutrition and Metabolic Care*, 14, 379–384.

Vermeij, G.J. (1987) *Evolution and Escalation. An ecological history of life*. Princeton, NJ: Princeton University Press.

3 Evolutionary psychological influences on the contemporary causes of terrorist events

Paul Ekblom, Aiden Sidebottom and Richard Wortley

Introduction

We write this chapter with some trepidation. The source of our concern lies in the knowledge that many researchers interested in terrorism will see little worth in exploring how evolutionary psychology (EP) attempts to make sense of terrorist behaviour. EP is a field unfamiliar to many. Some view it as controversial. It is regularly the subject of criticism, some valid and some misguided, but which taken together often results in its exclusion from scientific discussions on the causes of human behaviour. In the context of terrorist behaviour, there is little direct evidence with which to convince sceptics of its value, realized or nascent. Moreover, compared to other domains, it is often difficult to see how the task of preventing terrorism might be informed by insights from EP.

According to EP, the process of natural selection, originally described by Darwin (1859), has equipped humans with a set of evolved psychological mechanisms that conferred a survival and reproductive (or 'adaptive') advantage in our ancestral past and which, in combination with contemporary developmental and environmental factors, influence how we interpret and behave in different situations, whether those behaviours are currently advantageous or not (for an overview see Buss 2005). We refer to these species-wide adaptations that occurred in our historical environment as 'ultimate' causation. An evolutionary psychological analysis of terrorism focusing on ultimate causation differs from developmental approaches, which focus on 'distal' causal processes, namely, those events that occur over an individual's life-course that are judged to increase (or reduce) the likelihood of engaging in terrorist acts. At the opposite extreme of causal analysis is the applied approach most associated with environmental criminology and crime science (Laycock 2005). This considers how 'proximal' causal mechanisms in or near the immediate crime setting generate criminal or terrorist events through psychological (Clarke 2008) and ecological (Cohen and Felson 1979; Brantingham and Brantingham 2008) processes, and in particular how this understanding can be used to formulate situational interventions (see Clarke 1997).

For evolutionary psychologists, all three levels of causation – ultimate, distal and proximal – are seen to operate in conjunction with an individual's goals to generate purposive behaviour, with some adaptive function in the here-and-now (Tinbergen 1963; Davies *et al.* 2012). The individual may set out to behave with a specific purpose in mind, or he/she may encounter an unforeseen opportunity that activates a general readiness to pursue a particular goal.

The often used example concerns why we eat. The proximal causal explanation for why we eat is because we are hungry, and consuming food sates our appetite and assuages our hunger. Developmental mechanisms explain how food preference and food-acquisition abilities emerge from conception to maturity. Yet the ultimate explanation is that a preference to eat in our ancestral past would have increased the likelihood of surviving and reproducing compared to conspecifics with food apathy. The evolutionary functions of the conscious purposes may be hidden from the agent – for example, only after Darwin's insights in the nineteenth century did it become clear why we like sweet things.

In this chapter we integrate the concept of ultimate causation derived from EP with the proximal situational perspective of causal mechanisms and goals, with the view to better understand, predict and prevent terrorist behaviour and events. The developmental perspective, while important, is not central to our current analysis. Those working in crime science, and more especially situational crime prevention, have only recently begun to show an interest in terrorism (Clarke and Newman 2006; Freilich and Newman 2009; Roach *et al.* 2005) and EP (Ekblom, in press; Roach and Pease 2013; 2014), while to the best of our knowledge there appears to be little research linking situational theories, EP and crime or terrorist behaviour. It is our contention that EP has something useful to say about how we respond to and act on information in the immediate environment, and that a better appreciation of evolutionary influences on person-situation interactions might helpfully inform efforts to reduce the proximal causes of crime and terrorist behaviour or disrupt criminals'/terrorists' proximally active, tactical goals.

The chapter is structured as follows. We begin by setting out some prevalent misconceptions about EP that we argue account for the lack of interest in the approach among terrorist researchers, and that need to be dispelled before we can proceed with our proposed analysis. Next, we set out the parameters of our analysis, and describe terrorism in a manner that is amenable to an evolutionary perspective. Given the difficulties in defining terrorism, we select the concept of tribalism as a significant exemplar of a terrorism-supporting mechanism and our focus for analysis. We move then to the main goal of this chapter: integrating the proposed causes of terrorist behaviour, from ultimate causes rooted in our evolutionary past to proximal causes and goals in the immediate environment. This analysis is conducted within the framework of the 'conjunction of terrorist opportunity' (CTO) (Roach *et al.* 2005), a conceptual model that seeks to link a range of situational and offender-based, proximal causes of terrorist events. We conclude by reflecting on the implications of our exercise for research and prevention.

Clarifying misconceptions about evolutionary psychology

Evidence in support of evolution by natural selection is overwhelming (Coyne 2009; Dawkins 2009). Virtually all scientists accept that the anatomy and physiology of an organism, including humans, can be explained by natural selection. However, extending that logic to accept that human behaviour has similarly been shaped by selection pressures over evolutionary time is more controversial, even among ardent Darwinists. Acceptance of this premise requires that one also accept that human behaviour is, at some level, dependent upon hard-wired brain structures that have evolved in the same way as other physical attributes. Such a premise runs counter to the deeply rooted tradition in those fields most closely associated with the study of crime and terrorism – such as sociology and criminology – where a blank-slate model of human behaviour predominates (as with some learning theories, see Burgess and Akers 1966). From these perspectives, individuals are depicted as devoid of instincts – and the causes of criminal and terrorist behaviour, and the propensities that underlie it, are ascribed solely to social and developmental processes occurring over each individual's lifetime. Many social scientists are further offended by the associated challenge from EP to the concept of rationality and the disconcerting proposition that human beings perform many actions for 'ultimate' reasons that are hidden from them (Cosmides and Tooby 1997; Ekblom, in press).

Against the background of these concerns comes misunderstanding of the implications of EP for human behaviour in general and for crime and terrorism in particular. The misunderstanding can take several forms. At its most extreme is the assumption that EP depicts human behaviour as genetically determined, predestined at birth, insensitive to environmental inputs and in ignorance of human morality. This is clearly anathema to proponents of antisocial and violent behaviours as products of socialization and developmental experiences. It is also dangerously close to Lombroso's (1876) crude and widely discredited application of Darwinian theory in the context of criminal behaviour, namely that criminals constituted evolutionary throwbacks who could be reliably identified by virtue of physical characteristics such as asymmetrical facial features. One would struggle to find a contemporary card-carrying evolutionary psychologist who claims that everything in human psychology is genetically predetermined. As we will emphasize throughout this chapter, EP works off a biosocial model of human behaviour. Just as a fundamental component of evolutionary biology is that the expression of our genes (phenotype) is determined by environmental factors, so too do evolutionary psychologists hold that human behaviours are the product of internal (nature) and external (nurture) factors in complex and protracted interaction.

The charge of genetic determinism in part reflects a common misunderstanding of a core concept in EP, namely 'hard-wired'. EP suggests that the human brain is equipped with numerous evolved psychological mechanisms as a consequence of recurrent selection pressures that continue to inform contemporary human behaviour (see Table 3.1). These mechanisms are domain-specific: they are not generalized, pan-situational predispositions (e.g. aggression) but rather they are activated under certain conditions (e.g. aggression when insulted by a sexual rival). We are not consciously aware of these mechanisms and nor are we slaves to them. Hard-wired is often taken to mean permanency and behaviour fixity. This is incorrect. It is simply not possible for any biological process to provide us with a repertoire of preprogrammed responses to every situation we will encounter during our physically and socially complex lives – that is why we evolved intelligence. In any case, in any given situation there are usually multiple competing causes and goals influencing behaviour so the outcome is rarely a simple 'stimulus-evolutionary response' one. Moreover, the sorts of problems individuals must solve

Table 3.1 Ten 'hard-wired' psychological mechanisms and their hypothesized evolutionary function

Psychological mechanism	*Function*
Fear of snakes	Avoid poison
Superior female spatial-location memory	Increase success at foraging/gathering
Male sexual jealousy	Increase paternity certainty
Preference for foods rich in fats and sugar	Increase caloric intake
Female mate preference for economic resources	Provisioning for children
Male mate preferences for youth, attractiveness, and waist-to-hip ratio	Select mates of high fertility
Landscape preferences for savannah-like environments	Motivate individuals to select habitats that provide resources and offer protection appropriate to our physical and mental capabilities to exploit them and cope with hazards
Natural language	Communication/manipulation
Cheater-detection procedure	Prevent being exploited in social contracts
Male desire for sexual variety	Motivate access to more sexual partners thereby increasing the probabilty of reproductive success

Source: adapted from Buss (1995).

can vary depending upon whether they are male or female, rich or poor, or old or young. Evolved psychological mechanisms are *flexible* cognitive programmes that are responsive to individual circumstances and behavioural contexts, and provide for *adaptive* solutions to life's challenges. We can and often do act against our psychological mechanisms. Roach and Pease (2013) eloquently liken this to cutting wood:

> The notion that evolution makes for uniform behaviour is just wrong ... wood has a grain. Anyone who has worked with wood will tell you how much easier it is to work with the grain than across the gain. Evolution provides the grain for behaviour, but we don't have to work with it.
>
> (p. 3)

Some of us can resist the biscuits.

A related misunderstanding of EP that is central to this chapter is the view that a focus on ultimate causal processes might unhelpfully lead to a neglect of proximal causes of human behaviour. It is easy to see the origins of this misconception. Most EP research is interested in ultimate causes of human behaviour, to complement the proximal explanations that dominate the social and behavioural sciences. However, it is not practised in ignorance of proximal causation. Indeed, as indicated above, the chief message of EP is that hard-wired psychological mechanisms, including purposive ones, are contingent on stimuli in the proximal environment. This sort of gene-environment interaction is powerfully demonstrated in Caspi *et al.* (2002), who elegantly show that the probability of maltreated children developing violent and antisocial tendencies is mediated by the availability of monoamine oxidase A (MAOA) – an enzyme responsible for the breaking down of biochemicals such as dopamine. Higher levels of MAOA were found to suppress the criminogenic effect of child maltreatment. Yet the profound insight by Caspi and colleagues was that the apparent violence-promoting effect of low levels of MAOA is only initiated if individuals are subjected to maltreatment during childhood – a genetic effect contingent on proximal causes. Part of the motivation behind this chapter is that a focus on the proximal causes of crime and terrorist behaviour has meant crime science has yet to fully embrace an evolutionary perspective on person-situation interactions. But the evolutionary component is not a simple add-on. The 'preprogramming' to 'expect' and to be ready for the occurrence of certain stimuli emerges through protracted and cumulative interaction between human genes and environment throughout the process of development and learning. The bringing forth of particular behaviours in particular situations may be precipitated (Wortley 2001, 2008) in situ (as with instant provocations); it may also be potentiated by a short-term build-up of mood (Van Gelder 2013). Each of these processes takes in both evolutionary and environmental influences.

Setting out the parameters of our analysis

Before we can connect terrorism with evolution and situational causation we must take care to mark out the phenomena that our theories and research are intended to explain and practically influence. Terrorism comprises diverse aspects. It is variously: a strategy to achieve societal- or international-level goals; the recruitment, maintenance and operation of terrorist groups; the tactical terrorist behaviour committed by groups and individuals in support of strategy, including preparation, execution and post-event actions; the terrorist events resulting from those actions; and the climate of terror which terrorists seek to create and maintain (the inverse of community safety) as a means of influence. We can also distinguish, following Roach *et al.* (2005), two kinds of *target* of terrorist action: the tactical 'target vectors', i.e. immediate victims or people put in fear, and material assets damaged/disrupted, as instrumental means; and the strategic 'target audience', i.e. the government, or large company, say, that the terrorists want to influence as their ultimate end. The situation in turn comprises diverse entities and agents which the terrorists must cope with as threats or exploit as opportunities.

Within these diverse aspects of terrorism, crime science primarily focuses on criminal or terrorist events and their proximal causes (Clarke and Newman 2006). This analysis covers the tactical behaviour of terrorists leading to, during and immediately after those events, plus the immediate situation/s in which they occur. As will be seen, EP potentially informs our understanding of the perceptions, emotional/motivational reactions and behaviour of all the agents present in (and beyond) the proximal circumstances of terrorist events, both individually and as groups and societies. The proximal is therefore just our starting point from which we work back upstream, causally speaking, carefully seeking to identify emergent phenomena and processes on the way, and always looking for the possible contribution of evolutionary causes, including influences on offenders' and others' goals that are active before the crime situation, or activated in it.

We note the whole contextual array of causal mechanisms that start from immediate ecological interactions between offender and crime situation, and proceed in two interwoven branches. On the offender side they extend to the offender's tactical goals, decisions and reactions, to conditions firing up motivation and emotion over a longer timescale and perhaps greater physical distance, to more distal developmental processes, which contribute to an individual's predisposition to aggression, violence or destructiveness, to genetics. On the environmental side there extends a counterpart branch of opportunities, niches, habitats, markets, social structure/ecosystems and so forth. Connecting both sets of branches at the tips are the ultimate evolutionary causes – how the ancestral organisms adapted to ancestral environments. Such ultimate causes are at the very least ancient hominin prehistory and at most have operated in 'deep time' over hundreds of millions of years. But in the here-and-now, according to EP, they must act to influence the behaviour of offenders and other agents through genetic and developmental processes, and through the environments in large part created and maintained by other human agents.

The question remains, however: what behaviours are to be judged to be acts of terrorism? Defining terrorism has proven challenging wherever attempted (e.g. Bassiouni 2002; Saul 2006; Sosis and Alcorta 2008). The key *legal* quandary is how to characterize the phenomenon while avoiding, say, criminalization of violent resistance by freedom fighters to oppressive regimes, and while more generally separating the legal concept of proscribed and condemned harmful intent and behaviour from matters of politics and value. *Scientific* attempts to characterize terrorism encounter a similar problem, and indeed face the additional requirement of developing an objective viewpoint detached from the cultural and institutional assumptions in which even the most disinterested legal perspectives and discourses are inevitably steeped. From an evolutionary perspective it is yet more challenging to make connections between prehuman and early human behaviour and environments on the one hand, and the refined, culture-bound notions of crime, and even more so of terrorism, on the other. The hypothesized conditions under which our distinctively human mental adaptations arose – referred to collectively as the 'environment of evolutionary adaptedness' (EEA: Bowlby 1969) – are located mostly in the Pleistocene epoch (1.8m–11,000 BP). Modern humans and their predecessors lived in small hunter-gatherer tribes, all of whose members knew each other intimately; there was no permanent settlement, agriculture, private property, large interacting populations, or mass communication. Imagine, for example, trying to find a convincing counterpart of a contemporary terror attack in a group of Homo erectus or a band of modern humans roaming the tundra in the Paleolithic. Imagine, too, trying to find convincing homologous behaviour among a contemporary band of chimpanzees. Terrorism and terrorist behaviour have only emerged as complex societies have developed. While *cultural* evolution can contribute to our understanding of the origins and nature of terrorism per se, *biological* evolution can only suggest how humans, by virtue of their EEA, came evolutionarily predisposed to evolve the strategy and tactics of terrorism when the social environment was right for it; and as individuals *ready-prepared* to be motivated and capable of committing terrorism when this emerged.

One promising approach – which will be adopted here – is described by Sosis and Alcorta (2008) when endeavouring to find a similarly detached way of addressing the relationship of religion/religiosity and terrorism. Rather than trying to define religion directly, they avoid the quagmires concerning what constitutes religion by *delineating the core adaptive features of religion that facilitate cooperation*. 'This is important because we suspect that similar to their religious counterparts, successful secular terrorists employ some of these core features, such as emotionally evocative symbols, rituals and myths.' (pp. 116–17). In support of this they refer to the practices of the Tamil Tigers in Sri Lanka who employed (among other methods) secular suicide bombing.

They go on to say:

> The secular-religious distinction made by Western societies with institutionalized religious systems may not be a useful paradigm for examining the determinants of terrorist activity. Rather, analyses would be better served by concentrating on *how terrorist organisations use the particular characteristics of the human religious adaptive complex we outlined here to inspire group commitment and individual action.*
>
> (p. 117: our italics)

Our own approach, therefore, is to examine *terrorist-supporting behavioural, cognitive and motivational tendencies and capacities* originating in our adaptations to our EEA, and to explore how this adds to our understanding of people and groups playing various roles in today's world of terrorism – the offenders, target vectors, target audiences, preventers and others. Note that this is a broader focus than on the terrorist offender alone – understanding the *terrorized or terrorizable* is equally important.

The evolution of terrorism-supporting mechanisms: the case of tribalism

So what, then, are the evolved human behavioural patterns that support the development of terrorist behaviours and ideologies? As a starting point, we suggest the following non-exhaustive list of overlapping attributes:

- A capacity for aggressive behaviour as a means of exerting power and defending reputation and status, especially among adolescent males.
- A capacity for detecting cheating, attributing deservedness and for extracting vengeance or formal punishment.
- A capacity for distinguishing between human groups based on racial, linguistic, social, political, religious, etc. identifiers.
- A capacity for in-group solidarity/loyalty and a related capacity for emotional/motivational response to perceived attacks on in-group identity.
- A capacity for individual and collective feelings of territoriality.
- A capacity for seeing people as objects and suppressing empathy, often on the basis of out-group identifiers.
- A capacity for cooperation, enabling the development of collective responses to problems affecting the in-group.
- A capacity to maintain effective collaborative relationships with a finite yet substantial number of people, considerably more so than other primates (our so-called 'Dunbar number' is approximately 150 people (Dunbar 1992)).
- A capacity to organize in-groups along hierarchical lines and for members to assume leadership and follower roles.

- A capacity for moral belief systems that can define an in-group and justify action against out-groups in pursuit of a moral cause.
- A capacity for belief in, and motivation by, rewards distant in time and space, including after death.

We do not have the space in this chapter to set out the evidence and trace the evolutionary development of each of these attributes. However, many of them can be collected under the broader concept of tribalism. There is evidence that tribalism is a universal behavioural pattern across humans (McDonald *et al.* 2012; Tajfel *et al.* 1971) and it has also been observed in other primates (Mahajan *et al.* 2011). In a major review of the social psychological research, Van Vugt and Park concluded that

> humans have a pronounced tribal psychology, comprising tendencies to (a) quickly distinguish ingroup from outgroup members and prefer ingroup members, (b) form deep affections toward ingroups, (c) dislike disloyal ingroup members, (d) actively discriminate against outgroup members, and (e) engage in competition with outgroups.
>
> (2009, p. 9)

Intergroup conflict has been pervasive throughout human history. Most terrorist behaviour has a group dimension. The moral cause is usually a collective or group concern, which may involve conformity to particular practices and beliefs, and define group membership and by extension non-membership (e.g. co-religionists are in; others are to be influenced – maybe converted – or killed). Terrorists are driven by, and actively exploit, group processes in running their own organization or network, including using group symbols, language, religion and identity (Sosis and Alcorta 2008). Even so-called lone wolf terrorists typically identify with the cause of a wider group (Watts 2012). Group membership factors may supply or deny legitimacy to some counterterrorist actions, influencing whether they will be productive or counterproductive in their influence on particular audiences.

McDonald *et al.* (2012) succinctly summarise the ultimate explanation for tribalism. Group living afforded humans huge survival and reproductive benefits. These covered both strength in numbers, pooling of resources and scope for division of labour; also cooperative parenting, protection from predators and territorial defence. Such advantages could have created selection pressure for the evolution of psychological mechanisms favouring a desire to cooperate and our need to 'belong'. But there is still the need to explain 'why humans are so fiercely tribal in the sense that they are motivated to engage in discrimination and aggression against members of other groups.' (p. 671). This element is of central relevance to terrorism. McDonald *et al.* (2012) connect it to a wider pattern in which it is men who almost exclusively perpetrate aggression against members of other groups. Setting out (and adducing evidence for) this 'male warrior' hypothesis, they argue that this 'fierce' tribal inclination is an adaptive response to the threat of coalitional aggression and intergroup conflict perpetrated by 'warrior males' in both ancestral and modern human environments. The warrior male tendency in turn derives from the ultimate goal of acquiring or protecting reproductive resources.

Tribalism and contemporary proximal and distal processes

To recapitulate, the ultimate causes in evolutionary history can only influence here-and-now behaviour in the immediate terrorist-attack situation, and in the preparation for that attack, by influencing proximal causal mechanisms. But there is no 'action at a distance': the ultimate causes have to get to the proximal ones. It is *distal* processes, including psychological development, socialization and learning that connect the evolutionary history to the proximal. The major route is via information (knowledge for survival and reproduction in past environments) stored in our genes. But distal processes conduct evolutionary influences via other channels too, in particular through cultural (memetic) transmission from present and past society. Cultural and genetic evolution are hence intertwined, because that culture may itself have been shaped by genetic influences (the classic example is the retention of childhood lactase enzymes by adult Europeans and certain East Africans, enabling adults to digest milk, that co-evolved with dairying culture). All cultures will have elaborated on, and distinctively shaped, our universal genetically based human tendencies to tribalism, and it is these elaborations that are culturally transmitted.

Drawing a boundary between the proximal and the distal is somewhat arbitrary; moreover, the boundary depends on whether we are considering a group or individual perspective. For groups, we consider as distal the process of establishment of an interacting and collaborating group of individuals motivated by a common moral cause and seriously contemplating terrorist actions to further that cause. We consider as proximal for the group, all the actions of that established group in furthering its strategy (in our case specifically through the planning and execution of terrorist attacks). This will cover recruitment and socialization of new group members, including those member's own 'terrorism involvement' decisions. But while this is proximal for the *group* as just defined, it is distal for that *individual*. Given our psychological focus, where there is divergence between these perspectives we emphasize the individual over the group (and note there is still much controversy over the existence of group-level genetic selection – e.g. Dawkins 2006; Pinker 2012). We now review the field of proximal mechanisms in some depth. This is followed by coverage of distal processes, in a more limited treatment intended just to bridge the conceptual gap between ultimate and proximal causation.

Proximal processes

Proximal for our purposes covers the immediate causes operating within the terrorist attack situation during the event and shortly before it, including preparations. Conventionally, crime science has organized its understanding of the proximal causes of criminal and terrorist events via the ecological 'routine activities' perspective (Cohen and Felson 1979), where a likely offender encounters a suitable target in the absence of capable guardians. Also relevant is the environmental approach of crime pattern theory (Brantingham and Brantingham 2008), which suggests the places where likely offenders and suitable targets are most likely to converge, whether by deliberate planning by the former, or coincidence of offender and victim routines. To these has been added the psychological 'rational choice' perspective (Cornish and Clarke 1986) in which the immediate decision to offend is influenced by (perceived) opportunity in the shape of the risk of harm, effort and reward. A more recent addition, which takes us beyond rational opportunity factors in isolation, has been crime precipitation (Wortley 2001, 2008). This covers situationally induced perceptual, motivational, emotional and interpersonal processes (prompting, provocation, pressure and permission) in or near the proximal crime situation that may activate a goal, the search for an opportunity and its exploitation. Obviously, precipitation can only account for the triggering of impromptu attacks, but may also influence the manner in which planned attacks are conducted and escalate the severity of the response, for example, the beating of a recalcitrant hostage.

The conventional formulation has several shortcomings for present purposes. First, while the constituent perspectives cover most of the relevant field of causation equally well for terrorism as for crime, the situational orientation underlying them all has not traditionally focused on powerful and persistent ideologically based offender motivation of the kind that drives people to extremes such as suicide bombing, and accordingly to make great effort to circumvent barriers (i.e. displacement). Likewise, situational approaches generally assume the offender wishes to avoid bodily harm, which may not hold in suicide missions. More generally, the emphasis on the situational side and the deliberate 'cardboard cutout' offender (Cornish and Clarke 2008; Ekblom 2007), albeit understandable for historical reasons, leaves very little beside 'likely' or 'motivated' and 'rational' for EP to work with.

Calls to incorporate within a situational analysis of crime a more detailed and realistic picture of offender psychology – one that more fully recognizes the importance of the person-situation interaction that underpins the logic of ecological approaches (Wortley 2012) – would seem even more pressing when terrorists are the subject of the analysis. Although the emphasis on the situation remains, evolutionary psychological influences obviously have to come via the offender (and agents playing other roles in the event) before they can interact with the situation: a more detailed model is needed.

The 'conjunction of criminal opportunity' (CCO: Ekblom 2010, 2011) attempts to integrate these perspectives, plus more on the offender side, into a single, fine-grained, comprehensive and consistent set of causal elements with an equally consistent terminology. CCO covers *agents* occupying several active roles (offender, crime preventer, crime promoter) and *entities* (material or human target, target enclosure, wider environment, resources for offending that the agents have to cope with or exploit). Roach *et al.* (2005) adapted and extended this to the CTO, adding *offender* enclosures (e.g. hideouts) and dividing targets into target *vectors* (whose injury or damage is the message) and target *audience* (the recipients of the message whom the terrorists seek to influence). We shall use CTO here, modified as necessary with more recent thinking. CTO is summarized in Box 3.1 and described in more detail below.

Box 3.1 The conjunction of terrorist opportunity: proximal causes of terrorist events (modified from Roach et al. 2005)

Terrorist:

1 Predisposition
2 Lack of resources to avoid terrorism
3 Readiness to act
4 Resources for committing terrorist acts
5 The decision to act

Situation:

6 Presence of terrorist in situation
7 Target vectors and target audience
8 Target enclosure
9 Wider environment
10 Absence/incapacity of terrorism preventers
11 Presence/capacity of terrorism promoters

It should be noted that (like 'routine activities') CTO does not claim to be a theory of the causes of terrorist events, but a detailed description of the broad proximal elements – the offender in the situation – that come together to define such events, and through which the causes are channelled. As such, more specific theories and causal mechanisms can be arranged upon the framework (for example, what prompts people to perceive a terrorist opportunity, or how the executive function might inhibit a terrorist action). The theories can then be related to one another on the same conceptual 'workbench' in the search for gaps, overlaps and clashes; and a more consistent and comprehensive terminology developed to support thinking, communication, knowledge management and practical innovation. CTO makes no distinction between offender-centred causes that are common to all humans (e.g. the generic capacity for aggression) versus those that indicate individual differences (e.g. a person with a particular predisposition to be aggressive). The choice of perspective is up to the researcher: here, we emphasize the former, universal alternative.

CTO sets out 11 proximal causes of acts of terrorism (Box 3.1). We now consider the implications of evolutionary theory to each of these causes in turn, starting with the offender/terrorist side of CTO (1–5) and moving to the more ecological factors (6–11). Although the 11 proximal causes are intended to be an exhaustive list, within each cause, for reasons of space, coverage is just illustrative and at this stage in the development of crime science and EP, contains some speculation.

1 Predisposition

As already described, humans may be predisposed to form coalitions and groups; to possess a group identity or identities; to perceive/assign group membership of other individuals; to evaluate other groups for threats posed to their own group's interests (in terms of territory, resources, reproductive opportunity); and to take action to influence, harm or destroy groups thus perceived as threatening.

2 Lack of resources to avoid terrorism

Personal resources to avoid terrorism (and criminal behaviour more generally) include empathic ability (which may be species universal though subject to variation) and perspicacity/tact in handling others' group-related sensitivities and interests; also relevant is the ability to resist charismatic leaders, group pressures and permissions.

3 Readiness to act

Readiness refers to emotional/motivational states that can be triggered, boosted or diminished, and given direction (as goals) towards some target which may comprise members, or assets, of another group. The states may persist and be amplified especially if reinforced by group processes involving, for example, social judgement (Tajfel *et al.* 1971), which may nowadays be mediated over the Internet. Broader, less-immediate influences acting in earlier situations may potentiate the readiness over time, for example, a series of perceived insults from some out-group. Proximal influences awakening and directing readiness in the immediate attack situation may operate through provocation (e.g. perceived insults/strategic threats to group) or prompting (e.g. triggering recollections of resentment, enmity, etc.), although whether such 'spontaneous' attacks count as terrorism is unclear. There may be a similar readiness in relation to perceived betrayal or defection within the terrorist group.

4 Resources for committing terrorist acts

Resources (e.g. Ekblom and Tilley 2000; Gill 2005) may be psychological, or ecological ('out there' in the environment, such as weapons). Psychological resources include effectiveness at undertaking terrorist activity within a group, skill at mobilizing other group members or ability to identify members of opposing groups based on language, ethnic or religious symbols. The ability to inhibit empathy towards out-group members is a likely candidate for EP, as may be our ability to persuade others. The ability to self-justify may not be of EP origin however, though self-deception in general may be a specifically evolved capacity (Trivers 2011), as may be the generic capacities for communication and imitation that spread such justification, and the potency of group support in underwriting that justification.

The ability of humans to collaborate and cooperate is a highly evolved universal species characteristic; as said, a defining component of group life, closely connected with 'cooperation-for-conflict' whether with other humans or predatory/competing animals. As part of such collaboration, personal resources may be disseminated between group members, through teaching of skills and knowledge; likewise ecological resources are often shared.

Tool use is rare and limited among non-humans, but an evolved universal human characteristic. It is of practical importance in terrorism, especially where such activity is asymmetric – i.e. not just battle groups of similar size slogging it out, but smaller numbers on one side compensated by weaponry such as IEDs. The sight of weapons has been shown to prompt aggressive behaviour (Berkowitz and LePage 1967) though whether there is an evolutionary psychological component (which would relate to weaponry in general, since AK47s were seldom seen in the Pleistocene; or to an even more general tool-related priming) is uncertain.

5 The decision to act

Objective opportunity for a particular agent – say a terrorist – is a combination of some *goal*, favourable *situational conditions* (covering both the entities and the other agents identified in CTO) and the terrorist's *resources* to exploit the vulnerabilities and cope with the hazards in those conditions. There may not be any group-related EP contribution here, only a general – evolved – adaptability to *take* opportunities based on a more or less sophisticated capacity for quasi-rational choice, and sometimes to creatively *make* them. However, EP may come in more phenomenologically when we consider *perceived* opportunity. The capacity of *affordance* – involving the ability to see utility in items and places in the environment (Ekblom and Sidebottom 2008; Gibson 1950; Taylor and Currie 2012) where they relate to one's goals – is part of the same picture.

Precipitation is perhaps more fruitful as a locus of possible EP influences. Perception of threat may be prompted by sight of out-group members in particular places or doing particular things; and perceived insults may provoke retaliatory action. Humans may be evolutionarily predisposed to perceive, even to actively look out for, threats to group esteem or well-being and to respond aggressively, hence 'ready for readiness', in the same way it is proposed that we are primed to detect cheating (Tooby and Cosmides 1992). This overlap between predisposition, perception and readiness illustrates the challenge, but hints at the value, of making analytic distinctions within a holistic cognitive system.

Ecological factors are found in the immediate attack situation or in the broader proximal environment in which attacks are conceived, planned and prepared. They are often only indirect channels for potential EP mechanisms – it is how the terrorist is *primed* to perceive and respond to them that may be EP-mediated. The capacity of a swastika to provoke a socialist, say, and the capacity of the socialist to be provoked by the swastika are essentially two sides of a single coin (Ekblom 1994) combining objectivity and subjectivity; not independent properties. But given that the environment of the terrorist importantly includes people (and groups) playing other roles (preventer and promoter), and constituting human targets, the EP influences on *these* agents may be significant, whether those factors are serving to provoke the terrorist, say, or to make the targeted people respond the way the terrorists desire (intimidation or fleeing straight into a second bomb rather than defiance).

6 Presence of terrorist in situation

One or more terrorists has to be able to influence particular situations, whether these are the attack situation itself or prior scenes in a complex sequence of preparations, and whether the presence is the material or cyber version. Presence brings risks of identifiability/recognizability, and the scope for one group to exclude another from its territory. Group factors include ethnically distinct facial or other bodily features, which may be largely genetic, although non-psychological. Our ability to recognize a huge number of individuals, though imperfect, is a key evolved capacity. Our distinguishing features may be embellished or concealed by grooming, clothing and adornments, which may in turn be cultural in content but partly genetic in origin.

Group factors and collective territoriality may make it easy/difficult for visibly or audibly different groups to travel to and to get into particular situations and/or be perceived to fit in/not to fit in; and to be suspected of malintent through (prejudicial) stereotyping. Routine movement patterns exploited by terrorists as targets or cover may be group-related, e.g. pilgrimages or commuting, and may well relate to species-specific tendencies (imagine how a group of mutually unacquainted chimpanzees would get on packed into a commuter train).

7 Targets

Targets are of two main sorts. Target *vectors* are the direct object of the terrorist act. Crime science has generated a set of situational risk factors for the choice of target vectors for terrorism (Clarke and Newman 2006). EVIL DONE comprises exposed, vital, iconic, legitimate (in the eyes of the terrorists and their supporters), destructible, occupied (i.e. containing human targets), near and easy. How far any of these reflect a specific EP component, and in our current illustration, a tribalism/group-relevant one, is debatable: most may simply reflect the pragmatics/rationality of foraging tactics (e.g. *Near, Easy*) addressed by any roving animal. However, *Iconic* may reflect emotional/motivational properties of the target audience, namely what (the terrorists believe) the audience values in the target vector such as, say, Big Ben. Such valuation may partly derive intensity from their symbolic significance to the target audience group, and we seem to have evolved to react to collective symbols and especially threats to them. *Legitimate* is full of possibility for emotional/motivational factors and perception of threats from out-groups who thus 'deserve' attack, and there may be EP influences on these. 'Righteous' or 'vengeful' aggression may be inherently rewarding to express (McCullough 2008), whether it is the terrorists or their opponents who act it out. *Occupied* may reflect the presumed universal tendency of people to respond more to harm to humans than to property, and such responses may be stronger when it is members of our in-group who are harmed, especially but not exclusively kinfolk. Again this may indirectly determine what is rewarding to terrorists.

The target *audience* is the population that the terrorists wish to influence; often that population will be a group (community, country, company, etc.). Influence is attempted by threatening or attacking target vectors and creating pressures on the audience via a 'climate of fear'. Vector-audience interactions are important (and may be further complicated by being channelled through political processes involving leadership and coalitions). The reward-value to the terrorists of the target vectors depends partly on how they can be harmed and how they react, but also on the vectors' influence in turn (which sometimes may be posthumous) on the target audience. Humans' emotional reactions to the occurrence of bad events have evolved to awaken empathy and prompt assistance (a capacity shared with hominid apes), and being in an in-group with the target audience may boost this (or at least will not inhibit it). Astute terrorists are well aware and able to exploit this in seeking to influence the target audience; though they run the risk of inadvertently engendering *defiance*, which is of course antagonistic to the desired *intimidation*. Audience members, particularly leaders of groups such as nations, cities or non-geographical communities (e.g. religions) will seek in turn to foster defiance and buttress against intimidation. To the extent that this discourages terrorists from trying anything on a given population, this serves as a 'preventer' activity.

Extending Roach *et al.*'s (2005) analysis of targets, other foci of terrorist action may be distinguishable, such as those whom a terrorist group wishes to recruit, convert or prevent from leaving. Such targets may be subject to violent acts or threats of intimidation sometimes used to promote conformity and loyalty within a group. This is not specific to terrorism, being a feature of 'outlaw' groups more generally; but it may often be exploited by terrorist groups. The tribalism EP hypothesis does however note the special opprobrium people generally feel towards traitors and splitters within their group, and terrorists may use or consciously exploit this pressure.

8 Target enclosure

Terrorists are infamous for hideouts, caves, compounds, weapons stashes, etc., which may be owned for group benefit and managed via group processes. They can also take hostages and barricade themselves in 'offensible space' (Atlas 1991). Likewise targets of terrorism may be protected in similar enclosures, for equivalent tactical reasons. Whether this is anything more than the result of pragmatic adaptation to topological realities is unclear, as are any specifically group-related EP factors, although 'prospect-refuge' processes may be an EP candidate and buildings often have group-related emotional significance (as with the 'Iconic' risk factor).

9 Wider environment

The wider environment (which may contain enclosures) has two broad kinds of influence on criminal/terrorist behaviour:

1 tactical/logistical (where the lie of the land, built environment, etc. favour preventers over offenders or vice-versa in terms of 'script clashes' (Ekblom 2012) such as conceal vs. reveal, pursue vs. escape, use force vs. resist, etc.); and
2 motivational/emotional, which can relate to instrumental issues such as containment of attractive target vectors, or symbolization of group ownership or status.

Whether such territoriality is specifically EP-influenced in humans (as asserted in popular writing, e.g. Ardrey 1966) is debatable. Its apparent universality may simply stem from humans' generic adaptive response to universal features of two- or three-dimensional environments. However, there is a body of literature on humans' apparently evolved aesthetic preferences for certain types of environment (reviewed e.g. in Silverman and Choi 2005). Aesthetics is an evolved mechanism for guiding our preferences in the here-and-now environment; interestingly, the *emotional/motivational mechanism* currently active in proximal circumstances may have evolved to confer *tactical/logistical advantage* by attracting humans to those places to which they are best adapted to instrumentally cope with risk and exploit opportunity (hence the CTO elements of readiness, rational choice and resources for offending work together). Hypothesized preferences include, beyond the familiar 'savannah' landscape of the EEA, those for coherence, legibility, optimal complexity and mystery; and a balance between 'prospect and refuge' (Appleton 1996). According to the last, within a given landscape the preferred locations are vantage points combining unimpeded visual prospects with a ready scope for concealment or withdrawal to a safe refuge.

Whether such preferences interact with any EP tendencies towards our tribalism example is unclear, but more generally they do have interesting implications for the foraging and exploration of terrorists and criminals (e.g. when undertaking hostile reconnaissance). Within crime science, incorporating such ideas could enrich the 'awareness space' concept of crime pattern theory, and connect with 'exposed', 'near' and 'easy' of EVIL DONE.

10 Absence/incapacity of terrorism preventers, and 11 Presence/capacity of terrorism promoters

Preventers are people, organizations or groups who reduce the risk (probability and harm) of crime or terrorism events; promoters increase that risk. In both cases there are varying degrees of responsibility/culpability – ranging from the person whose mere act of passing by at the wrong moment disrupts an attack or blocks a surveillance camera, through to deliberate action in securing a control room door or in supplying terrorists with moral support, permissions and pressures, and logistical help.

Group membership in itself may influence whether individuals act as preventer or promoter; and groups (both members and leaders) may actively supply such influences in mobilizing such behaviour. Compliance and acceptance mechanisms may be in operation to support group norms and loyalty. Relevant to this is Felson's (1986) 'handler' role in which certain people exert a preventive influence over offenders – and as he states, the offenders need appropriate psychological 'handles', i.e. a 'receptor mechanism' for that influence. EP-enhanced tribalism may contribute both to the handles and the handlers. The 'anti-cheating' complex of detection and response (Tooby and Cosmides 1992) is an EP mechanism likely to motivate preventers' attempts to control crime; it may also drive offenders' and promoters' attempts to control fellow terrorists' disloyalty, free-riding and quitting or splitting the group. In all cases, we should note that prevention and promotion is relative to the norms and interests of particular groups: what is promotion of terrorism for wider society may be prevention of desertion or betrayal for the terrorist group.

Distal processes

As said, our review of distal processes is cursory and intended mainly to suggest links between ultimate and proximal causation. Fundamentally, from the moment of conception of a human individual the information/instructions stored in its human genotype – the product of biological evolution's experience for survival over millennia – has to feed into the developing body, which becomes the phenotype that endures for a single lifetime and generates our behaviour. Of special interest is the development of the brain.

Many of the contributions of evolution are transmitted from gene to body during the development phase from zygote to adult, controlling the development process (the study of this process is known as 'evo devo'). For example, a human gene variant for linguistic ability may kick in to cause particular parts of the brain to grow faster or for longer than their counterparts in chimpanzees. Such processes may simply 'unfold' or 'mature' with elementary material input from the environment (nutrients, oxygen, warmth) but limited informational input. In other cases, particularly after birth, genetic influences are combined with environmental inputs of a progressively more subtle kind. The combined product of this layer of gene-environment interaction in turn interacts further with the physical and social environment as the child develops. EP influences can thus exert themselves via a range of developmental processes. These are distal from terrorist acts and events but – with benefit of hindsight – in some individuals, in some circumstances, they can be shown to have led towards them. The distal-to-proximal processes operate over various timescales and include child development and maturation; socialization and enculturation; and learning of various kinds ranging from Pavlovian and operant processes to social learning; also inventiveness and problem-solving.

Learning continues throughout life, although with language acquisition for example, there may be critical periods of sensitivity to environmental inputs, followed by diminished flexibility. Socialization/enculturation in most cases are predominantly over by young adulthood, but never fully finish. Radicalization of adolescents or indeed of mature adults is one such process that is highly relevant to terrorism. EP influences may be incorporated at any of these stages and they may operate interactively – for example, priming certain experiences to be rewarding (which will then shape any learning that gives access to such rewards) or making certain connections or actions easier to learn than others, or harder to unlearn. In this connection Breland and Breland's (1961) famous 'On the Misbehavior of Organisms' article showed that what a given species was ready to learn was related to its ecological adaptations – thus, for example, pigs could not be stopped from rooting activity with their target objects (in this case, they had to place tokens in … a piggy bank) even if this was at the expense of reward (in the same way that the Ekbloms' pet rabbit remains impervious to vigorous and sustained attempts to teach him not to chew the furniture). Ecological factors, in the form of life circumstances and prior situations experienced by the growing individual, contribute to the learning, socialization and enculturation process. Some of these will be relatively 'timeless' (e.g. establishing relationships with siblings) while others will bear the imprint of history (e.g. growing up in a refugee camp, or in a particular war).

Group membership will supply and shape some of these experiences, and will also contribute influences such as whom to attend to and/or imitate and learn from. Whether we are evolutionarily primed specifically to attend to and learn from in-group members, or leaders/celebrities especially, is a possibility. Developmental processes are involved in the construction of individuals' identity, and frustrated or conflicting identity may be a developmental problem whose resolution can involve alignment with, and recruitment to, extremist groups and causes.

Implications for situational prevention

Although this chapter is primarily conceptual and exploratory in focus, in this final section we give some attention to the preventive implications of our analysis. Our intention is not to develop a catalogue of fully formed prevention strategies, but rather to suggest possible directions for further work in this area. We follow in the footsteps of Roach and Pease (2011) who similarly call for the development of an 'evolution-evidenced crime reduction programme'. Roach and Pease discuss diverse forms of crime prevention, although our focus here is largely confined to how insights from EP might inform situational crime prevention applied to the proximal environment of terrorist attacks or preparations for those attacks (e.g. obtaining explosives or undertaking hostile reconnaissance). Our argument is thus. EP suggests that the human brain contains numerous psychological mechanisms. These psychological mechanisms are present today because they initiated behaviours which increased the likelihood of solving *specific* adaptive problems in our ancestral past, irrespective of whether those problems are still with us today, or whether the evolved solutions remain appropriate in today's cultural and ecological context. Because these mechanisms are specialized, as opposed to 'general-purpose', they are only activated in particular conducive settings (Tooby and Cosmides 2005). The task of the evolutionary-minded practitioner of prevention is hence to identify those psychological mechanisms that might reduce the likelihood of someone engaging in criminal and terrorist behaviour (such as stimulating empathy) and the situational conditions in which these mechanisms are most likely to be activated. Doing so would inform the manipulation of contemporary environments. To this aim we suggest two avenues worthy of exploration, now discussed in turn: increasing the effectiveness of situational preventive interventions by manipulating the environment in ways that activate crime and terrorist-related psychological mechanisms; and avoiding the unintended consequences of such interventions. Finally, we briefly consider the EP implications for prevention as we trace back from the proximal dynamics of the terrorists event.

Boosting the effectiveness of situational prevention

Firstly, we consider the design of situational interventions, and in particular, designs that speak to the psychological mechanisms, which according to EP, are 'hard-wired' in our brains. To the best of our knowledge, there are currently no examples of counterterrorism strategies that have been explicitly inspired by EP. There is, however, a recent example concerning a situational crime prevention measure that was specifically designed with EP in mind and that serves to illustrate the concept. Nettle and colleagues (2012) report an evaluation of signage designed to deter cycle thieves. The signage being evaluated showed a pair of human eyes and contained the message 'cycle thieves, we are watching you'. The watching eyes signs were implemented across three sites at a British university campus. Compared to the rest of the campus, there was a 62% reduction in reported cycle thefts the year following intervention. As Nettle *et al.* (2012) describe, the design of watching eyes posters draws heavily on evidence from EP in two ways. First is the well-established finding that human decision-making is sensitive to situational contingencies and often decisions are made using 'fast and frugal' heuristics as opposed to slow deliberation in search for an optimal outcome (see Kahnemann 2011; Gigerenzer and Gaissmaier 2011; Todd 2000). This makes evolutionary sense: when faced with recurrent threats to survival, natural selection would favour those who responded quickly to pertinent stimuli and survived most of the time (so-called error management theory, Haselton and Buss 2000). Second is the influence on human decision-making of the presence of watching eyes. Studies in both laboratory and real-world settings demonstrate that the presence of images depicting watching eyes is reliably associated with more prosocial behaviours, from charity donations (Powell *et al.* 2012) to collecting litter (Ernest-Jones *et al.* 2011). This so-called 'watching eyes effect' is explained by recourse to our ancestral environment, as Nettle *et al.* (2012, p. 2) write:

> The rationale for the effect is that being observed committing an act is likely to lead to social repercussions, either positive or negative, and thus it makes sense that when observed, people tailor their acts so as to be more socially desirable. The watching eyes in the studies are always just images, and thus cannot in fact observe anything. The effect occurs nonetheless, since humans have fast, automatic psychological mechanisms which have evolved to respond to all eye-like stimuli.

Returning to terrorism, clearly the motivations for stealing a bike are likely to be very different from those underpinning terrorism. Nor do we claim that simple posters of the sort described by Nettle and colleagues (2012) will be sufficient to reduce the likelihood of terrorist events. Yet the watching eyes effect is considered to be a universal trait, applicable to prospective terrorists as it is to bike thieves or burglars. And we have research showing that powerful motivational states engendering behaviour can be beneficially influenced by situational factors, as with suicide (Clarke and Mayhew 1988) and violent assaults in bars (Graham and Homel 2008). Therefore, when implementing any situational measure designed to reduce the opportunities for behaviours associated with terrorist acts, such as entering a secure space or carrying weapons, there may be grounds to try and ensure the design and/or message is consistent with EP – going with the grain of the wood, and hopefully even exploiting it. And at the very least we can get a clearer idea of which kinds of intervention, in which contexts, may be the most difficult to get to succeed.

Most ways of organizing situational prevention knowledge build on the 25 techniques of situational crime prevention (Clarke and Eck 2003). These contain an assemblage of methods like 'target removal' or 'making compliance easier', arranged under generic rational-choice mechanisms such as reducing the risk, increasing the effort or reducing the reward. Taking evolutionary approaches further, we might ask what mechanisms in our EP influence the perception of and appetite for, risk, effort and reward? And what things, events or states are perceived as rewarding or aversive? Much has been written on evolution and rational choice (reviewed in Ekblom, in press) and clearly this is an avenue to explore. If specialized cognitive modules for dealing with, say, cheating, vengeance, insult, etc. are the order of the day in human minds, then this rather questions the validity of arranging the 25 techniques under universal generic columns (for example, reducing the value of *material* assets may need to work very differently from attempts to reduce the value of *human* targets).

A similar table of techniques has been developed by Wortley (2008) specifically focusing on situational precipitators, causal factors in the environment that awaken or intensify motivation or emotion in-situ through prompting, provocation, pressure and permission which then drive the search for, and exploitation of criminal opportunity. This is causally richer territory for exploring the implications of specialized, inherited, cognitive modules (and see Ekblom 2007). A third approach, developed in the context of applying situational prevention to the control of hostile reconnaissance by terrorists (Ekblom and Hirschfield 2014), and consistent with CTO, is the Ds framework. Currently 11 in total, these sharply focus on the mechanisms by which offenders might be influenced; the most relevant ones to investigate for evolutionary input comprise Deter (known and unknown), Discourage, Demotivate, Disconcert and Deceive.

Avoiding adverse consequences of situational prevention

It is well-known that ill-conceived and poorly managed attempts to control behaviour (including criminal behaviour) can provoke unintended backfire effects (e.g. Sherman 1993; Martin and Osgood 1987). Psychologists refer to this as reactance, which is thought to arise from a perceived curtailment of personal freedom (Brehm 1966), though how far this is a human universal or culture specific is not clear. Just as situations might be altered in a bid to stimulate psychological mechanisms that might reduce the probability of criminal behaviour, it is important to consider that some situational measures formulated in ignorance of these mechanisms might be counterproductive by precipitating these hard-wired responses (Wortley 2008). This can clearly be seen in the psychological mechanisms associated with tribalism described earlier. Disseminating messages that conform to or promote the delineation of an in- and out-group may boost a retreat to in-groups.

Similar mechanisms may operate regarding vengeance. (At the time of writing we have just learned of the 'vengeance' attack by the Taliban in Peshawar which killed 132 children and 9 adults.) Various studies have been conducted (e.g. Jaffe 2011; McCullough *et al.* 2010) but with as yet limited application to terrorism. Situational interventions to limit vengeance and its cycle might usefully be explored although the situations effectively changed by such measures might be way upstream of some terrorist events, and in the immediate aftermath of others.

Upstream of the proximal

Preventive interventions clearly go far beyond the proximal situation. Roach and Pease (2013) acknowledge a wider range, on the situational and offender sides. The CTO framework indicates how each of the causal elements can be followed up to understand the 'causes of the proximal causes', and identify interventions in these, covering earlier developmental experiences and life circumstance situations which influence mood and motivation of individuals and groups, radicalization, and the conflicts and competition which generate terrorism. But however remote and complex, all such influences have to end up as active causes in the heads of individual terrorists in the immediate situations of preparation and attack. EP can influence each of these processes, potentially at any stage. Embittered refugee parents, social reject-status at school, perceived attacks on cherished beliefs and customs, association and identification with a particular group, can in the wrong circumstances lead to a terrorist career. Potentially, evolutionary psychological influences can make these more or less likely to lead to terrorism – depending on context. And they offer 'handles' to manipulate through careful interventions. Situational prevention emerged partly as a result of problems with social engineering approaches (Clarke 1997). And current EP-based social engineering seems to have run into difficulties, especially that based on group-level selection theory (Coyne 2011). Our view is that while such approaches should continue to be explored, this should be done in ways that are the least likely to do harm. Meanwhile, the advantages of the situational approach in connecting highly specific situational stimuli to what may be evolved preparedness to respond to such stimuli offers, we believe, a much tighter linkage to explore and hopefully to exploit.

Conclusion

EP remains at the margins of the study of criminal and terrorist behaviour. This is attributed to concerns with EP more generally (such as the inability to directly observe our ancestral past) and the application of evolutionary thinking to crime in particular (where a blank slate model predominates). Our intention with this chapter was to continue the work of a small cadre of researchers who suggest that EP might usefully advance efforts to better understand, detect and prevent criminal behaviour. To this end, we attempted to connect the ultimate (evolutionary history) causation of human behaviour, which is the province of EP, with proximal (situational) causes which, to date, have successfully been applied in the service of situational crime prevention. We used the CTO as a framework to try and make these causal ends meet, focusing by way of example on tribalism as a terrorist-promoting attribute that has its origins in our ancestral past, where cultural/technological change has raced ahead of our biological tendencies, with serious threats to our well-being and perhaps survival.

As is the case with any branch of science attempting to encroach on a new domain, the acceptance of EP among terrorist scholars in general and in situational prevention in particular will in large part be determined by its ability to generate testable hypotheses – and some of these tests may well involve undertaking experimental preventive action. However, the rarity of terrorist events, while a blessing, does place serious challenges to our methods of evaluation, which have normally relied on the analysis of reliable statistical patterns. A possible research agenda for the future could be to establish evidentiary criteria and develop methodologies to satisfy them; identify tactical circumstances and psychological states relevant to various stages of terrorist activity, from recruitment to detonation: systematically chart possible examples of relevant evolutionary psychological causes (perhaps organizing these, and identifying gaps, using CTO, an exercise truncated here on space grounds); and where evidence of causation of terrorism or of effectiveness of interventions is missing, consider how we might validly transfer the knowledge we have of everyday crime prevention across to counterterrorism contexts. Much as we do with, say, mouse models for the testing of drugs prior to trying them on humans, it may even be possible to identify 'models' of elements of terrorist behaviour in more everyday equivalents, on which to test out causes and trial our interventions.

References

Appleton, J. (1996). *The Experience of Landscape*, revised edn. New York: Wiley.

Ardrey, R. (1966). *The Territorial Imperative: A Personal Inquiry into the Animal Origins of Property and Nations*. New York: Kodansha America.

Atlas, R. (1991). The other side of defensible space. *Security Management*, March, 63–66.

Bassiouni, C. (2002). Legal control of international terrorism: A policy-oriented perspective. *Harvard International Law Journal*, 43, 83–103.

Berkowitz, L. and LePage, A. (1967). Weapons as aggression-eliciting stimuli. *Journal of Personality and Social Psychology*, 7, 202–207.

Bowlby, J. (1969). *Attachment and Loss: Vol. 1. Attachment*. New York: Basic Books.
Brantingham, P.J. and Brantingham, P.L. (2008). Crime pattern theory. In R. Wortley and L. Mazerolle (eds), *Environmental Criminology and Crime Analysis*, 2nd edn. New York: Waveland Press.
Brehm, J. (1966). *A Theory of Psychological Reactance*. New York: Academic Press.
Breland, K. and Breland, M. (1961). The misbehavior of organisms. *American Psychologist*, 681–684.
Burgess, R. and Akers, R. (1966). A differential association reinforcement theory of criminal behavior. *Social Problems*, 14, 128–147.
Buss, D. (1995). Evolutionary psychology: A new paradigm for psychological science. *Psychological Inquiry*, 6, 1–49.
Buss, D. (ed.). (2005). *The Handbook of Evolutionary Psychology*. New York: Wiley.
Caspi, A., McClay, J., Moffit, T., Mill, J., Martin, J., Craig, I., Taylor, A. and Poulton, R. (2002). Role of genotype in the cycle of violence in maltreated children. *Science*, 297 (5582), 851–854.
Clarke, R. (ed.) (1997). *Situational Crime Prevention: Successful Case Studies*, 2nd edn. Harrow and Heston: Guilderland.
Clarke, R. (2008). Situational crime prevention. In R. Wortley and L. Mazerolle (eds), *Environmental Criminology and Crime Analysis*. New York: Waveland Press.
Clarke, R. and Eck, J. (2003). *Become a Problem Solving Crime Analyst in 55 Small Steps*. London: Jill Dando Institute, University College London.
Clarke, R. and Mayhew, P. (1988). The British Gas suicide story and its implications for prevention. In M. Tonry and N. Morris (eds), *Crime and Justice: A Review of Research*, 10. Chicago, IL: University of Chicago Press.
Clarke, R. and Newman, G.R. (2006). *Outsmarting the Terrorists*. New York: Praeger Publishers.
Cohen, L.E. and Felson, M. (1979). Social change and crime rate trends: A routine Activities approach. *American Sociological Review*, 44, 588–608.
Cornish, D. And Clarke, R.V. (ed.) (1986). *The Reasoning Criminal*. New York: Springer.
Cornish, D. and Clarke, R. V. (2008). The rational choice perspective. In R. Wortley and L. Mazzerolle (eds), *Environmental Criminology and Crime Analysis*, 2nd edn. New York: Waveland Press.
Cosmides, L. and Tooby, J. (1997). *Evolutionary Psychology: A Primer*. Retrieved on 20 December 2014 from www.cep.ucsb.edu/primer.html.
Coyne, J.A. (2009). *Why Evolution Is True*. Oxford: Oxford University Press.
Coyne, J.A. (2011). *Can Darwinism Improve Binghamton?* New York Times Sunday Book Review, 9 September. Retrieved on 22 December 2014 from www.nytimes.com/2011/09/11/books/review/the-neighborhood-project-by-david-sloan-wilson-book-review.html.
Darwin, C. (1859). *On the Origin of Species by Means of Natural Selection*. London: John Murray.
Davies, N., Krebs, J. and West, S. (2012). *An Introduction to Behavioural Ecology*, 4th edn. Oxford: Wiley-Blackwell.
Dawkins, R. (2006). *The Selfish Gene*, 30th anniversary edn. Oxford: Oxford University Press.
Dawkins, R. (2009). *The Greatest Show on Earth: The Evidence for Evolution*. New York: Free Press.

Dunbar, R.I.M. (1992). Neocortex size as a constraint on group size in primates. *Journal of Human Evolution*, 22 (6), 469–493.

Ekblom, P. (1994). Proximal circumstances: A mechanism-based classification of crime prevention. In R.V. Clarke (ed.), *Crime Prevention Studies*, vol. 3. Monsey, NY: Criminal Justice Press.

Ekblom, P. (2007). Making offenders richer. In G. Farrell, K. Bowers, S. Johnson and M. Townsley (eds), *Imagination for Crime Prevention: Essays in Honour of Ken Pease*. Crime Prevention Studies 21. Monsey, NY: Criminal Justice Press/Devon, UK: Willan Publishing.

Ekblom. P. (2010). The conjunction of criminal opportunity theory. *Sage Encyclopedia of Victimology and Crime Prevention*, 1, 139–146.

Ekblom, P. (2011). *Crime Prevention, Security and Community Safety Using the 5Is Framework*. Basingstoke: Palgrave Macmillan.

Ekblom, P. (2012). Happy returns: Ideas brought back from situational crime prevention's exploration of design against crime. In G. Farrell and N. Tilley (eds), *The Reasoning Criminologist: Essays in Honour of Ronald V. Clarke*, pp. 163–198. Crime Science series. Cullompton: Willan.

Ekblom, P. (in press). Evolutionary approaches to rational choice. In W. Bernasco, H. Elffers and J.-L. Van Gelder (eds), *The Oxford Handbook on Offender Decision Making*. Oxford: Oxford University Press.

Ekblom, P. and Hirschfield, A. (2014). Developing an alternative formulation of SCP principles – the Ds (11 and counting), *Crime Science*, 3 (2).

Ekblom, P. and Sidebottom, A. (2008). What do you mean, 'Is it secure?' Redesigning language to be fit for the task of assessing the security of domestic and personal electronic goods. *European Journal on Criminal Policy and Research*, 14 (1), 61–87.

Ekblom, P. and Tilley, N. (2000). Going equipped: Criminology, situational crime prevention and the resourceful offender. *British Journal of Criminology*, 40, 376–398.

Ernest-Jones, M., Nettle, D. and Bateson, M. (2011). Effects of eye images on everyday cooperative behavior: A field experiment. *Evolution and Human Behavior*, 32, 172–178.

Felson, M. (1986). Linking criminal choices, routine activities, informal control and criminal outcomes. In D. Cornish and R.V. Clarke (eds), The Reasoning Criminal: Rational Choice Perspectives on Offending. Springer-Verlag, New York.

Freilich, J.D. and Newman, G. (ed.) (2009). *Reducing Terrorism through Situational Crime Prevention*. Crime Prevention Studies, vol. 25. Boulder, CO: Lynne Rienner Publishers.

Gibson, J.J. (1950). *The Perception of the Visual World*. Boston, MA: Houghton Mifflin.

Gigerenzer, G. and Gaissmaier, W. (2011). Heuristic decision making. *Annual Review of Psychology*, 62, 451–82.

Gill, M. (2005). Reducing the Capacity to Offend: Restricting Resources for Offending. In N. Tilley (ed.), *The Handbook of Crime Prevention and Community Safety*. Cullompton: Willan.

Graham, K. and Homel, R. (2008). *Raising the Bar: Preventing Aggression in and around Bars, Pubs and Clubs*. Cullompton: Willan.

Haselton, M.G. and Buss, D.M. (2000). Error Management Theory: A new perspective on biases in cross-sex mind reading. *Journal of Personality and Social Psychology*, 78, 81–91.

Jaffe, E. (2011). The complicated psychology of revenge. *Observer*, 24, 8.
Kahneman, D. (2011). *Thinking Fast and Slow*. New York: Farrar, Straus and Giroux.
Laycock, G. (2005). Defining crime science. In M.J. Smith and N. Tilley (eds), *Crime Science: New approaches to preventing and detecting crime*. Crime Science Series. Cullompton: Willan.
Lombroso, C. (1876). *L'uomo delinquent*, English translation by M. Gibson and N.H. Rafter (2006) *The Criminal Man*. Durham, NC: Duke University Press.
Mahajan, N., Martinez, M., Gutierrez, N., Diesendruck, G., Banaji, M. and Santos, L. (2011). The evolution of intergroup bias: Perceptions and attitudes in rhesus macaques. *Journal of Personality and Social Psychology*, 100, 387–405.
Martin, F.P. and Osgood, D.W. (1987). Autonomy as a source of pro-social influence among incarcerated adolescents. *Journal of Applied Social Psychology*, 17, 97–107.
McCullough, M. (2008). *Beyond Revenge: The Evolution of the Forgiveness Instinct.* San Francisco: Jossey-Bass.
McCullough, M.E., Kurzban, R. and Tabak, B.A. (2010). Evolved mechanisms for revenge and forgiveness. In P.R. Shaver and M. Mikulincer (eds), *Understanding and Reducing Aggression, Violence, and their Consequences*, pp. 221–239. Washington, DC: American Psychological Association.
McDonald, M., Navarrete, C. and Van Vugt, M. (2012). Evolution and the psychology of intergroup conflict: The male warrior hypothesis. *Philosophical Transactions of the Royal Society B*, 367 (1589), 670–679.
Nettle, D., Nott, K. and Bateson, M. (2012). 'Cycle thieves, we are watching you': Impact of a simple signage intervention against bicycle theft. *PLoS ONE*, 7 (12), e51738.
Pinker, S. (2012). *The False Allure of Group Selection*. Retrieved on 22 December 2014 from http://edge.org/conversation/the-false-allure-of-group-selection.
Powell, K.L., Roberts, G. and Nettle, D. (2012). Eye images increase charitable donations: Evidence from an opportunistic field experiment in a supermarket. *Ethology*, 118, 1096–1101.
Roach, J. and Pease, K. (2011). Evolution and the Prevention of Violent Crime. *Psychology*, 2 (4), 393–404.
Roach, J. and Pease, K. (2013). *Evolution and Crime*. London: Routledge.
Roach, J. and Pease, K. (2014). Evolutionary perspectives on crime prevention. In G. Bruinsma and D. Weisburd (eds), *Encyclopedia of Criminology and Criminal Justice*. New York: Springer Verlag.
Roach, J., Ekblom, P. and Flynn, R. (2005). The conjunction of terrorist opportunity: A framework for diagnosing and preventing acts of terrorism. *Security Journal*, 18 (3), 7–25.
Saul, B. (2006). *Defining Terrorism in International Law.* Oxford: Oxford University Press.
Sherman, L. (1993). Defiance, deterrence and irrelevance: a theory of the criminal sanction. *Journal of Research in Crime and Delinquency*, 30, 445–473.
Silverman, I. and Choi, J. (2005). Locating places. In D. Buss (ed.), *The Handbook of Evolutionary Psychology.* New York: Wiley.
Sosis, R. and Alcorta, C. (2008). Militants and martyrs: Evolutionary perspectives on religion and terrorism. In R. Sagarin and T. Taylor (eds), *Natural Security: A Darwinian Approach to a Dangerous World*, pp. 105–124. Berkeley and Los Angeles: University of California Press.

Tajfel, H., Billig, M., Bundy, R. and Flument, C. (1971). Social categorization and intergroup behaviour. *European Journal of Social Psychology*, 2, 149–178.

Taylor, M. and Currie, M. (2012). *Terrorism and Affordance.* London: Bloomsbury.

Tinbergen, N. (1963). On aims and methods of ethology. *Zeitschrift für Tierpsychologie*, 20, 410–433.

Todd, P.M. (2000). The ecological rationality of mechanisms evolved to make up minds. *American Behavioral Scientist*, 43 (6), 940–956.

Tooby, J. and Cosmides, L. (1992). Psychological Foundations of Culture. In J. Barkow, L. Cosmides and J. Tooby (eds), *The Adapted Mind.* New York: Oxford University Press, pp. 19–136.

Tooby, J. and Cosmides, L. (2005). Conceptual Foundations of Evolutionary Psychology. In D. Buss (ed.), *Handbook of Evolutionary Psychology*, 5–67. Hoboken, NJ: Wiley.

Trivers, R. (2011). *Deceit and Self-Deception: Fooling Yourself the Better to Fool Others.* London: Penguin.

Van Gelder, J.-L. (2013). Beyond rational choice: The hot/cool perspective of criminal decision making. *Psychology, Crime and Law*, 19 (9), 745–763.

Van Vugt, M. and Park, J. (2009). The tribal instinct hypothesis: Evolution and the social psychology of intergroup relations. In S. Stürmer and M. Snyder (eds), *Psychology of Helping: New Directions in Intergroup Prosocial Behavior.* London: Wiley Blackwell.

Watts, C. (2012). *Radicalization in the U.S. Beyond al Qaeda: Treating the Disease of the Disconnection.* Program on National Security. Philadelphia: Foreign Policy Research Institute. Retrieved on 15 December 2014 from www.fpri.org/docs/media/PaperRadicalization_in_the_US_Beyond_al_Qaeda_Watts.pdf.

Wortley, R. (2001). A classification of techniques for controlling situational precipitators of crime. *Security Journal*, 14 (4), 63–82.

Wortley, R. (2008). Situational precipitators of crime. In R. Wortley and L. Mazerolle (eds), *Environmental Criminology and Crime Analysis.* Cullompton: Willan.

Wortley, R. (2012). Exploring the person-situation interaction in situational crime prevention. In N. Tilley and G. Farrell (eds), *The Reasoning Criminologist: Essays in Honour of Ronald V. Clarke.* London: Routledge.

4 Terrorism

Lessons from natural and human co-evolutionary arms races

Paul Ekblom

Introduction: Why take a co-evolutionary perspective on terrorism and counterterrorism?

The potential for violent, destructive and threatening behaviour against fellow humans seems to be inherent in our psychological and anatomical nature (the latter arguably evidenced by special adaptations of our fists, and fist-resistant faces (Morgan and Carrier, 2013; Carrier and Morgan, 2014)). This is true whether that behaviour concerns an argument over an insult, careless driving, domestic relations, religious beliefs and practices, or who governs Eastern Ukraine. The kinds of tactics and strategies classed, at times, as acts of terrorism, fall within this set. Fortunately equally inherent in us are cooperation, empathy and altruism, although in a conflict these can be selectively applied to one's own side, even by terrorists.

As Chapter 3 notes, we can look to our evolutionary origins to help understand, and hopefully to influence, what turns us – as individuals and groups – on and off violent conflict, who we target, over what moral/political causes and under what circumstances. This is the domain of beliefs, identities, ideologies and motivation.

But we can also take another perspective, which is *how* conflicts tactically and strategically unfold, and how this process can be influenced for the differential benefit of the 'good side'. The 'how' essentially concerns the process of *adaptation*, whereby organisms as individuals, groups or species change over some relevant timescale to become better fitted to survival, flourishing and reproduction in their habitual environment. Adaptation for potentially violent and destructive conflict such as carrying out terrorism or defending against it is the core concern of this chapter, although adaptation for cooperation and straightforward foraging with or without violence also play a part. The aim of the chapter as a whole is to explore the lessons for counterterrorism from evolutionary studies of adaptation in both human and natural domains. This is partly to come up with some practical suggestions at tactical and strategic levels; but partly also to foster a distinctive and, I will argue, promising way of thinking among policymakers, security services, engineers, planners and designers.

From bacteria to buffalo, conflict is an ecological fact of life. In most animals conflict is driven by scarcity of resources such as food and living space, or mating opportunities, and can range from tussles over food, say, to outright predation, where the conflict is over the fleshly assets of the prey. In humans, conflict extends to cover purely culturally mediated issues of ideology, belief and conformity to particular ways of doing things. In all cases, conflict can lead to violent behaviour although in certain circumstances, injury avoidance or minimization strategies have evolved such as ritualized combat between the males of certain species (e.g. stags), though even here fights to the death occur. Sport arguably plays a similar role in human culture. (This prompts speculation that a more civilized outlet for terrorist motives might be for the groups to enter teams in the Olympics rather than shoot the other competitors up; religiously motivated teams, anticipating divine help towards gold, should expect the effort rewarding.)

In most animals, conflict evolves slowly, as changes in anatomy and physiology (sharp fangs and claws, and powerful muscles versus armoured hide and rapid healing of wounds). Among more advanced animals evolution of *cognitive* contributions to conflict (e.g. ambush behaviour, vigilance, knowledge of opponent's moves and capabilities) proceeds faster as there are fewer constraints and trade-offs at the information-processing level. This is especially so if the animal has already evolved the capacity to learn at an individual level during its lifetime rather than the species learning at a genetic level over many generations. With certain limited exceptions, humans are the only species where cognition and our wider evolutionary psychology (EP) has led to extreme adaptability and *cultural* evolution.

Although intelligence has evolved in stages from the Cambrian Revolution (530my BP) to date, the increase in cognitive powers in hominins (the subfamily of ancestral human species that split from the other great apes) accelerated markedly in the evolutionarily recent past. Whiten and Erdal (2012) note the tripling of human brain size over the last 2.5 million years – a remarkable development, especially for an organ so expensive to grow and maintain, vulnerable to damage and hazardous in childbirth. They ask how it was possible for a moderately sized ape lacking the formidable anatomical adaptations of competing professional hunters like lions to compete over the same prey. Earlier authors (e.g. Tooby and DeVore, 1987) have focused on explanations in terms of the elaboration of a new cognitive niche based on intelligence and technology (for example the advanced inferential reasoning in tracking prey—how many, whether wounded, how long ago they passed; and the refinement of composite weapons for the kill). Whiten and Erdal argue, however, that cognition alone is insufficient. They present evidence that a fuller answer

> lies in the evolution of a new socio-cognitive niche, the principal components of which include forms of cooperation, egalitarianism, mindreading (also known as 'theory of mind'), language and cultural transmission, that go far beyond the most comparable phenomena in other primates.

> This cognitive and behavioural complex allows a human hunter-gatherer band to function as a unique and highly competitive predatory organism. (p. 2119)

Whiten (2006) termed the complex 'deep social mind' to emphasize the core features of mental interpenetration and adjustment of individual to group-level goals. The consequent fitness benefits, and positive feedback between the elements just described, are claimed to underlie our exploding brain size. Whether evolution proceeds at an anatomical, cognitive or cultural level (or as a mixture), certain influences act as potent accelerants, channelling and speeding the processes of change. These influences include *rapid environmental fluctuation* (as wet and dry conditions repeatedly alternated in our ancestral East African habitat, demanding hyper-adaptability to survive – Anton *et al.*, 2014); *sexual selection* (as in the creation of the male peacock's tail) and the more general case of *co-evolution.* All three of these still involve a given species adapting to survive, prosper and reproduce in its environment. But in the last two categories particularly, a key regularity of that other environment is *other organisms* in conflictual or competitive ecological relationships and the mutual feedback between those organisms over various timescales ranging from the evolutionary (over many generations) to the individual lifetime.

Co-evolutionary pairings can be mutually beneficial, as with meerkats and ground hornbills keeping a look out for each other, but those with a conflictual or at least a competitive dimension range from mates versus mates, predators versus prey, mothers and foetuses not just in collaboration on mutual survival but in competition over nutrition and energy, and parasites/pathogens versus hosts. Co-evolution can result in what appear to be equilibria between the two conflicting parties but in reality these are provisional, more like temporary standoffs until one party invents (in human culture) or 'invents' (in biological evolution) some new weapon, tool, poison, claw-sharpening process or similar, that for the time being at least, prevails over the other's kit or repertoire. Co-evolution, e.g. between predators and prey, is also considered to drive the formation of new species. In all these cases, individual species are locked into a *complex adaptive system,* where attempts by any one party to anticipate and control the course of adaptation and counter-adaptation are extremely challenging (Chapman, 2004).

Humans have evolved as intensely social animals, as described above: from early primate ancestors onward, the environments we have adapted to through biological and, increasingly, cultural evolution have always been made up to a significant degree by our conspecifics – nowadays, fellow humans. As populations have grown in historical times, and various technological revolutions such as agriculture have allowed for ever-denser living culminating in urbanization, phase-changes in social structure have meant that we humans, and our buildings, comprise an ever-higher proportion of our own environment. We are thus in a position of having to adapt ever better to living with, and unfortunately conflicting with, each other.

We have also had to adapt *to*, as well as *through*, changes in our own technology and consequent changes in our wider society and culture. Higher primates and certain bird groups have evolved the use and even the design and manufacture of tools (e.g. chimpanzees and termite-fishing sticks). Earlier human species like *Homo habilis* made slow technological progress. The 'Oldowan' flint-stones they shaped as flake tools and weapons kept the same form for 700,000 years. Only with the arrival of more advanced species did the capacity for design, development and improvement take off, marked by the emergence of sophisticated Acheulian core tools such as hand-axes and cleavers some 1.7 million years ago. And with the arrival of *Homo sapiens* development took place at an accelerating pace with only a few minor setbacks (such as the fall of the Roman Empire) up to the present day, where we routinely talk of 'future shock' (Toffler, 1970). New technology is disruptive: it perturbs human cultural, and natural ecosystems and upsets the provisional equilibria of conflict described above. It contributes to the 'disturbed ground' of rapidly changing habitat of the kind claimed to have driven the evolution of our intelligence and generic adaptability (in natural disturbed ground we encounter aggressively adaptive, generalist species like rats, and rapidly growing and breeding weeds). Thus change begets change: ever more adaptive cultures, or species, create the very conditions for further adaptability, opportunism and change.

Terrorist movements seek to violently impose change on fellow humans, or to reverse others' changes they do not like. The movements may be engendered by exogenous disruptions, may exploit them strategically and tactically, and may cause further disruptions in their turn. Terrorists, as individuals, are presumably no more adaptive than the rest of us (indeed some terrorist movements are in many ways highly conservative and internally conformist, though that constraint unfortunately seems not to apply to their innovativeness in technology or technique). But as groups, organizations, networks and movements they collectively possess some distinct adaptive properties which compare favourably (from their perspective), say, with organized crime and common-or-garden criminals. (Lone-wolf terrorists may either possess some of these properties as individuals or free-ride on those of others.) They are highly motivated to work hard to achieve strategic goals and intermediate ones such as the acquisition of logistical resources and weaponry, and the pursuit of innovative means. They may be persistent and consistent over years or even generations, unlike casual criminals, who are rarely displaced from immediate, easy opportunities to ones that are a bit harder, more risky and less rewarding (Guerette and Bowers, 2009). Terrorists may value risk and danger as a badge of commitment, or an emblem of intimidation. Their belief system (and system of self-justification) can overcome a range of psychological or societal constraints including the finality of death, and the deservingness of enemy groups for empathy, respect and humane treatment. They may develop such a level of fellow-feeling, centred on nationalism, religion or some other ideology, that interpersonal trust can flourish. These characteristics can give them adaptive advantages over everyday society.

When cultural or biological co-evolutionary struggles persist, they may develop into an *arms race*, where each party tries to out-evolve the other over some extended period (in biological evolution, 'tries' is of course used as shorthand for those parties that manage to out-evolve their enemies, and hence win out in survival and reproduction). In the natural world such races may continue for aeons (for example, between bacteriophage viruses and bacteria). In the human world it is rare that we can keep specific intergroup conflicts going in a consistent direction for more than a few decades. The Hundred Years' war between England and France is thus named as a rarity (and was, in fact, intermittent); the nineteenth/twentieth century naval arms race between Britain and Germany endured only a few decades; but a more generic race, between defensive and offensive arms manufacturers now continues on an indefinite basis in the global weapons market. Crime and its control have been described in arms race terms for some while (e.g. Ekblom, 1997, 1999; Sagarin and Taylor, 2008). The classic example is the safe (Shover, 1996). Here, the succession of moves and countermoves, against the background of emerging disruptive technologies like thermic lances and diamond-tipped drills on the one side, and manganese steel, copper laminates to conduct away heat and intelligent/internet-connected alarms on the other, has meant that what works for offence or defence at one point in time may cease working in future. Terrorist arms races include, for example, concealment versus detection of hand weapons and explosives, penetration versus resistance of physical barriers, concealment and booby-trapping of IEDs, and hacking versus security of IT systems and controls.

How, then, does legitimate society handle terrorists, who undoubtedly have a strong capacity and motivation to adapt and evolve? Until relatively recently, the consensus among evolutionary-minded commentators on security (whether crime or terrorism control) was summed up by Cohen *et al.* (1995, p. 216) who argued that 'contemporary crime control policies are hopelessly static'; by Ekblom (1997, 1999) in similar terms; and more recently by Dietl (2008) who argued that we need frameworks that do not 'freeze' change. And society's conventional legalistic response is notorious for being slow moving, although this is for quite understandable reasons: attempts to rush in legislation to address particular criminal or terrorist problems have tended to misfire and to have adverse and unforeseen side-effects, such is the complexity of the corpus of laws and of human lives they are intended to regulate. In fairness, there has been progress, particularly on the cybercrime front (where evolution of both attack and defence can be rapid). The 2010 UK National Security Strategy (UK Cabinet Office, 2010), for example, proposes that because 'we cannot prevent every risk as they are inherently unpredictable', there is a need to 'remain adaptable for the uncertain future' and to 'identify threats and opportunities at the earliest possible stage' (pp. 18–25). Situational crime prevention has been sensitive to the accusation of vulnerability to displacement from one well-protected place or target to another less so. Arguably, this has blocked any sustained interest beyond the short term

– when displacement is uncommon – to the longer term, when adaptation is more likely (e.g. Ekblom, 2008).

So, society is in a tactical co-evolutionary arms race with terrorists, against a wider backdrop of technological and social change that continually perturbs any balances of advantage that temporarily benefit one or other party, offering new opportunities for offence (weapons, tools and targets) and defence. How best, then, can society cope over the medium-to-longer term? Not by winning individual security battles, important though these are – indeed, some approaches that confer short-term gains in power and influence may be inconsistent with longer-term strategies of survival (Vermeij, 2008). Instead, we have *to gear up against terrorism* by playing the terrorists at their own game: through strategic, co-evolutionary thinking about arms races and how to run or sidestep them. This necessitates a closer look at evolution itself.

Vermeij (2008), like Roach and Pease (2013) suggests that lessons from biology and palaeontology have been overlooked by policymakers due to the widely held notion that human nature differs fundamentally from the adaptations of other life forms, not least because the problems faced by humans do not apply to other living things. He contends, by contrast, that humans have faced the *same* problems of limited resources and vagaries of climatic and geological upheaval and that 'the distinctive attributes of human individuals and groups are subject to the same rules of competition and cooperation that have governed the adaptation and evolution of organisms always and everywhere' (p. 26). He goes on to say (p. 27) that:

> This fundamental identity of human nature with the natures of other life forms opens the door wide to the principles and major findings of disciplines dealing with life's evolution in a challenging world. At the very least, this approach can help us identify solutions that have worked in the past for many forms of life over the long run, as well as point to responses that have proved less effective.

This neatly articulates the line taken in this chapter.

In the rest of the chapter, I first backtrack a little to summarize the key features of the process of biological evolution, and co-evolution. (A useful alternative account, with a discussion of how evolution and social science-based criminology can and should mix rather than mutually repel, is in Roach and Pease, 2013; an excellent account from the security world is in Schneier, 2012; and coming from biology to security is the book *Natural Security*, edited by Taylor and Sagarin, 2008.) Then, I show how closely related evolutionary processes apply to cultural (including technological) change, opening the knowledge-transfer process up to a range of natural, and human, co-evolutionary struggles. Following that, I show how such a widened perspective can apply to terrorism and counterterrorism in particular. Before concluding, I discuss a range of lessons for how to run terrorist arms races, drawing heavily on those most human of culturally evolved adaptive processes, design, research, theory and evaluation.

To avoid later disappointment, I should declare that adopting an evolutionary approach confers no clear ability to predict in detail what terrorists will do next (or what preventive measures will emerge). As Dietl (2008) states, the historically contingent nature of selection cannot be overemphasized. However, Vermeij (1999) holds that while the precise time course of history and the nature of the participants remain unpredictable, some universal rules governing participants and their actions enable us to discern underlying temporal patterns that *are* predictable and scientifically testable. He also (2008) contributes useful ideas on how organisms themselves have evolved to handle unpredictability in their lives and across generations. And abstract approaches to conceptualizing innovation in engineering can also offer some encouraging possibilities, as will be seen.

It is possible to undertake a completely detached and disinterested analysis of political and religious violence, and a significant degree of distancing from everyday perceptions, feelings and values is needed for social science to make an appropriate contribution. But where that contribution is a practical one, there is an inescapable value-choice, namely to come down on our own side – albeit in full acknowledgement of the difficult issues in defining crime and terrorism (Bassiouni, 2002; Ekblom, 2012a) and the troublesome trade-offs between, say, controlling terrorism and promoting privacy.

Evolution: key features

In this section I aim to cover first, the basics of evolution, and second, some more elaborated themes with relevance to co-evolution of terrorism and security.

The basics

As Darwin first proposed, and others have since developed, the basic process of evolution is threefold: *variation* (in some anatomical, physiological or behavioural trait of individual members of a living species); *selection* (differential survival and reproduction of the fittest, i.e. best-adapted variants of that species); and *transmission or inheritance* of the successful variations to successive generations. Given a consistent selection pressure, say for taller individuals, operating in the habitat of a particular species, the population of that species will come, over generations, to be dominated by the variants best adapted to that selection pressure. From time to time, a single species will split into two or more descendants.

The mechanisms of variation and inheritance are intimately linked – through the replication and storage of information mainly in the DNA of our genes. Variations come about through several kinds of error in copying the information from one generation to the next, and from the mixing of diverse contributions from both parents in sexual reproduction. Occasionally *symbiosis* will bring together more radically divergent sources of information/experience of how to survive, and this seems to have engendered major leaps forward in the success of the life forms combining in this way. For example, the incorporation by certain primitive single-celled organisms of oxygen-burning bacteria – ancestral mitochondria – provided a huge boost in the energy supply for what became our eukaryote forebears (eukaryotes being complex cells with nuclei and other organelles, contrasting with the simpler prokaryotes, namely Bacteria and Archaea). Without this facility, advanced life forms would not exist.

Selection may be the 'vanilla' version of hazards and challenges like climate change, meteorite impact, an unlucky local landslip, or invading species that are simply better-adapted to outcompete; or it may be specifically driven by sexual preference or wider co-evolutionary processes. Typically an organism must simultaneously contend with diverse selection pressures, so the result is usually some kind of compromise in 'fitness space'. This is a multidimensional manifold of possible variations characterized by peaks, plains and valleys. Dawkins's book *Climbing Mount Improbable* (1996) describes how variation and adaptive advantage in relation to selection pressures can, through gradual steps, ratchet a species up to a pinnacle of fitness. In nature, however, the variation is blind, and in the unbroken chain of living generations, every single heritable variation must either convey some immediate adaptive benefit or at least be neutral. Thus an organism may be marooned on a local peak and unable to move to a higher one just across the plain because to do so would require entering an intermediate state of maladaptation, hence diminished reproductive chances relative to predators, competing conspecifics etc. Leaps directly across space from one peak to another through 'lucky' mutations or other copying errors are extremely rare, but inter-species sharing of DNA (e.g. via viruses) can occasionally produce otherwise impossible advances, as can inheritable forms of symbiosis, as described.

By this simple and mindless process of variation, selection and transmission, nature generates 'endless forms most beautiful' (Darwin, 1859, p. 489) – and some pretty ugly ones too. Several elaborations deserve mention, which are now, or may be in future, useful for thinking about terrorism in co-evolutionary terms.

Evolution as learning and hypothesizing

Evolution has been described as a kind of *learning* process at the species level, wherein genetic variations can be viewed as 'hypotheses' about predictable elements of an organism's customary environment including dangers and risks, and of what works to enable an organism to survive and reproduce there (Vermeij, 2008). (An earlier and related formulation is Campbell's (1974) concept of 'evolutionary epistemology', where our academic theories are tested by practical implementation to see if they achieve the anticipated and desired changes in the real world.) The knowledge accumulated is not only about how to survive, but also by extension about the nature of the 'environment of evolutionary adaptedness' (EEA) (Bowlby, 1969) itself. Thus for example our genes have come to 'know' that we live on a planet with a certain strength of gravity, an oxygen atmosphere, dangerous predators, poisonous snakes, etc.

Niche construction and the 'extended phenotype'

A new basic evolutionary process, *niche construction*, has recently come to the fore (e.g. Laland *et al.*, 2009). This takes account of the fact that many species, perhaps most, do not simply adapt to their environment as it is, but in one way or another *shape* that environment. This may initially be accidental – for example some herbivores may graze plants down so only certain species survive (the familiar example being grass, adapted to being chopped off from above by growing from the base rather than the tips) so the landscape they occupy actually becomes a more suitable niche for their talents to exploit. (The grass example also exemplifies positive co-evolution.) Humans are, of course, the arch niche-constructors, whether those niches are in the material or social world, or both.

Evolution of evolvability

Co-evolution was earlier described as an accelerant of evolution. Another accelerant is the *evolution of evolvability* (Dawkins, 2003). This refers to the fact that some organisms, generally the more complex ones, evolve sets of genes that facilitate the generation of variety. Moreover this is not just random variety, where the chances are that such a spanner dropped into the works of a complex machine will be more likely to harm than help, but variants that have a good chance of survival and possibly of conferring benefit. Kirschner and Gerhart (2005) describe how vertebrates and other advanced animals have a well-organized suite of genetic switches (certain DNA sequences which turn genes on and off during development to guide the formation of limbs, body segments etc.). This is in effect a high-level computer language of structural design and development which sits on top of the fundamental code in 0s and 1s (or in DNA terms, codons of AAC, GTC, etc.). The upshot is that the organism in possession of such suites of genes and gene switches, can through mutation and sexual recombination of genes generate *orderly* variety of, say, limb length, shell shape, or neck musculature: candidates for adaptation that ab initio fit as a workable proposition with the rest of the body, rather than just a limp and squidgy mess. Kirschner and Gerhart entitle their book *The Plausibility of Life*, referring to the fact that the new proposals (or hypotheses) for survival are not nonsense strings but eminently sensible. A metaphorical way of looking at this is to consider how Mozart, even in his first drafts of pieces, could come up with beautiful music straight from the fingertips: he had the capacity to generate musically plausible variety.

Handling unpredictability

If biological evolution is about genetic learning, it can only learn about those aspects of the environment that stay constant over a long enough timescale to supply consistent selection pressures to shape the genes. Crude facts about the environment (such as the presence of gravity and the need to respect it by not falling out of tall trees) will be learned within a generation or two; subtler facts, or those which are stochastic and involve a lot of good or bad luck (such as how strong particular branches on particular types of tree are) will take longer. But however much invariance-knowledge the genes can extract from the environment, there will be sufficient 'slings and arrows of outrageous fortune' for the world to remain a very unpredictable place from the gene's eye view. *Cognitive* learning evolved to extract local invariances that remain valid for periods *less* than a generation – for example, that the trees around here (which grew rapidly in exceptionally warm conditions) are *not* to be relied on despite the superficially reassuring girth of their branches. Unsurprisingly, those species that invest in building and maintaining brains capable of supporting cognitive learning tend to live longer. But again, there is no escaping the huge amount of unpredictability that remains to challenge the chances of any individual, or species, surviving and reproducing. Some of this unpredictability revolves around 'known unknowns', such as whether there is a lion around the next rock (or an IED under the next culvert), where the prey can, through inductive learning at a cognitive or genetic level, estimate some prior probability; some will be nonlinear 'unknown unknowns', like the outbreak of an entirely new disease, or the arrival of a new predator species with exceptional night vision. In an arms race context, the co-evolutionary feedback between, say, predator and prey means that one source of unpredictability is how the predator will respond to one's own new defence. The implications of unpredictability for terrorism are pretty self-evident and will be revisited in detail below.

With certain rare exceptions, humans are the only species that has evolved the capacity to go beyond inductive learning to explicitly *anticipate* hazards including those that originate from enemy action (and indeed, from enemy countermoves to one's own first moves). Two facilities underlie this capacity: perception and modelling of *causation*, and *theory of mind* (e.g. Whiten, 2006) – involving the perception of other people's point of view and specifically of their intentions. More generally, humans can imagine their own actions and their consequences both regarding the material world; and the reactions of other people and groups (not that they always get it right). As Popper put it (1972), we humans can let our ideas die in our stead – in other words, we discover the flaws in some action by imagining doing it and seeing how it could go wrong, rather than always having to learn the hard way.

Humans, too, have evolved to be unpredictable predators par excellence. Tooby and DeVore (1987) argue that the evolution of human intelligence allows us to mount evolutionary 'surprise attacks' which escalate the arms race against prey, such that the latter cannot keep up through their own biologically evolving counter-adaptations which are more limited in scope and slower to emerge. When we try this against our human enemies, of course, the tactical advantage of surprise is still a potent one, but the enemy may be on the alert, may have anticipated some such move, and may have some surprises of their own in store.

The units of evolution

Terrorism and security are predominantly group-related activities. A major, unresolved argument in evolutionary science is over the existence of group-level selection. Early assumptions about particular adaptations being 'good for the *species*' were revealed as nebulous, a trend culminating in the perspective of adaptations being 'good for the selfish *genes*' (Dawkins, 1976). But authors including sociobiologist Edward O. Wilson (1975) argue for an independent, additional influence of group-level selection especially, but not exclusively, with reference to 'eusocial' species such as ants or humans where major manifestations of altruism seem to occur. Indeed, the more recent concept of multilevel selection (e.g. Okasha, 2006) covers not just evolution at the level of groups but incorporates a whole hierarchy of potential genetic/evolutionary units including also the intense symbiosis between the once-independent-living cellular components of eukaryote organisms (mitochondria and chloroplasts), and the functional interdependence of groups of genes. (To illustrate, the genes enabling perception and those enabling response are useless without one another, both being needed for their mutual survival and replication.) Recent arguments on the status of multilevel selection are at http://edge.org/conversation/the-false-allure-of-group-selection and by D. Sloan Wilson (2012). Whether or not it is profitable to apply multilevel selection within biological evolution, the case for it is rather clearer with cultural evolution, to which we shortly turn.

The evolutionary algorithm – universal Darwinism

Dennett (1995) describes the variation-selection-inheritance process as the *evolutionary algorithm*; and like all such abstractions, suggests it can be applied, in pretty much the same form, to understand a wide range of other 'substrate' processes including the functioning of the immune system, thinking processes in the brain and instrumental (trial and error) learning. The perspective now known as 'Universal Darwinism' (e.g. Dawkins, 1983; Dietl, 2008) addresses the wider applicability of the algorithm. Cultural evolution is one such extension. But such is the power of the concept that we can even see explicit, recursive uses *within* human scientific/technological culture, in the form of genetic algorithms for finding the best combinations of new materials out of vast numbers of alternatives, and for coming up with solutions to complex mathematical and practical problems that cannot be directly computed.

Some of these may even end up in the service of counterterrorism, as with developing armour and optimizing patrol/surveillance schedules.

'Darwinizing culture'

Human culture is an evolutionary invention which has transformed our evolutionary capabilities – an example of the evolution of evolvability at many levels (including the example just given). As a concept, culture itself is notoriously hard to define (Spencer-Oatey, 2012). However, Richerson and Boyd (2005, p. 5) offer a definition sufficiently generic and abstract to handle the diversity of human culture while meaningfully connecting with evolutionary concepts:

> Culture is information capable of affecting individuals' behavior that they acquire from other members of their species through teaching, imitation, and other forms of social transmission. By information, we mean any kind of mental state, conscious or not, that is acquired or modified by social learning, and affects behavior.

Transmission of information through culture can occur both vertically – as an extra-genetic storage-and-retrieval system for knowledge accumulated over generations – and horizontally – as in peer-to-peer sharing. The transmission process may differ in significant ways from the standard biological model – for example, we may well envisage Lamarckian inheritance of acquired characteristics. Verbal encoding of knowledge has meant that the inheritance of such information has progressed from the low-fidelity reproduction of photocopies-of-photocopies, which rapidly become a blur, to a digital level of precision (just like DNA).This is particularly so, when know-how is represented as instructional procedures (Blackmore, 1999), for example in *how to make* an origami boat rather than, say, a *description* of the end product.

Human culture is of course the substrate for evolution of both terrorist-type ideologies and motives and their antagonists, and the tactics of attack and defence that are the subject of this chapter. Human culture has undoubtedly *itself* been evolving, and authors (e.g. Richerson and Boyd, 2005) make the convincing case that the same evolutionary algorithm is at work (Aunger, 2000 entitles his anthology *Darwinizing Culture*). We can readily see processes of variation, selection and inheritance on scales ranging from catchy tunes, to designs for weapons, to religions. The concept of *memes* (Dawkins, 1976; Blackmore, 1999) treats such items and complexes of knowledge as replicators similar to genes, with ourselves and our technologies of information storage and dissemination as vehicles. From a meme's eye-view, we humans are their means of replication and memes are in competition with one another for brain-space and airtime. Sometimes, as with rival scientific hypotheses or extreme political ideologies, memes are in conflict. Mechanisms of cultural replication are diverse and operate on different scales. Godfrey-Smith

(2012) distinguishes: imitative selection from the population of intra-cultural variants of behaviour (i.e. individuals choosing what/who to copy); cumulative cultural adaptation (e.g. adjustments to climate change); and the most macro-level, 'cultural phylogenetic change'. The last, for example, comprises radical discontinuities like the Neolithic revolution shifting societies from hunting/gathering to farming; and industrialization.

The most recent such cultural phylogenetic change has arguably been the emergence of information technology, starting first with writing, moving on to printing, then to telecommunications, to computing and finally to the combined culmination of all these in the form of the Internet and other distributed systems. IT acts as a significant accelerant, in facilitating the development and dissemination of knowledge of terrorist and counterterrorist practice in the material world – for example, how to anonymously move funds, or obtain assets such as explosives or detonators online. It also is inherently faster to evolve, since what is changing is code and code-based systems, with far fewer constraints than the material world imposes. Both terrorists and security can swiftly upgrade their software or hardware.

A diversity of arms races

Extending the scope of the co-evolutionary process from biological to cultural domains enables us to consider, and learn from, adaptive strategies and tactics in a range of natural, human and mixed arms races. These are listed in Box 4.1.

Box 4.1 A diversity of arms races

The natural world

Prey versus predators (confronters, trappers, dupers), mainly resembling crimes against the person – assault, robbery, homicide

Plant versus herbivore grazing – taking stored energy and materials from plants, resembling theft

Host versus parasite parasitism by insects, tapeworms, etc. – resembling theft

Host immune system versus pathogen (overcoming host's defences) infection by bacteria, etc. – resembling robbery

Host immune system versus viral pathogen infection by viruses, resembling fraud or embezzlement in misappropriation of resources for and control of production; computer hacking (breaking access and control codes), and computer viruses themselves

Natural 'theft or robbery' within or between species – e.g. birds taking each other's nest sticks, or seizing others' food in mid-air attacks

Natural 'fraud' – e.g. birds taking nectar by pecking a hole in the side of the flower to avoid the effort required to pass on pollen, orchids pretending to be female wasps and cheating males of reproductive effort and opportunity

Natural 'threat, assault' or killing – conflict over territory, mates, food

Humanity versus nature

Disease control – hygiene, public health, inoculation, vaccination, antibiotics – resembling prevention of theft/robbery

Pest control – rats etc. spoiling/stealing crops or livestock, spreading human diseases, acting offensively – resembling prevention of theft/damage, disorder/nuisance

The human world

Military arms races and (counter)terrorism – arms versus armour, missiles versus electronic countermeasures, manoeuvrability – resembling assault and prevention of assault, homicide, disorder, theft of property, coercion, control of production

War-games and other simulation military training – e.g. evolution of new strategies in chess; computer-games of tactics and strategy

Economic warfare – outgrowing the enemy or disrupting their economy (shading into real crimes like forgery or extortion)

Hacking

Espionage military/industrial, to steal information on resources, products, tactics and strategy, shading into theft of information/obtaining it in preparation for crime.

(Adapted from Ekblom, 1999)

Military arms races demonstrate many examples of castles versus cannon, tanks versus bazookas, planes with electronic countermeasures versus missiles with counter-countermeasures. The military has only had a few millennia to evolve equipment and tactics but natural arms races rather longer. Co-evolution between predator and prey has at least 600 million years of experience to offer. The long struggle between pathogens and immune system has resulted in dynamic and adaptive strategies on each side. This has culminated in such sophisticated attackers as the HIV and smallpox viruses. Smallpox (Dunlop *et al.*, 2003) has over 80 genes that interact with human defence mechanisms. In fact it has evolved counter-countermeasures to cope for example with a 'virus alert' chemical produced by infected cells, whose function is to warn nearby uninfected cells to activate their defences against virus attack. At some stage the smallpox virus 'stole' a length of DNA from the human host, which coded for the host cells' receptor molecules for the virus alert chemical. When the smallpox virus invades a host cell it can therefore direct the cell to produce bogus receptor molecules which blot up the alert chemical. This masks the alarm signal so uninfected host cells are unprepared to resist the virus. It is ironic – but perhaps no coincidence – that one threat seriously considered by security services is that terrorists may acquire smallpox viruses from scientific repositories, the disease having been eradicated in the wild. Another interesting cross-link is the 'infection' model of the transmission of terrorist ideology or memes (Lafferty *et al.*, 2008).

Vermeij (2008), quoted at the beginning of this chapter, argues that there is enough in common to these co-evolutionary struggles for human security to learn many useful lessons. But what, exactly, is 'common'? Protracted competition and conflict between agencies which vary in their characteristics, adapt, differentially survive and replicate inherited or otherwise cumulatively developed characteristics. All the struggles (whether they are mediated by gene-based evolution or some other process such as rational thought) are pursued through development in tactics, strategy, and evolution of design. All involve exploitation of disturbances on one side and sufferance of their consequences on the other. The fundamental problem faced by the participants in each struggle is identical:

1 how to maximize positive consequences and minimize negative ones using the minimum of resources;
2 when enemies or rivals are doing the same;
3 against a background of disturbances which may favour, and/or be exploited, by one side or the other.

Co-evolution and terrorism

It's now time to connect the basics and the details of evolution as just described, to terrorism and security, drawing on the insights of both genetic and culturally mediated processes.

Beyond immediate survival

Arms races can seem an exercise in futility, an endless spiral of adaptation and counter-adaptation with first one party, then the other, gaining momentary advantage. Indeed, biological arms races have been described as a 'Red Queen's Game' (from Lewis Carroll's *Alice through the Looking Glass*), in which you must keep running merely to remain in the same place (van Valen, 1973; see also Schneier, 2012 for a detailed exploration of security implications). As Vermeij (2008) notes, in biology those lineages that cannot adapt to the latest weapons of predators are ecologically marginalized, though rarely completely extinguished (typically finding themselves modest niches as insectivores or bottom-feeders). A similar fate may await those societies that cannot, or will not, keep up in the arms race. At present, this may seem unlikely in Western industrial nations (although the rise of fascist dictatorships and communism in the twentieth century came close to eclipsing democracy) but in the long-term, who knows? And some human conflicts differ from natural ones in the deliberate pursuit of extermination of cultures or ethnic groups.

Unpredictability

According to Vermeij (2008) the greatest challenge to security, and the hardest to adapt to, is uncertainty. Terrorists readily exploit unpredictability in both their tactics and their strategic goals. That unpredictability relates to both 'known' and 'unknown' unknowns (respectively, for example, the time and place of the next AK47 attack, versus flying a passenger plane into a tall building). However, given the rapid horizontal spread of information among human groups the 'surprise attacks' rapidly cease to be surprising – silver bullets turn to lead. I previously referred to such episodes as 'breakouts with transient advantage' (Ekblom, 1999), like the invention of the tank in the First World War. In a related fashion, security measures also become obsolescent. The rate of obsolescence will depend on the kinds of offenders involved, their resources, and the kinds of social and technological changes that occur.

Variation, acceleration and the evolution of evolvability

Human ingenuity in generating variations, say, of methods of attack and defence is boundless. The 'dark side of creativity' is explored by Cropley *et al.* (2010; Cropley and Cropley, 2013). As in biological evolution, certain human inventions boost adaptive potential. Ekblom and Pease (2014) discuss this concept further in relation to adaptive criminals, citing for example 'script kiddies' (software kits enabling amateurs to generate effective computer viruses). Because of this acceleration in technologically induced change, the breathing space we get from a new preventive method, before it is bypassed, is tending to diminish. Other cultural phylogenetic changes coming up which are potentially equally momentous are in artificial intelligence/robotics and biotechnology/genetic engineering. Taylor (2008) notes that DNA synthesis became more than 500 times faster between 1990–2000; it also became more automated and black-boxed so progressively less tacit knowledge is needed to employ the technology of synthetic genomics, which could be misused, say, in producing crop-destroying or ethnically targeted pathogens.

Niche construction

Vermeij (2004) notes that all scales of economic life, from cells to ecosystems, from firms to states, influence their own evolution by being both the object of selection and the creator of the conditions of that selection. Terrorists and security organizations alike seek to foster supportive environments – whether this is for the ready provision of safe houses and moral support and the recruitment or corruption of security officials, or (on the opposing side) the public/political acceptance of intrusive surveillance.

Lessons from co-evolution

We are now in a position to draw together some lessons for how to handle the co-evolutionary nature of terrorism. As I previously observed (Ekblom, 1997, 1999) regarding crime in general, a perusal of natural history sources (and a long history of watching wildlife programmes by David Attenborough and others with a 'security affordance' mindset) revealed the difficulty of coming up with specific, tangible interventions from nature that humans had not already culturally reinvented for themselves. The classic example here is the lizard's detachable tail (e.g. see www.youtube.com/watch?v=rQkWn4jodbY), designed to distract predators: British police uniform ties detach at the neck to avoid strangulation by criminals.

More promising are lessons of biological and human design and engineering relating to use of materials, structures and mechanisms, and how to trade off the conflicting requirements between security and, say, effort in foraging or in constructing convenient but defensible buildings. These are explored below.

But the main theme of this chapter, and the most promising level of approach, is at the level of campaigns, not individual battles – where victories are soon eroded by adaptive terrorists and/or technological game-changers – but by running or avoiding arms races.

Running arms races

The following list of suggestions has developed from my own earlier thinking (Ekblom, 1997, 1999) and is significantly supplemented by other authors. Inevitably there is some overlap between the headings. In all that follows, similar opportunities and constraints apply to the terrorists and to the security sides: hence, we will be flipping perspectives quite often.

Before proceeding, I should emphasize that each human or human/nature struggle from which lessons may be drawn has its own ethical issues – what is acceptable in war, espionage or pest control is not necessarily appropriate for civil security. Application of transferred knowledge must therefore be sensitively done.

Handling unpredictability of terrorists

Terrorists have made a thing of unpredictability, both for good tactical reasons and also for wider strategic benefit to convey an image of superiority. How does biological evolution handle unpredictability? Vermeij (2008: 30–35), drawing on an encyclopaedic view of evolutionary strategies, lists the following, with my own interpretations in brackets:

- Passive tolerance
- Active engagement with the enemy
- Striving to increase predictability by observing the habitat over longer periods and wider spatial tracts, and investing in the intelligence to analyse a greater proportion of invariance (Likewise, the security side can limit observation of its own defensive tactics and assets. Users of online banking are familiar with the technique of partial use of passwords as in 'enter the third and sixth digits'.)
- Being unpredictable oneself (as with rarity, dispersal, the zigzag flights of moths aiming to confuse bats, or Hannibal Lecter's observation on the locations of the serial killer's victims in *The Silence of the Lambs* movie 'Clarice, doesn't this random scattering of sites seem *desperately* random?'. The accumulation of a diverse stock of 'silver bullets' on the security side may be useful here. The development of military counterparts by Lockheed's 'Skunk Works' design facility is described by Rich and Janos (1994).)
- Quarantine, isolation and starvation (e.g. Russia's scorched earth strategy against Napoleon's invading army, and 'hearts-and-minds' campaigns to deny terrorists support)
- Redundancy
- Adaptability, for example through semi-autonomous components under weak central authority, flexibility and rapid communication between parts, and combinatorial generation of variety

Prescott (2008) also suggests the importance of developing *flexible responses* which do not fire every time with consequent cost and disruption (thinking for example of the feed-or-flee choice that suspends foraging birds on a knife edge of decision-making between breadcrumbs and lurking cat). Also, of developing adaptive/security responses which are *generalized*, so they are less likely than a specialized defence, to be caught out by a new one-off attack (an example being our generalized 'innate immune system' which complements the highly specific antibody-based one that must learn about each individual pathogen).

Johnson and Madin (2008) note that *insurance* is an approach to mitigation of unpredictable disasters. In biological terms this is a form of 'preadaptation' to novel threats. In human terms, insurance can be both individualistic (e.g. storing food in case of an electricity disruption) or mutual. With the latter, however, insurance companies strongly prefer to cater only for those risks where past actuarial data is available, often excluding coverage of terrorist attack and leaving any compensation to governments.

Anticipation

Despite the challenging nature of terrorist unpredictability, 'investing in intelligence' enables humans to undertake some modest anticipation. Anticipation can cover both terrorists' first moves and their countermeasures, i.e. adaptations to the security response. It can also cover forecasting what might come up on the preventive side.

- The methods of foresight/horizon scanning (e.g. see DTI (2000) and Collins and Mansell (2004)) can be applied to terrorism and its control. Experience from that field indicates the risk of betting on very specific predictions; instead, the approach is to identify a wide envelope of possible futures and ensure security plans are valid across them all.
- Techniques like *technology road-mapping* can identify upcoming inventions, and the steps that still need to be taken before some tool or weapon becomes a practical proposition for terrorists or security. (The same applies to anticipating new viral infections – where health researchers have determined, say, that a particular pig-hosted virus strain is only two mutations away from acquiring human-to-human transmissibility.)
- The TRIZ approach to inventive principles, further discussed below, has accumulated a set of evolutionary trends in invention that may be used to identify where, in some specific engineering domain (e.g. armour), new inventions may be expected, and what kind of invention that might be (e.g. move from rigid connection to flexible link).
- *Crime impact statements* can be developed for proposed new tools, trading practices etc., identifying aspects which may supply new opportunities for terrorists and/or render existing preventive measures obsolete. These can be based on crime prevention theory (Ekblom, 2002b) or practice principles (Monchuk and Clancey, 2013).
- We can encourage a 'think terrorist' mindset to consider their next adaptive moves. The *Misdeeds and Security framework* (Ekblom, 2005, 2008) helps to systematically ponder ways in which new technology, systems, procedures etc. can generate opportunities for offending: misappropriation (theft), mistreatment (damage or injury), mishandling (e.g. smuggling), misbegetting (counterfeit), misuse (as tool or weapon) and mistake (e.g. false alarms or wrongful accusation). Counterpart categories enable similar anticipation of emerging opportunities on the security side.
- It is important to identify and block as many terrorist countermeasures as possible, perhaps through the use of 'attack trees' (e.g. Schneier, 1999), which tease out the widest range of alternative methods by which they can realize their attack), but beware diminishing returns and disproportionate 'over-engineering' of solutions.
- We must anticipate that even the best preventive method will have a limited lifespan, the aim being to develop ones slower to become obsolete. Military co-evolution supplies the concept of exploiting momentary advantage (e.g. that afforded by a new kind of fortification: useful for a while, even though it is soon countered by a new projectile).

Coping with the limits of anticipation

- Where anticipation fails, we should gear up for faster response to handle 'crime harvests' (Pease, 2001), by accelerating the learning curve for designers of preventive measures. Setting up learning paths, involving systematic assembly of attack incident information of the right kind (e.g. how the lock was broken/the security code was obtained/circumvented), can guide suitable adjustments. In effect this is quickly shutting the stable door before the *next* horse bolts.
- More generally, we should anticipate design failure or obsolescence by incorporating the possibility for remedy, making the inevitable retrofit solution easier, as discussed under design, below.

Adaptation in general

Having the capacity to evolve, learn and upgrade is as important as possessing any individual defensive feature which gives temporary advantage. Since adaptation, and the adaptability of both terrorists and the security side, are central to exploiting (co-)evolutionary perspectives on terrorism, we should understand how it works in some depth. Here are some aspects worth considering:

- Blumstein (2008) maintains that we must develop better understanding of how species respond to novel threats. In particular, do these require truly novel responses, or can we adapt responses that have evolved for some, possibly every day, purpose (the technical term is 'exaptation')? A similar point is made by Johnson and Madin (2008) who note that those adaptations that can be co-opted to alternative uses, protect against both commonplace and unpredictable threats. Counterterrorism strategies should likewise seek versatility rather than pared-down specificity to known threats.
- Adaptation often involves knowledge spread, or its equivalent, and the appropriate defence is to minimize opportunities for offenders to learn or pass on that learning. In biological evolution, exchange of plasmids enables bacteria to horizontally swap DNA 'knowledge', including that coding for antibiotic resistance. Whether any bacteriologists have discovered inhibitors of such transfers would be interesting to discover.
- Technology transfer in particular may be prevented by 'capture-proofing' equipment. The equipment is made difficult to operate without training; spares are difficult to obtain; it self-destructs, or stops working without authorization. This strategy applies to the literal transfer of military weapons to terror attacks. It could also apply to the 'hacking' of everyday equipment and applications which could be converted to terrorist misuse.

- Given that knowledge of target and procedural vulnerabilities, and of methods of attack, once developed, are likely to proliferate rapidly over the Internet, it is necessary, further, to devise preventive measures that are difficult for offenders to overcome, even if they know how they work (some encryption systems rely on offenders not possessing massive computing power and/or infinite time, although quantum computing may invalidate this).
- Security measures should not be specified as fixed construction standards, like incorporating particular types of lock or using particular resistant materials, but to *performance* standards (e.g. 'the lock must withstand 20 Newton force and resist expert picking for 20 minutes'). This slows obsolescence, and frees designers to devise diverse solutions rather than constraining them to a single one whose vulnerabilities can quickly be transmitted among attackers. It also prevents manufacturers from absolving themselves from responsibility by 'designing down' to minimum construction specifications. Terrorists faced with uncertainty about what preventive systems they may find in the next place they reconnoitre or attack, are at a tactical and psychological disadvantage. Ekblom and Hirschfield (2014), in identifying 11 generic mechanisms of influencing terrorists at an attack site, thus distinguish between 'deter-known' and 'deter-unknown'.
- Adaptability also implies avoidance of *phylogenetic constraint* (Raup, 1993). This is where an evolved security or defence system becomes so complex and integrated, that radical redesign is impossible, only minor adjustment. A related issue is developing ways to cope with rapid change. In both cases, we must discover which kinds of security adaptations have preserved flexibility, and which have led to rigidity and constraint (Vermeij, 2004). More generally, we on the security side want to avoid evolutionary blind alleys of prevention; or conversely, exploit those blind alleys by shaping offenders into them, causing them to specialize in ways which are slow and costly to reverse (but we should also beware of *adverse* shaping of terrorists towards more harmful methods of attack).
- Unfortunately, the 'plus ça change' hypothesis (Sheldon, 1996) suggests that the kind of rapidly changing social/technological environment humans have now created, is more likely to favour generalist rather than specialist adaptive strategies – a lesson that applies to both sides.
- Another constraining factor is *field obsolescence* – that is, where we have developed a new, more secure product or system but it takes time and money for the current, less secure, versions to be replaced. The classic example is the older generation of cars lacking steering locks (Webb, 1994), where the half-life for replacement was about a decade. Tackling this problem can involve a switch from vertical to horizontal transmission of change such as 'broadcast' security upgrades of the kind we get with our software operating systems, or product recalls for cars. With

material products like buildings, we can design-in the capacity for easy upgrades such as more secure door fittings. Rather than over-engineering the doors on every school or government office, say, we can design the door frames to swap-out higher-security fittings only where and when necessary, in the light of threat assessments.

- A strategic point on *resources* is made by Johnson and Madin (2008), who argue that adaptations require substantial allocation of energy and time, constraining competing functions under a fixed budget. A complementary strategy to the 'exaptation' of routine security measures to extreme but rare terrorist attacks, mentioned above, is to ensure that security measures designed to address these should also confer more day-to-day benefit in, say, crime control or transportation safety. Another resource management strategy Johnson and Madin identify derives from the immune system's ability to tick over at a low level of energy expenditure until it encounters a threat, when it can rapidly ramp up a highly targeted response. This fits nicely with attempts to provide graduated 'bronze, silver and gold' responses to repeat victimization (Chenery *et al.*, 1997). They also note the dangers of inappropriate or overreaction, where immune responses can drain the organism's resources, with obvious lessons for security and life in general. The balance between active and passive resistance is therefore tricky to determine (Vermeij, 2008).
- Johnson and Madin further state the importance of allocating *rolling budgets*, rather than one-off lump sums, to security. This is part of a wider evolutionary/ecological analysis of the sources of resistance to adaptive change: we humans normally wait for a disaster to trigger significant action rather than anticipate and avoid it. In this connection, Johnson and Madin's contribution deserves close attention if we wish to avoid anticipation failure and/or implementation failure. Rolling budgets support ongoing anticipation, maintenance of expertise and information flows, and perhaps '*pipelines*' of a succession of new security measures ready to put into place in the expectation that current ones are a wasting asset and will soon become outdated. This approach is well-developed in, for example, the domain of credit cards and pay-tv services.

Adaptation: redundancy and resilience

Sagarin and Taylor (2008), Prescott (2008) and especially Vermeij (2008) identify several interlinked principles from evolutionary history which confer resilience. These include redundancy; distributed rather than centralized functions, with diffuse control relying on multiple, semi-autonomous units rather than hierarchy; integration; and flexibility. Likewise Edwards's (2009) review of resilience calls for society not just to resist and respond to current challenges, but to anticipate, and be ready to adapt to, future ones.

Adaptation: the importance of variety

Variety of preventive measures, and the ability to generate *plausible* variations (see next section), is a vital challenge to terrorist tactics. Uniform security systems or devices are often installed for reasons of economy of funds and effort, but – like crop monocultures facing a new mutant fungus – this could be a case of 'crack one security measure, crack them all'. The more genetically *diverse* the potential hosts of disease, the more restricted is the scope for any one type of pathogen to attack them (Wills, 1996; Colinvaux, 1980).

To further exploit variety, it is useful to act on several fronts simultaneously (like multiple antibiotic regimes), such as hardening target assets while improving surveillance, to introduce some redundancy and/or synergy into security measures.

Adaptation: design, innovation, creativity and anti-creativity

Producing variety equates to innovation. Arms races seek to out-innovate the opposition. Innovation is about the successful exploitation of new ideas; creativity is the generation of new ideas; and design is what links creativity and innovation, shaping ideas to become practical and attractive propositions for users or customers, that is, creativity deployed to a specific end (HM Treasury, 2005, p. 2). We have already seen how natural systems can generate plausible designs, and noted the contribution of theory (specifically, crime science theory) in supplying that plausibility. This is irrespective of whether that theory originates in a human scientific process, or as accumulation of genetic hypotheses about what works for this species in this habitat. We have also acknowledged the significance of the evolution of evolvability: the human capacity to innovate through design is an example of this bootstrapping process, supported by a combination of genetic and culturally mediated accumulation and transmission of knowledge and know-how.

Unfortunately innovative capacity is as much available to terrorists as to the security side (Ekblom and Pease, 2014). But innovative capacity is best exploited through the consistent employment of the design *process*, not by lifting individual innovations off-the-shelf as products to deploy in individual evolutionary surprise attacks; and here, the security side should be able to gain intellectual advantage if it applies sufficient, sustained attention and resources to design.

In biological evolution, the exploration of fitness space is constrained to the local and the immediately advantageous, as described. Only human learning and cultural evolution are capable of looking, and leaping, across the valley separating a local fitness maximum from a far higher peak. We are able to do this because we can take the generation of variety, and the testing of possible responses, 'offline' from immediate biological survival (a rephrasing of Popper's point cited above) and into an imaginary and/or otherwise protected world. Here, evolution still operates, with our theory, and our prototype practical realizations, exposed to the selection pressure of searching appraisal and rigorous evaluation; but with a degree of tolerance that allows failures to be resurrected and modified rather than having to be reinvented all over again. Only when such innovations have reached a certain level of plausibility are they deployed in the field and exposed to real-world selection pressures (or not, as the discussion of evaluation reveals, below). Design embedded in a research and development process offers a systematic way of doing this.

Of course, the richer the stock of theoretical principles to draw on, and the more readily these can be accessed and recombined, the better-equipped are designers to generate plausible candidate innovations. This is equivalent to the diversity of genes we enjoy for protection against pathogens – and those they possess against us, as already described for smallpox. Theoretical frameworks, especially those that are comprehensive, integrated and well-articulated, can be useful here. Examples aspiring to these standards are the 'conjunction of terrorist opportunity' (CTO) on causes and interventions against terrorist events (Roach *et al.*, 2005; and see Chapter 3 in this volume by Ekblom, Sidebottom and Wortley); the 'misdeeds and security framework' (Ekblom, 2005) for identifying generic crime/terrorism risks involving designed products/technologies; the risk factors approach of terrorist target selection known as EVIL DONE (exposed, vital, iconic, legitimate, destructible, occupied, near and easy) (Clarke and Newman, 2006); and the theoretical/practical 'security function framework' for specifying security designs (Meyer and Ekblom, 2011). Most are summarized in Ekblom (2014).

Many terrorist groups allow themselves a free hand with violence and intrusion on people's lives. But the actions, and defensive equipment, open to the security side to create and deploy, are far more constrained. We must respect diverse 'requirements tradeoffs' between security and human rights, sustainability, aesthetics, economic growth, and avoidance of fear and fortification. The essence of design is to identify and creatively resolve such tradeoffs. (The huge metal 'Arsenal' sign at London's Emirates football stadium is the classic example, being designed to covertly protect against explosive-laden trucks ramming into the stadium.) This echoes a similar process in biological evolution: Prescott (2008) notes that extant organisms are descendants of those that got the balance right between security and other survival priorities. High-performance natural predators like cheetahs must trade off speed against the strength/weight to fend off hyenas wishing to steal their kill. Likewise such tradeoffs routinely occur in commercial and military engineering. Military aircraft require a combination of offensive and defensive capabilities, and face severe and complex tradeoffs of weight/manoeuvrability/damage resistance/damage tolerance/reliability/cost.

Articulating and resolving tradeoffs is highly developed in engineering design, for example through TRIZ, the theory of inventive principles (Ekblom, 2012b; and see www.triz-journal.com/triz-what-is-triz). This has identified some 39 generic 'contradictions,' and 40 'inventive principles' previously used to resolve them; and through 'optimization algorithms' (e.g. *Science Daily*, 2015). The identification of 'script clashes' (Ekblom, 2012b), generic procedural conflicts between offenders and preventers (e.g. pursue versus escape, conceal versus reveal, ambush versus alert) is another potentially useful approach for focusing design.

One specific way design can address the need to favour the good guys over the bad is in making products, places and procedures capable of *differentiation* – i.e. 'user-friendly, abuser-unfriendly'. The capture-proofing of weapons, previously described, is one such instance. The most strategic differentiation of all is to find ways of making it hard for terrorists to undertake design and innovation without putting brakes on the security designers and indeed those aiming to design for the rest of civil society. Space precludes coverage of how to block the dark side of creativity (e.g. see Dolnik, 2011), but essentially the strategy is to differentially throw into reverse, all those aspects of business and society that encourage and support design.

Design, however, goes beyond the steady generation and improvement of plausible ideas – important though this is – and, rather than remain satisfied with compromise, makes intuitive, ingenious leaps out of the initial frame of thinking to overcome requirements conflicts and bypass or relax tradeoffs. Sometimes this draws on new technology. An example is the arrival of the internal combustion engine, which enabled warfare to be conducted using armour *and* mobility combined (the tank), whereas in the horse-powered era it was one *or* the other. A 'jumping' strategy that occasionally occurs in the natural world is, as mentioned, through new symbiotic relationships that radically improve the resources available to a duo of species. Partnerships in the human world, of course, also bring together diverse resources and we must foster those on the security side while seeking to disrupt those on the terrorist side, for example by sowing distrust.

Designers also tend to question the assumptions behind the problem as put to them, by the clients. They advocate *reframing* of problems and solutions (see Lulham *et al.*, 2012 on reframing the anti-terrorist litter bin). This is related to the 'system operator/nine windows' technique within TRIZ that encourages engineers to look beyond the immediate problem domain to consider intervening at an earlier or later point in time, up a level to a super-system or down to a subsystem. At a strategic level, we might wish to avoid becoming locked into a pointless competitive loop of design and counter-design, for example in surveillance, counter-surveillance, counter-counter-surveillance. Therefore, we should prepare to deliberately jump out of the loop. Where technology currently favours terrorists, deliberate switching of security effort to conventional investigative security/law enforcement, man-guarding and offender-oriented approaches may be more appropriate until the balance of power reverts.

A last point about design is the utility of investing in the *infrastructure* of design against terrorism and crime. This involves creating an environment of theory, knowledge gathering and dissemination, understanding, and perhaps, even, the law which can empower designers more generally to gear up to tackle new problems as they emerge, and hopefully anticipate them too. However, as usual we must beware design infrastructure which offenders can misuse. The 3D printer, originally a design prototyping tool, has been misused to boost criminals' own capacity in, say, manufacturing accurately fitting and realistic-looking scanning mouthpieces for ATMs to read/transmit customers' card details; and in rapidly updating the shapes as soon as the bank security team modify the ATM front panel (Krebs, 2011).

Knowledge and evaluation

Knowledge-related processes play a significant part in the success, or otherwise, of security activity. Variety of response can derive from the richness of generative theory – theory which is plausible because it has been tested across a diversity of contexts. Variation also derives from empirical research, for example on the decision-making, scripts and perpetrator techniques of terrorists and other offenders, and an understanding of the mechanisms of attack and resistance, whether in humans, bacteria or larger pests like rodents. Integrated frameworks, as discussed above, draw theories together for users and designers.

A vital domain of knowledge, relevant to anticipation of attack methods and design of preventive measures, is *knowing the terrorists.* This may range from understanding their likely choice of targets, through to the constraints they operate under, to the *resources for offending* (Ekblom and Tilley, 2000; Gill, 2005) that terrorists have access to now or that they may acquire in future. Resources may range from mental (courage, skill and tactical procedures, techniques for 'neutralization' (Sykes and Matza, 1957) of norms or empathic processes) to material (weapons, logistics, etc.) and social (moral and material support).

But it is pointless risking the cost and effort we invest in developing, producing, implementing and using security-oriented designs if their principles are not *evidence-based.* Applied researchers set up their own selection pressures in the form of *evaluation* and evaluation criteria to test the fitness of particular practices (and perhaps of the theories that have generated those practices). Unfortunately, in the 'what works?' literature, a systematic review (Lum *et al.*, 2009) of over 20,000 accounts of anti-terrorist strategies, implemented at some unknown but doubtless enormous total cost, yielded only *seven* moderately rigorous evaluations from which policy-relevant conclusions might be drawn.

Of course, there is unique difficulty in applying traditional social/operational research methods to evaluate interventions intended to block extremely rare events; but there is no escaping that this is shameful neglect. It misses an enormously significant opportunity for exploiting the advantages of the 'big' side in asymmetrical conflict over the 'little' side, namely systematic research and the development of advanced, rational approaches to counterterrorism, much as science is the only hope we have for keeping up with the evolution of antibiotic resistance. (The significance of that particular arms race, and the need for a sustained and sophisticated drive to implementation, has recently been acknowledged at high level in society in the shape of the £10m 2014 Longitude Prize (www.bbc.co.uk/news/science-environment-28027376).)

It is vital nonetheless to develop alternatives to conventional evaluation. Red teaming and attack testing, including through simulations rather than the (often expensive) field exercise, are important to continue to develop, helping both to identify possible offender countermeasures and to assess the performance of security systems against them. But these tend to be rather atheoretical, so boosting them with crime science theory, attention to the detailed causal mechanisms (Tilley, 2006; Ekblom, 2011) of failure and success, and deep understanding of the tactical procedures and goals of terrorists ('scripts' – Cornish, 1994) is a necessary extension.

Beyond variation, *replication and inheritance* are difficult issues for preventive knowledge. Even when copying preventive 'success stories' as judged by good-quality evaluations, overemphasis on *literal* fidelity in replicating the action precisely is actually quite poorly adaptive to new contexts. Unfortunately, this is amply illustrated by the literature on 'implementation failure' in crime prevention (Tilley, 2006; Ekblom, 2002a, 2011). Successful replication – and innovation, where there is nothing in the trusted knowledge bank to copy – depends more on fidelity of generative *principles* of the kind based on theoretical knowledge of causal mechanisms.

As a final point it may well be easier to identify 'What *doesn't* work' – certainly every successful terrorist attack (or successful subsidiary step in such an attack) should be as instructive as it is unwelcome for the security side. And bearing in mind the turnover of the arms race we must continually test and weed even those security measures that have worked up to now (Blumstein, 2008).

Conclusion

Threats from lethal, destructive terrorist attacks will never go away, and no adaptations to them can be perfect, nor predictions reliable. The 'War on Terror' can never be won. But however futile the Red Queen's Game seems, we cease to run it at our peril. Studying evolution, and more specifically co-evolution, gives us access to knowledge of generic solutions to conflict and competition that have been tried and tested (and had their limitations and contextual supporting conditions revealed) in the very long run, over a wide range of 'universal' ecological problems faced by natural organisms of all kinds; and recapitulated over a far shorter timescale by humans in conflict with 'nature' and each other. Crime science, engineering science and design together with attention to evaluation of effectiveness, and sophisticated knowledge management, can all contribute to this repertoire through which we can hopefully out-innovate adaptive terrorists while preserving our cherished values and serving the widest range of societal priorities in a proportionate way. As noted, studying co-evolution across a range of natural, human and mixed Darwinian struggles may or may not generate specific preventive tactics and strategies. But as a fresh way of thinking about the problem of terrorism and how to combat it in the medium-to-long term, derived from some 600 million years of experience, it is surely worth adopting.

But we must also develop, and exploit, our unique ability to jump out of the loop. Solving intergroup conflicts politically is a strategy probably not found outside the realm of advanced primates. Unlike pretty much all other living creatures, we humans do have another avenue to pursue in parallel to, but not instead of, the counterterrorism arms race.

References

Anton, S., Potts, R. and Aiello, L. (2014). Evolution of early Homo: An integrated biological perspective. *Science*, 345/6192.

Aunger, R. (ed.) (2000). *Darwinizing Culture: The Status of Memetics as a Science.* Oxford: Oxford University Press.

Bassiouni, C. (2002). Legal control of international terrorism: A policy-oriented assessment. *Harvard International Law Journal*, 43 (1), 83–104.

Blackmore, S. (1999). *The Meme Machine.* Oxford: Oxford University Press.

Blumstein, D. (2008). Fourteen security lessons from antipredator behaviour. In R. Sagarin and T. Taylor (eds), *Natural Security: A Darwinian Approach to a Dangerous World.* Berkeley: University of California Press.

Bowlby, J. (1969). *Attachment and Loss.* New York: Basic Books.

Campbell, D. (1974). Evolutionary epistemology. In P. Schlipp (ed.), *The Philosophy of Karl Popper*, pp. 413–463. LaSalle, IL: Open Court.

Carrier, D. and Morgan, M. (2014). Protective buttressing of the hominin face. Biological Reviews. DOI: 10/1111/brv.12112. Available at: http://onlinelibrary.wiley.com/doi/10.1111/brv.12112/full, accessed 22 May 2015.

Chapman, J. (2004). *System Failure: Why Governments Must Learn to Think Differently.* London: Demos.

Chenery, S., Holt, J. and Pease, K. (1997). *Biting Back II: Reducing Repeat Victimisation in Huddersfield.* Crime Detection and Prevention Series Paper 82. London: Home Office.

Clarke, R. and Newman, G. (2006). *Outsmarting the Terrorists.* London: Praeger Security International.

Cohen, L., Vila, B. and Machalek, R. (1995). Expropriative crime and crime policy: An evolutionary ecological analysis. *Studies on Crime and Crime Prevention*, 4, 197–219.

Colinvaux, P. (1980). *Why Big Fierce Animals Are Rare.* Harmondsworth: Penguin.

Collins, B. and Mansell, R. (2004). *Cyber Trust and Crime Prevention: A Synthesis of the State-of-the-Art Science Reviews.* London: Department for Business, Innovation and Science. Available at: www.foresight.gov.uk/Cyber/Synthesis of the science reviews.pdf, accessed 21 January 2015.

Cornish, D. (1994). The procedural analysis of offending and its relevance for situational prevention. In R. Clarke (ed.), *Crime Prevention Studies 3.* Monsey, NY: Criminal Justice Press.

Cropley, D. and Cropley, A. (2013). *Creativity and Crime: A Psychological Analysis.* Cambridge: Cambridge University Press.

Cropley, D., Cropley, A., Kaufman, J. and Runco, M. (2010). *The Dark Side of Creativity.* Cambridge: Cambridge University Press.

Darwin, C. (1859). *On the Origin of Species*. London: John Murray.

Dawkins, R. (1976). *The Selfish Gene*. Oxford: Oxford University Press.

Dawkins, R. (1983). Universal Darwinism. In D. Bendell (ed.), *Evolution from Molecules to Man*. Cambridge: Cambridge University Press.

Dawkins, R. (1996). *Climbing Mount Improbable*. New York: Norton.

Dawkins, R. (2003). The evolution of evolvability. In S. Kumar and P. Bentley (eds), *On Growth, Form and Computers*. London: Academic Press.

Dennett, D. (1995). *Darwin's Dangerous Idea.* London: Penguin.

Dietl, G. (2008). Selection, security and evolutionary international relations. In R. Sagarin and T. Taylor (eds), *Natural Security: A Darwinian Approach to a Dangerous World*. Berkeley: University of California Press.

Dolnik, A. (2011). *Understanding Terrorist Innovation*. London: Routledge.

DTI (2000). *Turning the Corner: Report of Foresight Programme's Crime Prevention Panel.* London: Department of Trade and Industry.

Dunlop, L., Oehlberg, K., Reid, J., Avci, D. and Rosengard, A. (2003). Variola virus immune evasion proteins. *Microbes and Infection*, 5 (11), 1049–56.

Edwards, C. (2009). *Resilient Nation*. London: Demos.

Ekblom, P. (1997). Gearing up against crime: A dynamic framework to help designers keep up with the adaptive criminal in a changing world. *International Journal of Risk, Security and Crime Prevention*, 214, 249–265. Available at: www.veilig-ontwerp-beheer.nl/publicaties/gearing-up-against-crime/at_download/file, accessed 17 January 2015.

Ekblom, P. (1999). Can we make crime prevention adaptive by learning from other evolutionary struggles? *Studies on Crime and Crime Prevention* 8 (1), 27–51. Available at: www.veilig-ontwerp-beheer.nl/publicaties/can-we-make-crime-prevention-adaptive-by-learning-from-other-evolutionary-struggles/at_download/file, accessed 17 January 2015.

Ekblom, P. (2002a). From the source to the mainstream is uphill: The challenge of transferring knowledge of crime prevention through replication, innovation and anticipation. In N. Tilley (ed.), *Analysis for Crime Prevention*, Crime Prevention Studies 13, pp. 131–203. Monsey, NY: Criminal Justice Press/Devon: Willan Publishing.

Ekblom, P. (2002b). Future imperfect: Preparing for the crimes to come. *Criminal Justice Matters*, 46, 38–40. London: Centre for Crime and Justice Studies, Kings College.

Ekblom, P. (2005). How to police the future: Scanning for scientific and technological innovations which generate potential threats and opportunities in crime, policing and crime reduction. In M. Smith and N. Tilley (eds), *Crime Science: New Approaches to Preventing and Detecting Crime*. Cullompton: Willan.

Ekblom, P. (2008). Designing Products against Crime. In R. Wortley and L. Mazerolle (eds), *Environmental Criminology and Crime Analysis*. Cullompton: Willan.

Ekblom, P. (2011). *Crime Prevention, Security and Community Safety Using the 5Is Framework.* Basingstoke: Palgrave Macmillan.

Ekblom, P. (2012a). Book review of 'Liars and Outliers: Enabling the Trust that Society Needs to Thrive' by Bruce Schneier (Wiley). *Criminal Law and Criminal Justice Books*, September. Available at: http://clcjbooks.rutgers.edu/books/liars_and_outliers.html, accessed 19 January 2015.

Ekblom, P. (2012b). Happy returns: Ideas brought back from situational crime prevention's exploration of design against crime. In G. Farrell and N. Tilley (eds), *The Reasoning Criminologist: Essays in Honour of Ronald V. Clarke*, pp. 163–198. Cullompton: Willan.

Ekblom, P. (2014). Design and security. In M. Gill (ed.), *The Handbook of Security*, 2nd edn, pp. 133–156. Basingstoke: Palgrave MacMillan.

Ekblom, P. and Hirschfield, A. (2014). Developing an alternative formulation of SCP principles – the Ds (11 and counting). *Crime Science*, 3, 2.

Ekblom, P. and Pease, K. (2014). Innovation and crime prevention. In G. Bruinsma and D. Weisburd (eds), *Encyclopedia of Criminology and Criminal Justice*. New York: Springer.

Ekblom, P. and Tilley, N. (2000). Going equipped: Criminology, situational crime prevention and the resourceful offender *British Journal of Criminology*, 40, 376–398.

Gill, M. (2005). Reducing the capacity to offend: Restricting resources for offending. In N. Tilley (ed.), *Handbook of Crime Prevention and Community Safety*. Cullompton: Willan.

Godfrey-Smith, P. (2012). Darwinism and cultural change. *Philosophical Transactions of the Royal Society B*, 367, 2160–2170.

Guerette, R. and Bowers, K. (2009). Assessing the extent of crime displacement and diffusion of benefit: A systematic review of situational crime prevention evaluations. *Criminology*, 47 (4), 1331–1368.

HM Treasury (2005). *The Cox Review of Creativity in Business.* London: HM Treasury.

Johnson, D. and Madin, E. (2008). Paradigm shifts in security strategy: Why does it take disasters to trigger change? In R. Sagarin and T. Taylor (eds), *Natural Security: A Darwinian Approach to a Dangerous World.* Berkeley: University of California Press.

Kirschner, M. and Gerhart, J. (2005). *The Plausibility of Life: Resolving Darwin's Dilemma.* New Haven, CT: Yale University Press.

Krebs, B. (2011). http://krebsonsecurity.com/2011/09/gang-used-3d-printers-for-atm-skimmers, accessed 22 January 2015.

Lafferty, K., Smith, K. and Madin, E. (2008). The infectiousness of terrorist ideology: Insights from ecology and epidemiology. In R. Sagarin and T. Taylor (eds), *Natural Security: A Darwinian Approach to a Dangerous World.* Berkeley: University of California Press.

Laland, K., Odling-Smee, J., Feldman, M. and Kendal, J. (2009). Conceptual barriers to progress within evolutionary biology. *Foundations of Science*, 14 (3), 195–216.

Lulham, R., Camacho Duarte, O., Dorst, K. and Kaldor, L. (2012). Designing a counterterrorism trash bin. In P. Ekblom (ed.), *Design Against Crime: Crime Proofing Everyday Objects.* Boulder, CO: Lynne Rienner.

Lum, C., Kennedy, L. and Sherley, A. (2009). *The Effectiveness of Counter-Terrorism Strategies: A Campbell Systematic Review.* Oslo: Campbell Collaboration.

Meyer, S. and Ekblom, P. (2011). Specifying the explosion-resistant railway carriage – a desktop test of the Security Function Framework. *Journal of Transportation Security*, 5, 69–85.

Monchuk, L. and Clancey, G. (2013). A comparative analysis of crime risk assessments and their application in Greater Manchester and New South Wales. *Built Environment*, 39, 74–91.

Morgan, M. and Carrier, D. (2013). Protective buttressing of the human fist and the evolution of hominin hands. *Journal of Experimental Biology*, 216, 236–244.

Okasha, S. (2006). *Evolution and the Levels of Selection*. Oxford: Clarendon.

Pease, K. (2001). *Cracking Crime through Design*. London: Design Council.

Popper, K. (1972). *Objective Knowledge: An Evolutionary Approach.* Oxford: Clarendon.

Prescott, E. (2008). Corporations and bureaucracies under a biological lens. In R. Sagarin and T. Taylor (eds), *Natural Security: A Darwinian Approach to a Dangerous World.* Berkeley: University of California Press.

Raup, D. (1993). *Extinction: Bad Genes or Bad Luck?* Oxford: Oxford University Press.

Rich, B. and Janos, L. (1994). *Skunk Works*. London: Warner Books.

Richerson, P. and Boyd, R. (2005). *Not by Genes Alone: How Culture Transformed Human Evolution*. Chicago, IL: University of Chicago Press.

Roach, J. and Pease, K. (2013). *Evolution and Crime*. London: Routledge.

Roach, J., Ekblom, P. and Flynn, R. (2005). The conjunction of terrorist opportunity: A framework for diagnosing and preventing acts of terrorism. *Security Journal*, 18 (3), 7–25.

Sagarin, R. and Taylor, T. (eds) (2008). *Natural Security: A Darwinian Approach to a Dangerous World.* Berkeley: University of California Press.

Schneier, B. (1999). Attack trees. *Dr. Dobb's Journal*, December. Available at: www.schneier.com/paper-attacktrees-ddj-ft.html, accessed 21 January 2015.

Schneier, B. (2012). *Liars and Outliers: Enabling the Trust That Society Needs to Thrive.* New York: Wiley.

Science Daily (2015). Optimizing optimization algorithms: Getting best results when approximating solutions to complex engineering problems. Available at: www.sciencedaily.com/releases/2015/01/150121155545.htm, accessed 22 January 2015.

Sheldon, P. (1996). Plus ça change – a model for stasis and evolution in different environments. *Palaeogeography, Palaeoclimatology, Palaeoecology*, 127, 209–227.

Shover, N. (1996). *Great Pretenders: Pursuits and Careers of Persistent Thieves.* London: Westview Press/Harper Collins.

Spencer-Oatey, H. (2012). What is culture? A compilation of quotations. GlobalPAD Core Concepts. Available at: http://go.warwick.ac.uk/globalpadintercultural, accessed 15 January 2015.

Sykes, G. and Matza, D. (1957). Techniques of neutralization. *American Sociological Review*, 22, 664–670.

Taylor, T. (2008). Living with risk. In R. Sagarin and T. Taylor (eds), *Natural Security: A Darwinian Approach to a Dangerous World.* Berkeley: University of California Press.

Tilley, N. (2006). Knowing and doing: Guidance and good practice in crime prevention. In J. Knutsson and R. Clarke (eds), *Putting Theory to Work: Implementing Situational Prevention and Problem-Oriented Policing*, Crime Prevention Studies 20. Monsey, NY: Criminal Justice Press.

Toffler, A. (1970). *Future Shock.* New York: Random House.

Tooby, J. and DeVore, I. (1987). The reconstruction of hominid behavioral evolution through strategic modelling. In W. Kinzey (ed.), *The Evolution of Human Behavior: Primate Models*, 183–227. New York: SUNY Press.

UK Cabinet Office (2010). *UK National Security Strategy 2010*. Available at: www.gov.uk/government/publications/the-national-security-strategy-a-strong-britain-in-an-age-of-uncertainty, accessed 15 January 2015.

van Valen, L. (1973). A New Evolutionary Law. *Evolutionary Theory*, 1, 1–18.

Vermeij, G. (1999). Inequality and the directionality of history. *American Naturalist*, 153, 243–253.

Vermeij, G. (2004). *Nature: An Economic History*. Princeton, NJ: Princeton University Press.

Vermeij, G. (2008). Security, unpredictability and evolution: Policy and the history of life. In R. Sagarin and T. Taylor (eds), *Natural Security: A Darwinian Approach to a Dangerous World*. Berkeley: University of California Press.

Webb, B. (1994). Steering column locks and motor vehicle theft: Evaluations from three countries. In R. Clarke (ed.), *Crime Prevention Studies*, 2, pp. 71–89. Monsey, NY: Criminal Justice Press.

Whiten, A. (2006). The place of 'deep social mind' in the evolution of human nature. In M. Jeeves (ed.), *Human Nature*, pp. 207–222. Edinburgh: Royal Society of Edinburgh.

Whiten, A. and Erdal, D. (2012). The human socio-cognitive niche and its evolutionary origins. *Philosophical Transactions of the Royal Society B*, 367, 2119–2129.

Wills, C. (1996). Safety in diversity. *New Scientist*, 23 March, 38–42.

Wilson, D. S. (2012). Clash of paradigms: Why proponents of multilevel selection theory and inclusive fitness theory sometimes (but not always) misunderstand each other. Available at: http://socialevolutionforum.com/2012/07/13/david-sloan-wilson-clash-of-paradigms-why-proponents-of-multilevel-selection-theory-and-inclusive-fitness-theory-sometimes-but-not-always-misunderstand-each-other, accessed 15 January 2015.

Wilson, E. O. (1975). *Sociobiology: The New Synthesis*. Cambridge, MA: Harvard University Press.

5 Why terrorism terrifies us

Jordan Kiper and Richard Sosis

Introduction

Over the past decade, evolutionary scientists have provided many theoretical and practical insights to understanding the social dynamics and underlying motivations that foster terrorism. Several researchers have shown, for instance, that contrary to most criminological models of violent groups, such as gangs, the strongest predictors of terrorist recruitment are neither poverty nor lack of education (e.g. Atran, 2009; Hafez, 2009). Rather, would-be terrorists are often compelled by feelings of victimization and revenge on behalf of one's kin, motivations that are likely "instinctual" and evolved to deter intergroup violence (see McCullough, 2008). Evolutionary perspectives have also complemented rational choice models of political violence by showing that seemingly irrational violent-behaviors, such as suicide bombings, are parochially altruistic (Ginges et al., 2009; Qirko, 2009; Victoroff, 2009). This means that terrorists can elicit suicide bombings from otherwise normal (i.e. nonpsychotic) recruits by promising benefits to their kin and manipulating cues of genetic relatedness among group members (Atran, 2004; 2012; Azam, 2005). Additionally, evolutionary scholars have shown that terrorist organizations do not use religion simply to brainwash recruits (vs., Harris, 2004), but to provide systematic organization for group activity. For religion aids in forming coalition identities (Graham & Haidt, 2010), strengthening cooperative bonds (Sosis & Alcorta, 2008; Sosis et al., 2012), and strengthening group commitments to extreme acts, including violence (Atran, 2003; Norenzayan & Shariff, 2008).

Despite these insights, evolutionary scholars have rarely considered why terrorism terrifies us. At first glance, asking why we respond to terrorism as we do may seem like a trivial question, but it is not. Because exposure to violence influences reproductive decision-making (Wilson & Daly, 1997), migration (Knauft, 1987), and revenge (McCullough, 2008), terrorism must entail fitness consequences for survivors (Sharma, 2003). Furthermore, because exposure to terrorism results in approach and avoidance behaviors (e.g. increased anxieties, in-group identification, vigilance toward out-groups, etc.), which are evident in numerous communities after attacks (e.g. Fischer et al., 2006; Rogers et al., 2007; Yehuda & Hyman, 2005), terrorism must exploit a psychological system dedicated to extreme threats and uncertainties. However, understanding those responses would be incomplete without the methods employed by evolutionary scientists for identifying the mental algorithms or behavioral strategies that undergird them. Likewise, no evolutionary approach to terrorism would be complete without considering the effects of terrorism itself.

In the U.S., pneumonia, infections, and even lightning strikes result in much higher fatality rates than terrorism, yet these and countless other causes of death do not elicit the fear and attention that terrorism does. And this response is not unique to U.S. citizens. Even at the height of the Second Palestinian Intifada, Israelis were more likely to die in an automobile accident than a terrorist attack (Stecklov & Goldstein, 2004). Yet while many Israelis exhibited caution when riding on buses and going about their business in public spaces, similar concerns were not elicited by driving a car (Klar et al., 2002; Sosis, 2007). Why do we have this apparently non-rational response to terror?

The main purpose of this chapter is to use insights from the evolutionary study of human behavior to answer this query and explain why terrorism terrifies us. In so doing, we bring together several disparate strands of research. *Terrorism responses* are understood rather broadly as the psychological and behavioral patterns that result from directly or indirectly witnessing a terrorist attack, and the outcomes of various coping practices thereafter (e.g. Sinclair & Antonius, 2012, pp. 4–30). We link the broad spectrum of terrorism responses to the threat-compensation strategies of an anxiety module comprised of the anterior cortex and septo-hippocampal circuit (SHC). We hypothesize that terrorism is terrifying because, among other things, it exploits a number of uncertainties that activate, amplify, and sustain the activity of this module.

Our discussion will proceed as follows. We begin by defining terrorism and briefly differentiating modern terrorism from other forms of political conflict throughout history. After that we review the spectrum of psychological and behavioral responses to terrorist attacks. We then consider the evolutionary significance of such responses and connect them to an anxiety module that underlies threat-compensation strategies. We locate the module that responds to terrorism among several other anxiety modules in the brain's precaution system. Hence, what we propose here is a synthesis of material and a proposed module that has not been previously discussed in evolutionary psychology (EP).

Terrorism

Primoratz (2013, p. 24) defines terrorism as "the deliberate use of violence, or threat of its use, against innocent people, with the aim of intimidating some other people into a course of action they otherwise would not take." Indeed, as many scholars observe (e.g. Hudson, 1999), the keys to terrorism are

1 the spread of fear in a community by
2 targeting civilians with
3 shocking, unexpected, and unlawful violence in order to
4 intimidate or coerce a government or civilian population into political demands that are desirable for the terrorists.

This fourfold combination of terrorism is itself terrifying because it violates established norms more than any previous form of political conflict, even those witnessed in civil wars, making it truly one of the scourges of modernity (Cooley, 2000). Given the combination of the four, many scholars (e.g. Iviansky, 2009) agree that modern terrorism is a rather unprecedented form of violence in world history, employing divergent methods from previously known political conflicts.

To illustrate, unlike previous political conflicts and social struggles, such as nationalist movements, which generally struck at regimes somewhat narrowly by eliminating leading figures, contemporary terrorists frequently employ new tactics to strike at governments or communities in unpredictable ways. This is one of the reasons why terrorism is so terrifying—it is virtually unlimited in terms of what or whom it can target (Crenshaw, 2000, p. 412). Evolutionarily speaking, this lack of constraint also gives terrorism a high mutation rate: like an evolving virus, it can perpetually change to strike its target, namely, governments or communities, in new ways. Such mutability has entailed that potential targets develop, in turn, an immune system, which eliminates threats or prevents them from reoccurring.

Despite this, two mechanisms have facilitated the intensification of terrorism over the last decade. The first is the modern media: the media magnifies the effects of terrorism by exposing millions to attacks, and thus amplifying perceived threats and exacerbating traumatic impacts (Sinclair & Antonius, 2012, pp. 89–91). The second is religion: albeit not the cause of terrorism, religion facilitates improbable behaviors, such as suicide bombings, by framing conflicts as ultimate struggles, justifying terrorist acts, and imbuing terrorism with emotional and moral significance (Sosis & Alcorta, 2008, pp. 106–108). Given the media's capacity to spread images of terrorist attacks worldwide and religion's ability to turn political struggles into cosmic wars (Juergensmeyer, 2003), it is no wonder that terrorism is increasing and becoming more lethal (Pape, 2005).

The effects of terrorism

Although evolutionary approaches to terrorism have converged on the causes and motives of terrorists, they have not examined the psychological and behavioral effects of terrorism on targets. It remains an open question, then, as to why we respond to terrorism as we do (e.g. Bleich et al., 2003; Sinclair, 2010; Sinclair & Antonius, 2012). To illustrate another angle at why this matters, consider that our ancestors were not exposed to indiscriminate suicide bombings, barrages of terrorist images in the media, and globalized settings where terrorist attacks were even possible. Furthermore, terrorist attacks everywhere evoke panic, existential anxiety, prolonged stress, and psychopathological symptoms. Understanding why people respond in this manner, especially the "mental powers" and "capacities" that enable these responses, demands an evolutionary analysis (Darwin, 1859, p. 449). Specifically, one that analyzes the selective pressures that have shaped the underlying neuropsychology that elicits our responses to terror.

To be sure, studies indicate that people are as fearful of terrorism as they are of snakes, spiders, and public speaking—in fact, terrorism outranks all other fears for America's youth (see Gallup Poll, 2005). Given that fear circuits are conserved in mammalian brains (LeDoux, 2012), terrorism must trigger a circuit designed to detect and respond to fearful stimuli (Tritt et al., 2012). Although neglected by evolutionists, this potential circuit, along with terrorism responses, has received a good deal of attention from psychologists since 9/11. While we obviously cannot review all of those studies, we can highlight the most prominent discoveries. Accordingly, we synthesize four areas of research (viz., studies on PTSD (post-traumatic stress disorder), existential anxiety, vicarious stress, and resilience) and organize terrorism responses along a theoretical spectrum.

In a review of disaster costs, Bonanno et al. (2010) proposed that responses to terrorism fall into one of three categories, from most to least traumatic:

- Elevated stress and anxieties that do not dissipate, often resulting in psychopathological symptoms, such as catastrophizing and overgeneralizing or even PTSD.
- A delayed response, where the person initially shows few signs of distress but then develops potentially long-standing anxieties, especially about violence and death.
- Heightened levels of distress immediately after the attack, which may lead to ruminations about violence and death, but the person eventually experiences full recovery.

These effects can be summarized as an elevation in stress (viz. fast-acting epinephrine) and/or anxiety (viz. slow-acting corticotropin) that, depending on the individual and environment, lead to prolonged anxiety (e.g. hippocampal changes, immune system suppression, inhibition of reproductive functions, growth hormone inhibition, and gastrointestinal shutdown; see Sapolsky, 2003). These effects translate into forms of avoidance coping (depression, panic, withdrawal) and/or threat-compensation strategies (e.g. agoraphobia, vigilance, out-grouping), and sometimes even extreme distress (e.g. isolation, violence or suicide; see Madux & Winstead, 2005). Most remarkably, a single terrorist attack can bring about these effects and traumatize any individual, regardless of whether he or she experienced the attack directly or indirectly through media coverage (Sinclair & Antonius, 2012, p. 134).

Terrorism, therefore, can result in a kind of trauma and, as such, requires time and social support for recovery. Recovery is understood as returning to pre-trauma levels of functioning (Sinclair & Antonius, 2012 p. 134). Resiliency, on the other hand, is the ability to endure stress and make quick transitions from trauma to normal life (p. 135). With these distinctions in mind, we wish to examine the above spectrum, giving special attention to the outcomes of psychopathological symptoms and long-standing anxieties about violence and death.

Psychopathological symptoms

At its most extreme, terrorism traumatizes individuals and therein causes psychopathological symptoms, such as anxiety, depression, and even PTSD. This is perhaps not surprising when it comes to survivors who directly experience an attack and thus face intense confusion, insecurity, and disillusionment for months to years afterward (e.g. Shalev & Freedman, 2005). Perhaps more surprising, however, are the number of persons who show signs of psychopathology and PTSD after simply witnessing an attack or experiencing it indirectly through media coverage. For example, the lifetime prevalence rate of PTSD across the United States is 8 percent (see DSM-IV). However, a survey by Schlenger et al. (2002) found that PTSD symptoms, such as violent ideations, public avoidances, and anxieties about death, spiked across the U.S. to 18 percent after the 9/11 terrorist attacks. In Spain, too, roughly 20 percent of persons sampled in Madrid after the 2004 train bombings showed signs of PTSD, despite not being direct survivors of the bombings (Miguel-Tobal et al., 2005). Likewise, after the 2005 attacks on the London underground, 31% of surveyed Londoners reported experiencing elevated fears and stress that lasted for months after the attacks (Rubin et al., 2007). Accordingly, it is safe to say that terrorism, albeit limited in terms of the number of persons it affects directly, inflicts a widespread trauma on communities that is akin to full-fledged PTSD.

As surprising as it may be, then, few studies have investigated the long-term effects of PTSD on attacked communities. However, we can infer from other studies what the long-term effects are. Building on the studies of Bessel Van der Kolk (1987, 1996), researchers consistently find that persons with PTSD show two major neurological changes over time. Within weeks after the event, persons excrete lower levels of serotonin and cortisol, resulting in dramatic changes to neurotransmitter systems and long-term depression or anxiety, which in turn can trigger additional stress responses (e.g. Strickland et al., 2002). Months after the event, however, persons develop smaller hippocampal volume, leaving them more pathologically vulnerable to psychological trauma and stress-related psychopathologies (e.g. Gilbertson et al., 2002). Due to the seriousness of these possibilities, Rubin and Wessely (2013) recently resurveyed Londoners about the 2005 London bombings. While only 11 percent still reported PTSD-like symptoms—a 20 percent drop since 2007—those who required clinical interventions for such symptoms never received them. Thus post-terrorist attack communities require the same level of outreach as victims of natural disasters to provide effective psychiatric care for PTSD (Rubin & Wessely, 2013).

Another psychological syndrome prevalent after terrorist attacks is catastrophizing: the incessant fear that another terrorist attack will occur or that similar violence is imminent (e.g. Beck, 1995; Fremont, 2004). According to Sinclair and Antonius (2012), catastrophizing often entails persistent feelings of vulnerability, changes in beliefs about out-groups, and ideations about death. Respectively, it leads to long-standing magnifications of environmental risks, ruminations about would-be attackers, and overall feelings of helplessness (p. 95). Yet catastrophizing goes beyond mere shifts in cognitive style and constitutes a manifestation of psychopathology. This is due to the fact that catastrophizing often persists even when individuals are confronted with evidence to the contrary (Beck, 1995). For instance, the most common forms of catastrophizing are agoraphobia, vigilance toward out-groups, and trusting solely with one's immediate in-group (e.g. Hirschberger et al., 2009). As a result, catastrophizing persons are similar to people with PTSD insofar as they get locked into a state of recalling the experienced trauma attempting, consciously or unconsciously, to prevent similar traumas from reoccurring (e.g. Holbrook et al., 2011).

Before going further, we pause here to note that despite the similarities in responses to terrorism, there are nevertheless variations in responses among individuals and communities. For instance, internal factors that influence responses to trauma or social stress of any kind include genetics, temperament, and social skills (Yehuda & Hyman, 2005). Environmental factors that increase the impact of terrorism on anxiety, depression, and social phobias include the frequency of experiencing aversive social experiences in early development, and negative life events in adulthood (Rapee & Spence, 2004). Furthermore, anxiety levels vary according to place, revealing that regions with histories of conflict and injustices have higher anxieties than others, including Zimbabwe, Central African Republic, and the Gaza Strip (Bateson et al., 2011).

Existential anxieties

A moderate yet common response to terrorism, especially for those who witness it indirectly, is showing no immediate distress but developing long-standing anxieties thereafter. In most cases these anxieties differ in magnitude from catastrophizing and involve slight ruminations about violence and death, including one's own. This phenomenon is a manifestation of what is known as mortality salience (MS) (Pyszcynski et al., 2003). At its simplest, MS is the distinctly human fear of death, which supersedes all other anxieties and underlies many human compulsions, such as the need for certainty, meaning, and control (Greenberg & Arndt, 2011). In its broadest sense, MS influences human beings to attach themselves to cultural worldviews, self-esteem bolstering activities, and having children, which serve as buffers against the fear of death (Pyszcynski et al., 1999). The upshot is that defending one's worldview and contributing to meaningful activities allows one to culturally survive death, just as having children provides one with genetic immortality. However, there is a downside to these fear-of-death minimizers. When confronted with death, humans not only embrace and defend their worldviews but also derogate persons dissimilar to themselves (Harmon-Jones et al., 1997). According to Pyszcynski et al. (2003), this was evident after 9/11 when images of terror prompted fears of death and defenses against cultural worldviews, such as widespread patriotism and an unfortunate slew of prejudices and attacks against Muslims.

Such reactions are known as threat compensation behaviors: the affirmation of alternative goals in the face of some other threatened goal. To illustrate, a common threat compensation behavior is for someone to affirm control over X after his or her control for Y has been threatened (Proulx, 2012). With regard to terrorism, Pyszcynski et al. (2003) find that most people, when exposed to a terrorist attack, experience existential threats, such as the realization of mortality, the loss of social order, and challenges to life's meaning. Indeed, the indiscriminate and unpredictable violence of terrorism threatens the view that the world is imbued with order, stability, and permanence (p. 16). As a result, most people compensate by engaging in the following: investing in kith and kin (Du et al., 2013), defending cultural worldviews (Pyszcynski et al., 2003), and committing to the social goals of their own in-group (Florian & Mikulincer, 2004).

The theoretical framework for explaining the above phenomena is known as terror management theory (TMT). TMT posits that the cognitive process of being threatened by death and maintaining psychological equanimity is undertaken by a form of dual-processing, where thoughts of death are suppressed through conscious beliefs that affirm the social order and both unconscious motivations and behaviors that provide symbolic immortality (Pyszcynski et al., 1999). When it comes to terrorism, this dual-process consistently translates into an increased commitment to, identification with, and defense of one's in-group (Pyszcynski et al., 2003). Indeed, exposure to images of terror has been shown to correlate with extreme in-group commitments, such as: escalating military intervention in the Middle East (Pyszcynski et al. 2006), using violence to solve international problems (Hirschberger et al., 2009), seeing the in-group's values as absolute (Tremoliere et al., 2012), and defending the in-group itself (Yen & Lin, 2012). Likewise, exposure to terror has been shown to correlate with prejudices toward out-groups (Das et al., 2009) and vigilance against anyone who threatens the in-group (Hayes et al., 2010).

From an evolutionary standpoint, these reactions are significant, for they illustrate how the threat of violence or death serves as a proximate mechanism for in-group behaviors. Consider, for instance, the fact that exposure to terrorism increases concern for one's neighbors and especially one's kin—even to the point of desiring more offspring after witnessing violence or death (e.g.

Fritsche et al., 2007; Wisman & Goldenberg, 2005). Exposure to terrorism also prompts individuals to evaluate physically dissimilar people more negatively and familiar people more positively than otherwise (Greenberg et al., 1992). Along the same lines, images of terrorism increase vigilance toward cultural norms (Greenberg et al., 1995) and disapproval of out-group symbols (Cohen et al., 2013), and motivate persons to strengthen social networks (Schmeichel et al., 2009). Hence, the existential anxieties brought about by terror not only touch upon an internal drive to minimize the fear of death, as TMT posits, but also to engage in behaviors that are relevant to in-group commitments and fitness itself.

Of course, this is not to say that such reactions are good. For doing so would commit the naturalistic fallacy and overlook the latent problems of in-group favoritism, vigilance against out-groups, and so forth. What is more, the behaviors associated with existential anxieties may, in fact, be an impetus for terrorism. According to McBride (2011), "people support or engage in terrorism to alleviate existential anxiety but ultimately find this anxiety exacerbated in the wake of the violence they create or sanction" (p. 560). As a result, terrorist attacks perpetuate violence, leading to retribution and sanctions against the very communities they stand for, which intensify existential frustration (see also Cottee & Hayward, 2011). Consequentially, deterring terrorism may require policies that not only provide self-determination, but also aspire to mitigate existential anxiety, a point we shall revisit in a coming section.

Vicarious stress

The most widespread effect of terrorism is vicarious stress: a mild form of distress brought about by images of terrorism conveyed through the media (Marshal et al., 2007). At its extreme vicarious stress can lead to avoidance behaviors, ruminations about the attack, and increased arousal symptoms, such as cortisol release (Sprang, 2001). More typically, however, vicarious stress simply leaves individuals fearful of other attacks and striving to avoid them. For instance, Pyszcynski et al. (2003) found that the majority of Americans experienced vicarious stress a year after 9/11, with roughly 74% of the country believing another attack was imminent and taking some kind of precaution to avoid it. According to Fremont (2004), while vicarious stress is often interpreted as being a common and somewhat innocuous response to terrorist attacks, it can nevertheless have profound effects on communities: if attacks are particularly destructive or frequent, they can lead to a continuous state of fear, where vicarious stress exacerbates anxieties in already distressed individuals. Hence, vicarious stress can easily give way to existential anxieties and psychopathological symptoms. For that reason, North and Pfefferbaum (2002) recommend that individuals limit media consumption after terrorist attacks, which prevents vicarious stress from giving way to full-fledged anxiety.

The evolutionary psychology of responses to terrorism

An evolutionary psychological perspective can make sense of the above response spectrum. To begin, each phase of the spectrum is an expression of fear, which is itself an adaptation but not always beneficial for the organism. As observed by Darwin in *The Expressions of the Emotions in Man and Animals* (1872), fear is a universal emotion and physiological experience brought about by external stimuli interacting with internal systems, often resulting in adaptive responses. However, as Darwin also observed, sustained fear often leads to mental exhaustion, a point at which the "mental powers fail" (p. 292). Nearly a century later, Selye (1956) postulated that organisms exposed to frightful stimuli go through three phases: alarm, resistance, and exhaustion. While alarm is responding by fight-or-flight, resistance is managing environmental threats and stress, which, if unmanaged, result in exhaustion. Following Selye, Sapolsky (1994) recognized that fear in humans, although adaptive, can result in stress, obsessive behaviors, and ultimately psychophysical illnesses, if triggered by extensive trauma or repeated stressors. Hence, fear is one of evolution's double-edged swords: it is an adaptation that is undoubtedly necessary for survival, but it often leads to adverse consequences, especially when it progresses from stress and resistance to psychophysical illness, such as PTSD.

In line with Darwin, we wish to inquire about the internal systems that interact with external stimuli, namely, exposure to terrorism, to produce the spectrum of responses. Specifically, we wish to consider whether the spectrum originates from an evolved psychological mechanism. That is to say, obviously not a mechanism designed for terrorism per se, but rather designed to respond to threatening stimuli, which terrorism exploits.

It should be noted that an evolutionary approach to anxiety is not new. Both Marks and Nesse (1994) and Cosmides and Tooby (1999) offered what are now classic expositions, showing that anxieties and fears are ultimately adaptive. Several evolutionists have recently developed these outlooks in what might be called the "evolutionary psychology of anxiety." Bateson, Brilot, and Nettle (2011) have shown the adaptive value of several anxious behaviors—for instance, that insomnia provides alertness, restlessness is the body prepared for action, and ambiguity aversion is the avoidance of threats (p. 711). Along these lines, Grinde (2012) has proposed that happiness itself may be the product of several mood modules, including a "low mood" module associated with anxiety and depression, which is activated during times of uncertainty to decrease activity and thus the likelihood of risks. There is an additional literature discussing the natural selection of various mood disorders and anxieties (e.g. Bateson et al., 2011; Hagen, 2011; Nesse, 2011). What is more, several theorists have proposed distinct anxiety modules for such things as social phobias (Rapee & Spence, 2004), snake-detection (Ohman et al., 2001), and more (for a review of evolved fear-circuitry see Bracha, 2006).

What we propose here is an additional module—a "terror module"—that has not been discussed in EP, namely one designed to detect and respond to extremely threatening stimuli, such as signs of death or violence. By identifying its circuitry, we show that the module embodies the neural connections responsible for responses to death and existential anxieties, as recently identified by Tritt, Inzlicht, and Harmon-Jones (2012). Moreover, by identifying its neighboring circuitry, we show that the module is one of several designed for uncertainty and part of the brain's precaution system, as proposed by Boyer and Lienard (2006).

Identifying the terror module

Because the core response to terrorism is existential anxiety, it is appropriate to consider first what TMT says about the matter. For most TMT theorists, the affective state and behaviors caused by terrorism are instances of MS, which are unique threat-defense mechanisms that develop within the lifespan of the individual (e.g. Greenberg & Arndt, 2011). In other words, because humans come to realize the inevitability of their own deaths, they come to invest in behaviors that render life meaningful (Pyszcynski et al., 1999). However, several theorists have recently qualified this outlook by associating MS with the broad spectrum of mammalian fear responses, which progress from fight-or-flight to exhaustion, as Selye (1956) observed. For instance, many suggest that MS is simply one mode in which the mind deals with fear and uncertainty, making it akin to cognitive dissonance, entropy management, and inconsistency compensation (e.g. Holbrook et al., 2011). Related to this view, Tritt, Inzlicht, and Harmon-Jones (2012) have observed that MS is the product of a specific "internal system," as Darwin would say, which deals with extreme uncertainties and threats.

Building on these observations, we suggest that the effects of terrorism are not only threat-compensation strategies but also fear responses designed to orient the individual's cognition to violent environmental threats. However, when these responses are amplified or prolonged, they give way to psychopathological symptoms. In what remains of this section, we spell out this idea in greater detail, defending the possibility of a distinct anxiety module—among other such modules in the precaution system of the brain—that responds to terrorism, as well as other threatening stimuli.

As evolutionary psychologists observe, the human mind is not a blank slate but rather an evolved organ with multiple innate modules, each designed for an adaptive problem, such as acquiring mates, finding resources, and so on (e.g. Cosmides & Tooby, 1992). These modules are domain-general processors that respond to different sets of phenomena and specific phenomenon therein (Karmiloff-Smith, 2000). For example, humans have a module designed for responding to animals that is flexible enough for any four-legged creature, such as a dog (Sperber, 1994). With regard to responses to terror, if any sign of violence or death elicits stress, anxiety, and MS, as many argue (e.g. Greenberg & Arndt, 2011), then it is possible that an underlying module regulates all of these responses. Accordingly, the module would be flexible enough to respond to a broad range of threatening phenomena but specific enough to respond to the phenomenon of terrorism.

Several lines of evidence support this possibility. Logically, it is unlikely that humans are unique among species in terms of responding to violence or signs of death, since doing so is essential for survival. Moreover, given the fact that fear systems in the brain are conserved, that is, built from ancient systems (see LeDoux, 2012), it is unlikely that humans evolved a unique module dedicated exclusively to death anxiety, as TMT suggests (e.g. Greenberg et al., 1986). What is more likely is that humans inherit a primitive anxiety system that is designed to detect and respond to extreme threats (e.g. expectancy violations, uncertainties, and dangerous stimuli). After all, when confronted with extreme threats, children, monkeys, and rats, like adult humans, respond in a similar way: they evade the situation or stimuli; avoid unfamiliar objects, places, or conspecifics; and/or consort with familiar conspecifics (Tritt et al., 2012, p. 722). Equally as remarkable, when primates are confronted with dangerous stimuli, they show a spectrum of fear reactions that parallel those of terrorism responses, progressing from stress to PTSD-like symptoms (e.g. see Cohen et al., 2006).

Still, this raises an important question: why a module? In other words, why wouldn't a primitive brain system alone, such as the amygdala circuit, be enough to explain such responses? In addressing this inquiry, we arrive at four additional lines of evidence.

The first is that threat-compensation strategies are too complex for a single fear system, especially a primitive one. Many threat-compensation strategies, such as the fear of snakes or spiders, are not only regular and innate—and thus modular—but also complex insofar as they detect a single stimulus and respond with similar behavioral patterns. This is due to the fact that such threat-compensation strategies derive from modules comprised of distinct association areas in the brain and primitive brain systems. Ethical behaviors, for instance, stem from moral modules comprised of association areas, such as the prefrontal cortex, and primitive brain systems, such as the disgust mechanism of the insula (e.g. Olatunji et al., 2008). The threat-compensation strategies caused by terrorism are similar in that they involve association areas, such as the prefrontal cortex and temporal lobes, and primitive nuclei, such as the amygdala (McGregor et al., 2009). Given this complexity of brain circuits, it is very likely that terrorism responses stem from a module as opposed to a single primitive fear system.

The second line of evidence is that researchers (Tritt et al., 2012, pp. 722–723) have recently mapped out the physiology of a potential module that controls threat-compensation strategies. The starting point of that map is the SHC, which compares mental schemas about the world and its proper ordering with incoming sensory information about the environment. When extreme misrepresentations are detected, such as dangerous stimuli, the SHC activates the anterior cingulate cortex (ACC), which in turn gives off a "cortical alarm" that triggers the sympathetic nervous system and orients cognition toward resolving higher-order inconsistencies in the environment. To resolve those inconsistencies, the SHC and ACC also activate the septal area and basal ganglia, which jointly control goal-oriented behaviors and actuate prefrontal systems and left cortical hemispheres. The prefrontal systems and left cortical hemispheres, in turn, control approach and avoidance behaviors. When this entire system is activated and sustained, as with the observance of violence or signs of death, the individual experiences heightened vigilance, increased goal-directed cognition, and amplified motivation to approach the familiar and avoid the unfamiliar. Because this process captures the psychological and behavioral patterns caused by extreme threats, such as terrorism, it underscores the likelihood of a distinct underlying anxiety module (Tritt et al., p. 715).

Following the last point, the third factor is that a modular account can explain the spectrum of terrorism responses in one fell swoop. As the work of Tritt, Inzlicht, and Harmon-Jones (2012) illustrates, the stress and anxiety caused by terrorism is obviously attributable to the SHC and ACC circuit. However, because the SHC and ACC regulate the limbic system, which is the central circuit for stress and anxiety in the brain, the SHC and ACC can cause psychopathologies, including PTSD. This happens when the circuit in question is amplified and sustained, usually due to an extensive trauma or repetitive exposure to traumatic events (e.g. Canteras et al., 2010). This of course explains how a module designed to respond to threats can nevertheless bring about mental exhaustion, as Darwin observed—put simply, when the SHC and ACC remain "turned on," the limbic system cannot be "turned off," resulting in a runaway stress response that leads to hippocampal cell loss and thus psychopathology (Sapolsky, 2003). Further, because the SHC and ACC wire to the prefrontal systems and left cortical hemisphere, they trigger goal oriented behaviors if moderately activated. This may explain why images of violence and death prompt the desires to sire kin (e.g. Fritsche et al., 2007), defend one's culture (e.g. Pyszczynski et al., 2004), and achieve personal goals (Kasser & Sheldon, 2000). Further still, recall that the SHC and ACC activate approach and avoidance behaviors, which demonstrates a conserved aspect of the mammalian fear response, but also accounts for the fact that threatening stimuli induce in-group loyalty and out-group exclusion (e.g. Das et al., 2009). Hence, the SHC and ACC circuit can account for each point in the spectrum of terrorism responses, rendering it a likely module for such responses.

The fourth point to consider is that a module along these lines makes evolutionary sense. While we cannot demonstrate that such a module indeed contributes to fitness, we can identify several facets that would render it potentially fitness enhancing. First, the spectrum of behaviors it produces—namely, approach and avoidance—would be adaptive in moments of threats and uncertainties (Tritt et al., 2012). Second, the fact that it heightens vigilance would be enough to minimize possible risks in times of distress (Slovic & Peters, 2006). Third, although it motivates in-group favoritism and out-group prejudice, the former could marshal social support and encourage in-group cooperation in times of vulnerability (Navarrete et al., 2004), while the latter kept out-group threats at bay in ancestral environments. Finally, it should not be overlooked that episodic stress and anxiety are themselves adaptive defenses against threats (Vaillant, 2000).

Activating the terror module

The proposed terror module is activated by expectancy violations, uncertainties, and threatening stimuli (Tritt et al., 2012). Indeed, in slight cases, anything unfamiliar, unknown, or intimidating could activate the system (p. 723). However, the key here is not so much what activates it but rather what amplifies and sustains its activity. By amplification we mean the marked intensification in the neural activity of the SHC and ACC circuit, and by sustained we mean that which causes it to be prolonged for an extended period of time. According to Gray and McNaughton (2000), the SHC and ACC circuit is amplified by noxious stimuli, violence, and war, and is likewise sustained by traumatic events involving such stimuli, especially if exposure is repeated.

With this in mind, it is no wonder that terrorism activates the module. Terrorism is both the use of militaristic violence (e.g. mass shootings, bombings, gassings, etc.) against non-combatant targets and the attempt to bring war-like conditions to civilian environments. While violence and war are necessary for amplifying the SHC and ACC circuit, they are not sufficient for sustaining it. To sustain the SHC and ACC, terrorists maximize trauma by repeating belligerent attacks that consistently employ shocking, unpredictable, and indiscriminate violence. This not only violates mental schemas of peace and social order, but also exposes communities to seemingly incessant traumas. Of course, the impact of such trauma is further compounded by media coverage of terrorist attacks, which expose individuals to repetitive images of terrorist violence. Hence, terrorism is terrifying because it activates, amplifies and sustains an internal system—what we have identified as a module—that is designed to respond to extreme threats.

We pause here to consider a relevant inquiry: is the terror module akin to, say, a war module? We do not think so. For it is unlikely that humans have evolved a war module per se, since war is, in fact, a highly complex cultural activity. And though human beings frequently engage in aggressive behaviors, they are nevertheless ambivalent about war and express natural inhibitions against conspecific-killing, suggesting that war is not as innate as some evolutionists have presumed (Smith, 2007; van der Dennen, 2008). Furthermore, what we are proposing is rather modest compared to positing a complex behavioral module, such as one for warfare. Recognizing that the human brain is equipped with anxiety modules, we suggest that it includes one designed to respond to extreme threats, such as portents of death and violence, which terrorist attacks inadvertently exploit. This module may indeed contribute to impulses for out-grouping, which in turn contribute to warfare, just as modules for aggression, resource acquisition, kin altruism and several others do; but the terror module would not be—nor would any other be—the sole module for war.

Locating the terror module in the brain's precaution system

Given the circuitry outlined in the last section, we are now in a position to make connections with other anxiety modules. The most relevant is the precaution system and its relation to pathological and ritualized behaviors, as discussed by Boyer and Lienard (2006). When humans are confronted with uncertainties, such as vulnerable life-stages or the birthing process, they not only experience anxiety, but also produce action-ritualizations—that is, stereotyped and repetitive behaviors, such as obsessions about contaminations and contagions, and avoidance, behaviors that resemble psychopathologies. According to Boyer and Lienard (pp. 2–5), these obsessions and behaviors are the output of a psychological immune system or "precaution system" comprised of two underlying cognitive subsystems:

1 an "action parsing system" that divides incoming sensory information and outgoing behavior into meaningful units, and
2 a "motivational system" that detects and reacts to potential threats to fitness.

The latter subsystem, which is most pertinent to our discussion, is further divided into a variety of circuits that include the frontal cortices, striatum, globus pallidus, and ACC. The result of this vast circuitry is that the motivational system controls a rather broad set of habitual responses and motor habits, and an extensive set of cortical alarms.

Granted this much, we can locate our proposed module within the motivational system. Boyer and Lienard (2006) speculate that the motivational system is designed to detect environmental errors of many kinds, including highly salient conditions that would have been dangers in our evolutionary past: reproductive risks, predation, pathogens, social harm, and possibly more (p. 8). Critically, each of these would have evolved as its own module, detecting certain manifest-threats (e.g. signals about the source of danger) and inferred-threats (e.g. when potential danger is likely), thereby initiating different decision rules (e.g. IF x triggers disgust, THEN reject x as pathogen; e.g. see Fessler & Navarrette, 2003). Accordingly, Boyer and Lienard (2006, p. 9) suggest that each of these devices would have evolved slightly different circuitry within the motivational system in order to detect threats of different kinds (e.g. cheaters, predators, pathogens, and the like).

We thus speculate that the terror module is one of the various devices in the motivational system. For it embodies some of the motivational system's circuitry designed for responding to environmental uncertainties, yet it is unique enough to react to the specific uncertainties involving death. By way of example, recall that humans are especially sensitive to any sign of death and violence, which trigger a spectrum of responses, from stress to PTSD. In line with Boyer and Lienard (2006), those signs are manifest and inferred-threats, and the responses are decision rules, thus underscoring that the underlying circuitry for them is part of the motivational system.

Conclusion

With increasing levels of destruction, terrorism continues to impact various communities and individuals across the globe. However, its alleged threat may not be as lethal as it seems. According to Mueller and Stewart (2011), despite the political rhetoric and news footage concerning terrorist attacks, terrorism poses a rather minimal risk for most persons and communities. In fact, compared to other threats, such as accidents or diseases, terrorist attacks are rather infrequent, and the majority of attempted attacks fail. Moreover, while terrorism inflicts millions of dollars in damages each year, the U.S. alone has spent over one trillion dollars since 9/11 to combat terrorism (p. 1). This discrepancy has led Mueller and Stewart to question why people overestimate the capacity of terrorists, inflate the vulnerability of targets, and neglect the probability of successful attacks. We suggest that it is due to the activation of a terror module, which, like the human reaction to spiders or snakes, responds strongly to extreme signs of death or violence, regardless of the actual threat posed by the stimuli. Indeed, such reactions, despite the reality of terrorism, underscore the importance of finding adaptive ways to cope with terrorist threats.

Even though communities have developed ways of coping with terrorist threats (e.g. Sosis, 2007; Sosis & Handwerker, 2011), the uncertainties of attacks, media coverage of terrorist carnage, and religious zeal of would-be attackers continue to cause distress among targeted individuals and witnesses. While this distress often results in vicarious stress and existential anxiety, it often produces psychopathological symptoms akin to PTSD. Thus any scholarly work that helps us get a handle on these responses is valuable for treatments in particular, and contributes to the ongoing conversation about dealing with terrorist threats in general. Along these lines, clinical psychology has developed rigorous means of identifying responses to terror, but by identifying the selective pressures that shape the neuropsychology of such responses we may be able to develop more efficacious coping strategies. Indeed, EP has extended approaches to clinical psychology by generating specific hypotheses about underlying modules, which have led to a more complex and interesting picture of human psychology over the last two decades. In this chapter, we have engaged in that ongoing conversation, hypothesizing that a distinct anxiety module in the brain's precautionary system, among others, operates over the spectrum of terror responses. The more we understand the EP of human anxiety, especially with regard to terrorism, the better we will be at managing responses to terror, which will contribute to resolving the threat of terrorism in the twenty-first century.

Acknowledgements

This work was supported by an ESRC Large Grant (REF RES-060-25-0085) entitled "Ritual, Community, and Conflict" and the James Barnett Endowment for Humanistic Anthropology.

References

Atran, S. (2003). Genesis of suicide terrorism. *Science*, 299, 1534–1539.

Atran, S. (2004). *Trends in Suicide Terrorism: Sense and Nonsense*. Presented to World Federation of Scientists Permanent Monitoring Panel of Terrorism, Eric, Sicily, August 2004.

Atran, S. (2009). Soft power and the psychology of suicide bombing. In J. Victoroff & W. Kruglanski (eds), *Psychology of Terrorism: Key Readings: Classic and Contemporary Insights* (pp. 441–445). New York: Hove Psychology Press.

Atran, S. (2012). War, martyrdom, and terror: Evolutionary underpinnings of the moral imperative to extreme group violence. In S.C. Roberts (ed.), *Applied Evolutionary Psychology* (pp. 222–238). New York: Oxford University Press.

Azam, J.P. (2005). Suicide-bombing as inter-generational investment. *Public Choice*, 122, 177–198.

Bateson, M., Brilot, B., & Nettle, D. (2011). Anxiety: An evolutionary approach. *Canadian Journal of Psychiatry*, 56(12), 707–715.

Beck, J.S. (1995). *Cognitive Therapy: Basics and Beyond*. New York: Guilford.

Bleich, A., Gelkopf, M., & Solomon, Z. (2003). Exposure to terrorism, stress-related mental health symptoms, and coping behaviors among a nationally representative sample in Israel. *Journal of the American Medical Association*, 290, 667–670.

Bonanno, G.A., Brewin, C.R., Kaniasty, K., & La Greca, A.M. (2010). Weighing the costs of disaster: Consequences, risks, and resilience in individuals, families, and communities. *Psychological Science in the Public Interest*, 11(1), 1–49.

Boyer, P., & Lienard, P. (2006). Why ritualized behavior? Precaution systems and action parsing in developmental, pathological and cultural rituals. *Behavioral and Brain Sciences*, 29, 1–56.

Bracha, H.A. (2006). Human brain evolution and the 'neuroevolutionary time-depth principle:' Implications for the reclassification of fear-circuitry-related traits in DMS-V and for studying resilience to warzone-related posttraumatic stress disorder. *Progress in Neuro-Psychopharmacology & Biological Psychiatry*, 30, 827–853.

Canteras, N.S., Resstel, L.B., Bertoglio, L.J., Carobrez, A.P., & Guimares, F.S. (2010). Neuroanatomy of anxiety. In M.B. Stein & T. Steckler (eds), *Behavioral Neurobiology of Anxiety and its Treatment*, pp. 77–96. New York: Springer Heidelberg Dordrecht.

Cohen, F., Soenke, M., Solomon, S., & Greenberg, J. (2013). Evidence for a role of death thought in American attitudes toward symbols of Islam. *Journal of Experimental Social Psychology*, 29, 189–194.

Cohen, H., Mater, M.A., Richter-Levin, G., & Zohar, J. (2006). The contribution of an animal model toward uncovering biological risk factors for PTSD. *Annual New York Academy of Science*, 1071, 335–350.

Cooley, J.K. (2000). Terrorism: Continuity and change in the new century. *Global Dialogue*, 2(4). Retrieved February 2014 from www.worlddialogue.org/content.php?id=109.

Cosmides, L., & Tooby, J.H. (1992). Cognitive adaptations for social exchange. In J.H. Barkow, L. Cosmides, & J.H. Tooby (eds), *The Adapted Mind* (pp. 163–228). Oxford: Oxford University Press.
Cosmides, L., & Tooby, J. (1999). Toward an evolutionary taxonomy of treatable conditions. *Journal of Abnormal Psychology*, 108(3), 453–464.
Cottee, S., & Hayward, K. (2011). Terrorist (e)motives: The existential attractions of terrorism. *Studies in Conflict & Terrorism*, 34, 963–986.
Crenshaw, M. (2000). The psychology of terrorism: An agenda for the 21st century. *Political Psychology*, 21(2), 405–420.
Darwin, C. (1859). *On the Origin of Species*. London: John Murray.
Darwin, C. (1872). *Expression of the Emotions*. London: John Murray.
Das, E., Bushman, B.J., Bezemer, M., Kerkhof, P., & Vermeulen, I.E. (2009). How terrorism news reports increase prejudice against out-groups: A terror management account. *Journal of Experimental Social Psychology*, 45, 453–459.
Du, H., Jonas, E., Klackl, J., Agroskin, D., Hui, E.K.P., & Ma, L. (2013). Cultural influences on terror management: Independent and interdependent self-esteem against anxiety. *Journal of Experimental Social Psychology*, 49, 1002–1011.
Fessler, D.M.T., & Navarrete, C.D. (2003). Meat is good to taboo: Dietary proscriptions as a product of the interaction of psychological mechanisms and social processes. *Journal of Cognition of Culture*, 3(1), 1–40.
Fischer, P., Greitemeyer, T., Kastenmuller, A., Jonas, E., & Frey, D. (2006). Coping with terrorism: The impact of increased salience of terrorism on mood and self-efficacy of intrinsically religious and non-religious people. *Personality and Social Psychology Bulletin*, 32, 365–377.
Florian, V., & Mikulincer, M. (2004). A multifaceted perspective on the existential meanings, manifestations, and consequences of the fear of personal death. In J. Greenberg, S.L., Koole, & T. Pyszcynski (eds), *Handbook of Experimental Existential Psychology* (pp. 54–70). New York: Guilford.
Fremont, W.P. (2004). Childhood reactions to terrorism-induced trauma: A review of the past 10 years. *Journal of the American Academy of Child and Adolescent Psychiatry*, 43, 381–392.
Fritsche, I., Jonas, E., Fischer, P., Koranyi, N., Berger, N., & Fleischmann, B. (2007). Mortality salience and the desire for offspring. *Journal of Experimental Social Psychology*, 43, 753–762.
Gallup Poll (2005). What frightens America's youth, gallup.com (29 March).
Gilbertson, M.W., Shenton, M.E., Ciszewski, A., Kasai, K., Lasko, N.B., & Pitman, R.K. (2002). Smaller hippocampal volume predicts pathological vulnerability to psychological trauma. *Nature Neuroscience*, 5(11), 1242–1247.
Ginges, J., Hansen, I., & Norenzayan, A. (2009). Religion and support for suicide attacks. *Psychological Science*, 20, 224–230.
Graham, J., & Haidt, J. (2010). Beyond beliefs: Religions bind individuals into moral communities. *Personality and Social Psychology Review*, 14(1), 140–150.
Gray, J.A., & McNaughton, N. (2000). *The Neuropsychology of Anxiety: An Inquiry into the Function of the Septal-Hippocampal System* (2nd edn). New York: Cambridge University Press.
Greenberg, J., & Arndt, J. (2011). Terror management theory. In A.W. Kruglanski, P.A.M. Van Lange, & E.T. Higgins (eds), Handbook of Theories of Social Psychology (vol. 1, pp. 399–415). New York: Sage.

Greenberg, J., Pyszczynski, T., & Solomon, S. (1986). The causes and consequences of the need for self-esteem: A terror management theory. In R.F. Baumeister (ed.), *Public Self and Private Self* (pp. 189–212). New York: Springer-Verlag.

Greenberg, J., Simon, L., Harmon-Jones, E., Solomon, S., Pyszcynski, T., & Lyon, D. (1995). Testing alternative explanations for mortality effects: Terror management, value accessibility, or worrisome thoughts? *European Journal of Social Psychology*, 25, 417–433.

Greenberg, J., Simon, L., Pyszcynski, T., Solomon, S., & Chatel, D. (1992). Terror management and tolerance: Does mortality salience always intensify negative reactions to others who threaten one's worldview? *Journal of Personality and Social Psychology*, 63, 212–220.

Grinde, B. (2012). An evolutionary perspective on happiness and mental health. *Journal of Mind and Behavio*r, 33(2), 49–68.

Hafez, M.M. (2007), *Suicide Bombers in Iraq: The Strategy and Ideology of Martyrdom*. Washington, DC: United States Institute of Peace.

Hagen, E.H. (2011). Evolutionary theories of depression: A critical review. *Canadian Journal of Psychiatry*, 56(12), 716–726.

Harmon-Jones, E., Simon, L., Greenberg, J., Pyszczynski, T., Solomon, S., & McGregor, H. (1997). Terror management theory and self-esteem: Evidence that increased self-esteem reduces mortality salience effects. *Journal of Personality and Social Psychology*, 72, 24–36.

Harris, S. (2004). *The End of Faith: Religion, Terror, and the Future of Reason*. New York: W.W. Norton.

Hayes, J., Schimel, J., Arndt, J., & Faucher, E.H. (2010). A theoretical and empirical review of the death-thought accessibility concept in terror management research. *Psychological Bulletin*, 136(5), 699–739.

Hirschberger, G., Pyszcynski, T., & Ein-Dor, T. (2009). Vulnerability and vigilance: Threat awareness and perceived adversary intent moderate the impact of mortality salience on intergroup violence. *PSPB*, 35(5), 597–607.

Holbrook, C., Sousa, P., & Hahn-Holbrook, J. (2011). Unconscious vigilance: Worldview defense without adaptations for terror, coalition, or uncertainty management. *Journal of Personality and Social Psychology*, 101, 451–466.

Hudson, R.A. (1999). The sociology and psychology of terrorism: Who becomes a terrorist and why? A report prepared under an interagency agreement by the Federal Research Division, Library of Congress, September 1999. Retrieved December 2011, from http:///www.loc.gov/rr/frd/pdf-files/Soc_Psych_of_Terrorism.pdf.

Iviansky, Z. (2009). Individual terror: Concept and typology. In J. Victoroff & W. Kruglanski (eds), *Psychology of Terrorism: Classic and Contemporary Insights: Key Readings in Social Psychology* (pp. 9–22). New York: Psychology Press.

Juergensmeyer, M. (2003). *Terror in the Mind of God: The Global Rise in Religious Violence*. Berkeley: University of California Press.

Karmilof-Smith, A. (2000). Why babies brains are not like Swiss Army knives. In H. Rose & S. Rose (eds), *Alas, Poor Darwin: Arguments against Evolutionary Psychology* (pp. 144–156). London: Jonathan Cape.

Kasser, T., & Sheldon, K.M. (2004). Non-becoming, alienated becoming, and authentic becoming: A goal-based approach. In J. Greenberg, S. Koole, & T. Pzcyzynski (eds), *Handbook of Experimental Existential Psychology*. New York: Guilford.

Klar, Y., Zakay, D., & Shavrit, K. (2002). If I don't get blown up ...: Realism in face of terrorism in an Israeli nationwide sample. *Risk, Decision and Policy*, 7, 203–219.

Knauft, B.M. (1987). Reconsidering violence in simple human societies: Homicide among the Gebusi of New Guinea. *Current Anthropology*, 28, 457–499.

LeDoux, J.E. (2012). Evolution of human emotion: A view through fear. *Progress in Brain Research*, 195, 431–442.

Maddux, J.E., & Winstead, B.A. (eds), (2005). *Psychopathology: Foundations for a Contemporary Understanding*. New York: Lawrence Erlbaum Associates.

Marks, I.M., & Nesse, R.M. (1994). Fear and fitness: An evolutionary analysis of anxiety disorders. *Ethology and Sociobiology*, 15(5), 247–261.

Marshall, R.D., Bryant, R.A., Amsel, L., Suh, E.H., Cook, J.M., & Neria, Y. (2007). The psychology of ongoing threat: Relative risk appraisal, the September 11 attacks, and terrorism-related dears. *American Psychologist*, 62, 304–316.

McBride, M.K. (2011). The logic of terrorism: Existential anxiety, the search for meaning, and terrorist ideologies. *Terrorism and Political Violence*, 23, 560–581.

McCullough, M. (2008). *Beyond Revenge: The Evolution of the Forgiveness Instinct*. San Francisco, CA: Jossey-Bass.

McGregor, I., Nash, K., & Inzlicht, M. (2009). Threat, high self-esteem, and reactive approach motivation: Electroencephalographic evidence. *Journal of Experimental Social Psychology*, 45, 1003–1007.

Miguel-Tobal, J.J., Can-Vindel, A., Gonzalez-Ordi, H., Iruarrizaga, I., Rudenstine, S., Vlahov, D., & Galea, S. (2005). PTSD and depression after the Madrid March 11 train bombings. *Journal of Traumatic Stress*, 19, 69–80.

Mueller, J., & Stewart, M.G. (2011). Balancing the risks, benefits, and costs of homeland security. Homeland Security Affairs, 7(16). Retrieved February 2014 from www.hsaj.org.

Navarrete, C.D., Kurzban, R., Fessler, D.M., & Kirkpatrick, L.A. (2004). Anxiety and intergroup bias: Terror management or coalition psychology? *Group Processes & Intergroup Relations*, 7(4), 370–397.

Nesse, R.M. (2011). Why has natural selection left us so vulnerable to anxiety and mood disorders? *The Canadian Journal of Psychiatry*, 56(12), 705–706.

Norenzayan, A., & Shariff, A.F. (2008). The origin and evolution of religious prosociality. *Science*, 322, 58–62.

North, C.S., & Pfefferbaum, B. (2002). Research on mental health effects of terrorism. *Journal of the American Medical Association*, 288, 633–636.

Ohman, A., Flykt, A., & Esteves, F. (2001). Emotion drives attention: Detecting the snake in the grass. *Journal of Experimental Psychology: General*, 131, 653–663.

Olatunji, B.O., Haidt, J., McKay, D., & David, B. (2008). Core, animal reminder, and contamination disgust: Three kinds of disgust with distinct personality, behavioral, physiological, and clinical correlates. *Journal of Research in Personality*, 42, 1243–1259.

Pape, R. (2005). *Dying to Win: The Strategic Logic of Suicide Terrorism*. New York: Random House.

Primoratz, I. (2013). *Terrorism: A Philosophical Investigation*. Cambridge: Polity Press.

Proulx, T. (2012). Threat-compensation in social psychology: Is there a core motivation? Social *Cognition*, 30, 643–651.

Pyszczynski, T., Abdollahi, A., Solomon, S., Greenberg, J., Cohen, F., & Weise, D. (2006). Mortality salience, martyrdom, and military might: The great Satan versus the axis of evil. *Personality and Social Psychology Bulletin*, 32, 525–537.

Pyszcynski, T., Greenberg, J., & Solomon, S. (1999). A dual-process model of defense against conscious and unconscious death-related thoughts: An extension of terror management theory. *Psychological Review*, 106, 835–845.

Pyszczynski, T., Greenberg, J., Solomon, S., Arndt, J., & Schimel, J. (2004). Why do people need self-esteem? A theoretical and empirical review. *Psychological Bulletin*, 130, 435–468.

Pyszcynski, T., Solomon, S., & Greenberg, J. (2003). *In the Wake of 9/11/2001: The Psychology of Terror*. Washington, DC: American Psychological Association.

Quirko, H.N. (2011). Fictive kinship and induced altruism. In C.A. Salmon & T.K Schackleford (eds), *The Oxford Handbook of Evolutionary Psychology* (pp. 310–328). New York: Oxford University Press.

Rapee, R.M., & Spence, S.H. (2004). The etiology of social phobia: Empirical evidence and an initial model. *Clinical Psychology Review*, 24, 737–767.

Rogers, B., Amlot, R., Rubin, G.J., Wessely, S., & Krieger, K. (2007). Mediating the social and psychological impacts of terrorist attacks: The role of risk perception and risk communication. *International Review of Psychiatry*, 19(3), 279–288.

Rubin, G.J., & Wessely, S. (2013). The psychological and psychiatric effects of terrorism: Lessons from London. *Psychiatric Clinics of North America*, 36, 339–350.

Rubin, G.J., Brewin, C.R., Greenberg, N., Hughes, J., Simpson, J., & Wessley, S. (2007). Enduring consequences of terrorism: 7-month follow-up survey of reactions to the bombings in London July 7, 2005. *British Journal of Psychiatry*, 190, 350–356.

Sapolsky, R. (1994). *Why Zebras Don't Get Ulcers*. New York: Holt Paperbacks.

Sapolsky, R. (2003). Stress and plasticity in the limbic system. *Neurochemical Research*, 28(11), 1735–1742.

Schlenger, W.E., Caddell, J.M., Ebert, L., Jordan, B.K., Rourke, K.M., Wilson, D., Thalji, L., Deniis, J.M., Fairbank, J.A., & Kulka, R.A. (2002). Psychological reactions to terrorist attacks: Findings from the national study of Americans' reactions to September 11. *Journal of American Medical Association*, 288, 581–588.

Schmeichel, B.J., Gailliot, M.T., Filardo, E., McGregor, I., Gitter, S., & Baumeister, R.F. (2009). Terror management theory and self-esteem revisited: The roles of implicit and explicit self-esteem in mortality salience effects. *Journal of Personality and Social Psychology*, 96, 1077–1087.

Selye, H. (1956). *The Stress of Life*. New York: McGraw-Hill.

Shalev, A.Y., & Freedman, S. (2005). PTSD following terrorist attacks: a prospective evaluation. *American Journal of Psychiatry*, 162(6), 1188–1191.

Sharma, D.P. (2003). *Victims of Terrorism*. New Delhi: APH Publishing.

Sinclair, J., & Antonius, D. (2012). *The Psychology of Terrorism Fears*. New York: Oxford University Press.

Sinclair, S.J. (2010). Fears of terrorism and future threat: Theoretical and empirical considerations. In D. Antonius, A.D., Brown, T. Walters, M. Ramirez, & S.J. Sinclair (eds), *Interdisciplinary Analyses of Terrorism and Aggression* (pp. 101–115). Cambridge: Cambridge Scholars Publishing.

Slovic, P., & Peters, E. (2006). Risk perception and affect. *Current Directions in Psychological Science*, 15, 322–325.

Smith, D.L. (2007). *The Most Dangerous Animal: Human Natures and the Nature of War*. New York: St. Martin's Press.

Sosis, R. (2007). Psalms for safety: Magico-religious responses to threats of terror. *Current Anthropology*, 48, 903–911.

Sosis, R., & Alcorta, C. (2008). Militants and martyrs: Evolutionary perspectives on religion and terrorism. In R. Sagarin & T. Taylor (eds), *Natural Security: A Darwinian Approach to a Dangerous World* (pp. 105–124). Berkeley: University of California Press.

Sosis, R., & Handwerker, P. (2011). Psalms and coping with uncertainty: Israeli women's responses to the 2006 Lebanon War. *American Anthropologist*, 113, 40–55.

Sosis, R., Philips, E., & Alcorta, C. (2012). Sacrifice and Sacred Values: Evolutionary Perspectives on Religious Terrorism. In T. Shackelford & V. Weeks-Schakelford (eds), *Oxford Handbook of Evolutionary Perspectives on Violence, Homicide, and War* (pp. 233–253). New York: Oxford University Press.

Sperber, D. (1994). The modularity of thought and the epidemiology of representations. In L. Hirschfeld & R. Gelman (eds), *Mapping the Mind* (pp. 39–67). Cambridge: Cambridge University Press.

Sprang, G. (2001). Vicarious stress: Patterns of disturbance and use of mental health services by those indirectly affected by the Oklahoma City bombing. *Psychology Reports*, 89, 331–338.

Stecklov, G., & Goldstein, J. (2004). Terror attacks influence driving behavior in Israel. *Proceedings of the National Academy of Sciences, USA*, 14551–14556.

Strickland, P.L., Deakin, W., Dixon, J., & Gater, R.A. (2002). Bio-social origins of depression in the community: interactions between social adversity, cortisol and serotonin neurotransmission. *British Journal of Psychiatry*, 180, 168–173.

Suris, A.M., & North, C.S. (2012). Mental health preparedness for terrorist incidents. In I. Marini & M. Stebnicki (eds), *The Psychological and Social Impact of Illness and Disability* (pp. 461–479). New York: Springer.

Tremoliere, B., De Neys, W., & Bonnefon, J.F. (2012). Mortality salience and morality: Thinking about death makes people less utilitarian. *Cognition*, 124, 379–384.

Tritt, S.M., Inzlicht, M., & Harmon-Jones, E. (2012). Toward a biological understanding of mortality salience (and other threat compensation processes). *Social Cognition*, 30(6), 715–733.

Vaillant, G.E. (2000). Adaptive mental mechanisms: Their role in a positive psychology. *American Psychologist*, 55(1), 89–98.

Van der Dennen, J. (2008). Ambivalent war-lovers? *Evolutionary Psychology*, 6(1), 3–12.

Van der Kolk, B. (1987). The separation cry and the trauma response: Developmental issues in the psychobiology of attachment and separation. In B. van der Kolk (ed.), *Psychological Trauma* (pp. 31–62). Washington, DC: American Psychiatric Press.

Van der Kolk, B. (1996). The body keeps score: Approaches to the psychobiology of post-traumatic stress disorder. In B. van der Kolk, A. McFarlane, & L. Weisaeth (eds), *Traumatic Stress: The Effects of Overwhelming Experience on Mind, Body, and Society*. New York: Guilford Press.

Victoroff, J. (2009). Suicide terrorism and the biology of significance. *Political Psychology*, 30(3), 397–400.

Wilson, M., & Daly, M. (1997). Life expectancy, economic inequality, homicide and reproductive timing in Chicago neighborhoods. *British Medical Journal*, 31(4), 1271–1274.

Wisman, A., & Goldenberg, J.L. (2005). From the grave to the cradle: Evidence that mortality salience engenders a desire for offspring. *Interpersonal Relations and Group Processes*, 89(1), 46–61.

Yehuda, R., & Hyman, S.E. (2005). The impact of terrorism on brain, and behavior: What we know and what we need to know. *Neuropsychopharmacology*, 30(10), 1773–1780.

Yen, C.L., & Lin, C.Y. (2012). The effect of mortality salience on escalation of commitment. *International Journal of Psychology*, 47(1), 51–57.

6 Terrorism as an act-in-context

A contextual behavioral science account

Akihiko Masuda, Matthew R. Donati, L. Ward Schaefer, and Mary L. Hill

There is general consensus that terrorism, however we define it, is a distressing global phenomenon (Eidelson & Eidelson, 2003; Moghaddam, 2005b; Morgan et al., 2011). Through human symbolic processes and advancing media technology, an act of terrorism in one part of the world now affects people and societies in many other parts of the globe. Another established view is that terrorism is a behavioral process, whether viewed at the individual or group level, and no sophisticated technology or increased military force will end terrorism in the long run (Moghaddam, 2005b). To better understand terrorism in hopes of promoting effective preventive solutions, experts in diverse disciplines, including psychology, have provided numerous theoretical accounts of terrorism.

Experts also note that many of the extant conceptual accounts of terrorism have shortcomings (Moghaddam, 2009; Taylor & Horgan, 2006). A major shortcoming is that these models do not necessarily lead to practical solutions for effectively preventing and reducing acts of terrorism. According to Moghaddam (2009), this limitation is due in part to the fundamental assumption that terrorism is a somewhat fixed phenomenon, whether it is attributed to dispositional or contextual events. As argued elsewhere (Moghaddam, 2005a; Taylor & Horgan, 2006), there is increasing awareness that terrorists are not born but made. In other words, by interacting in and with his or her sociocultural and symbolic context, an ordinary person could evolve into a terrorist. As such, terrorism (e.g. terrorist events and terrorist involvement) seems to be best understood as an evolving process of the behaviors of individuals interacting in and with their context, viewed historically and situationally (Moghaddam, 2009; Sidman, 2003; Taylor & Horgan, 2006).

As the present volume points out, in recent years there has been a growing interest in theorizing terrorism and related phenomena within a framework of evolutionary science. It is important to note that, while classical evolutionary models are generally gene-centric, some contemporary evolutionary models (Jablonka & Lamb, 2005; Wilson et al., 2014) theorize that evolutionary processes occur and interact at multiple levels, including genetic, epigenetic, behavioral, and symbolic levels. Within this framework, we present contextual behavioral science (CBS; Hayes et al.,

2012a; Hayes et al., 2013; Vilardaga et al., 2009) as a distinct extension of evolutionary science, approaching terrorism as an evolving process of contextually situated behavior of whole organisms at multiple-levels, especially at the levels of behavioral and symbolic processes (Hayes et al., 2002; Hayes & Toarmino, 1995). Given its contextual, pragmatic, and process-focused features, we find CBS to be particularly suitable for providing a better understanding of key issues related to terrorism and presenting potential solutions for these issues.

Evolutionary paradigm

In regard to human psychological and behavioral processes, early approaches to evolutionary psychology (EP) were generally gene-centric, positing that the mind is composed of specialized cognitive systems, each the product of *genetic evolution,* to solve specific problems faced by the ancestors of present-day humans (Buller, 2005). However, this dominant EP paradigm has significant shortcomings; most of the theories struggle to explain behavior change within the lifespan of an individual human. Terrorism may be influenced by genetically evolved modules, such as those that create a propensity for adherence to religious or political extremist ideology or by modules specific to group-based violence. However, many of the most socially significant questions surrounding terrorism, such as why terrorist behavior may occur more frequently in particular communities, or how and why an individual may be drawn into increasingly extreme forms of terrorist participation, cannot be answered by a strictly gene-centered evolutionary perspective. In addition, from a pragmatic standpoint, the causal factors identified by a gene-centric evolutionary perspective—genes and ancestral environment—are not directly manipulable targets for intervention in the present day.

An alternative evolutionary perspective

An alternative exists to the predominant gene-centric perspective on evolution. While individual theories may differ in some respects, they all begin from Darwin's observation that evolutionary change requires three elements: a mechanism for variation, an inheritance system for variations, and a mechanism by which these variations are selected according to certain fitness criteria. Classical genetic evolution clearly meets these criteria. Genes vary due to DNA mutation and recombination; organisms pass these changes on when they reproduce; and genotypic variation is selected for on the basis of its phenotypic effects on reproductive fitness. However, as Jablonka and Lamb (2005) argue in *Evolution in Four Dimensions*, change at the epigenetic, behavioral and symbolic levels also meets these three criteria. For our purposes, we will address epigenetic processes but focus more intently on the latter two dimensions of inheritance and evolution and its philosophical, conceptual, and strategic links to CBS (Hayes et al., 2012a; Hayes et al., 2013).

In evolution at the epigenetic level, environmental conditions lead to molecular changes, such as DNA methylation and histone acetylation that activate or inactivate particular genes. Epigenetic changes effectively modulate the expression of an individual organism's genotype, imposing a form of selection on particular patterns of gene activation. These changes can also be inherited by subsequent generations, allowing for epigenetic evolution at a rate far faster than possible through simple variation and selection at the genetic level. Epigenetic mechanisms have been implicated in the lifelong effects of a traumatic childhood on an individual's stress response and the predisposition towards obesity of children whose mothers experience famine during a critical period of gestation (Carey, 2012).

Epigenetic change and inheritance are relatively recent discoveries in the biological sciences, but as Roach and Pease (2013) argue, these processes have profound implications for the study and prevention of criminal behavior. By linking the distal genetic determinants of behavior and the more proximal environmental conditions in which individual humans currently live, epigenetics brings more rapidly appearing and changing human behavior within reach of an evolutionary analysis. As our knowledge of epigenetic processes grows, this level of evolution will likely become a crucial site of research and intervention around socially problematic behaviors like terrorism. However, the behavioral dimension of evolution, while often neglected, arguably offers more opportunity for direct intervention in the present day.

To say the behavior of humans and other organisms exhibit variation is hardly controversial. As Jablonka and Lamb (2005) point out, however, the nature of that variation is less often purely random, as with genetic mutation, and more often linked to prior learning. A bird attempting to crack a nut to obtain food will tend to try techniques that have helped it obtain food in other instances. The heritability of behavior is a more significant argument. Jablonka and Lamb point to the literature on observational learning and imitation as evidence that individual organisms can acquire—or "inherit"—novel behaviors without first experiencing the direct environmental contingencies in which those behaviors first developed. A classic example of this phenomenon is found in a colony of Japanese macaques on Koshima island, successive generations of which have continued to wash sweet potatoes before eating them, following the example of a single female (Kawai, 1965).

Behaviors that vary and are inherited are also subject to selection (Jablonka & Lamb, 2005). Through operant conditioning (Skinner, 1974, 1981), behaviors that bring an organism into contact with contextual and reinforcing stimuli will increase in frequency in the future, while those that bring the organism into contact with punishing stimuli will decrease. Framing operant conditioning as one form of a general principle of *selection by consequences*, Skinner (Skinner, 1971, 1981) proposed that behavior and cultural practices change according to the same evolutionary principles of selection that guide genetic evolution. Just as the reproductive consequences of a particular genetically determined phenotype shape the future frequency of that genotype, so too do the consequences of a particular behavior or cultural practice determine the future extent of that behavior or practice.

The symbolic dimension of inheritance and evolution is most clearly identified with human verbal behavior, especially language, but also music, art and gesture (Jablonka & Lamb, 2005). These symbolic systems all have unlimited capacity for variation: new words can be coined to refer to any object, and words can be combined to represent novel thoughts. Through speech, written language and recordings, symbolic information can be transmitted between individuals and inherited by future generations. It has been repeatedly argued that the open-ended capacity to relate and transmit symbols distinguishes humans from other species and is responsible for the proliferation of human cultural practices (Deacon, 1997; Penn et al., 2008).

Jablonka and Lamb (2005) and Skinner (1981) also identify forms of selection operating on the variation in symbolic behavior. We relate novel symbolic information that we acquire from other people to existing symbolic systems, and some symbols or relations between symbols are more likely to be successfully integrated than others. Often this process involves social reinforcement. For example, a normal child learning to speak will eventually begin using words metaphorically, perhaps by calling his mother, "sweet mummy" (Jablonka & Lamb, 2005, p. 199). Such a metaphor is likely to bring a child into contact with reinforcers such as attention, affection, and verbal responses from his mother. Consequently, the relations between those symbols will be strengthened, so that both mother and child will be more likely to use and respond to such metaphors in the future. By contrast, a metaphor such as "transparent mummy" is less likely to bring the child into contact with such social reinforcement.

At a larger scale, cultural practices that are embedded in symbols can be said to be selected by their consequences for the group. A particular method of farming, transmitted between individuals by language, may result in positive social consequences, such as improved farming yields, that select for that practice in the future (Skinner, 1981). Similarly, selection can act on abstract ideas, such as notions of political or religious utopias, changing their form, or increasing or decreasing their frequency within a culture, based on the consequences associated with transmitting and behaving in accordance with them (Jablonka & Lamb, 2005). The spread of a particular political ideology, a defining feature of terrorism, could thus be conceptualized as an indication of evolution at the level of behavior and symbols, in which variation and selection by consequences have selected for symbolic or overt behavior associated with that ideology.

Contextual behavioral science

CBS (Hayes et al., 2012a; Hayes et al., 2013; Vilardaga et al., 2009) is a human enterprise seeking the development and refinement of basic and applied scientific concepts and methods for the pragmatic purpose of *predicting-and-influencing* the contextually embedded actions of whole organisms, individually and within groups, with precision, scope, and depth. According to Hayes and colleagues (Hayes et al., 2012a; Vilardaga et al., 2009), CBS can be viewed as a distinct extension of Skinner's evolutionary science. What differentiates it from Skinner's account is a knowledge base about the principle of *arbitrarily applicable derived relational responding* (please see below) as the core of human symbolic/verbal learning and its impact on behavior. More specifically, CBS consciously commits to the agenda of linking knowledge about behavioral and symbolic development to other dimensions of human inheritance and development, such as genetic and epigenetic factors, biological and behavioral developmental plasticity, and cultural extensions of behavioral and symbolic development, in service of creating a behavioral science more adequate to the challenges faced by humans, including terrorism.

Assumptions of contextual behavioral science

CBS is based on a philosophy of science, called functional contextualism (Biglan & Hayes, 1996; Hayes et al., 1988). The fundamental perspective of functional contextualism is *the behavior of organisms interacting in and with a context, viewed both situationally and historically*. Functional contextualism chooses to view the world this way in order to understand why a behavioral phenomenon of interest occurs and the purpose of the behavior. The purpose and function of a given behavior is not defined by the behavior itself but by its interaction in and with the context (Hayes et al., 1988). As such, the functional contextualist view is that an act of a whole organism cannot be understood separate from the context in which it occurs.

The framework of an *act-in-context* is applicable not only at the individual level but also at the group level (Biglan, 2009; Hayes & Toarmino, 1995). Within this framework, acts of an individual terrorist, acts of a terrorist organization (Moghaddam, 2005b; Taylor, 2010), and people's reactions to terrorism (Dixon et al., 2003; Morgan et al., 2011) are all conceptualized as contextually situated actions. For example, the sarin attack on the Tokyo subway that occurred at the peak of morning rush hour on Monday, March 20, 1995 can be conceptualized at an individual level as the unfolding and purposeful, contextually situated behavior of an individual member of a cult group, Aum Shinrikyo, or it can be viewed at the group level as a cultural practice of a coordinated attack by the cult organization. Once again, the essence of functional contextualism is to explicate the purpose and maintaining function of a given act by seeking a causal link with the systematically manipulable context of that behavior.

The analytic goal of functional contextualism is *prediction-and-influence* of behavior by explicating a causal pattern between behavior and the context (Biglan & Hayes, 1996; Hayes et al., 1988). This pragmatic goal distinguishes it from other worldviews that are more descriptive in focus. For example, while it is important to accurately *describe* an act of terrorism (e.g. "The member of the cult group punctured a bag of sarin and exited the train at 8:40 am"), solely descriptive approaches do not necessarily help to address the problems that terrorism causes, nor do they fully address why this behavior occurs, or how we can prevent similar incidents in the future (Taylor, 2010; Taylor & Horgan, 2006). To do so, it is crucial to identify causal and buffering factors that can be systematically manipulated. According to Hayes and Brownstein (1986), at psychological and group levels of analyses, the contextual factors are the only causal factors that can be intentionally arranged and rearranged in service of influencing the behavior of interest.

The truth criterion of functional contextualism is *successful working*, which defines truth based on whether one's knowledge and strategy meet the predetermined purposes (Biglan & Hayes, 1996; Hayes et al., 1988). In other words, "truth" for functional contextualism is not an ontological matter but a functional one. Suppose that one is going to build a theory for terrorism for the purpose of developing feasible and effective strategies to reduce the incidence of future terrorist attacks. He then crafts a model of terrorist behavior. No matter how sophisticated it appears, the model is said to be untrue if it does not meet the goal of developing effective prevention strategies.

Contextual behavioral science as an evolutionary science

In a recent article, D. S. Wilson and colleagues (2014) offer a synthesis of CBS and multilevel selection theory and employ two terms for conceptualizing the simultaneous operation of genetic, behavioral and symbolic selection. The first, the "Darwin Machine," was originally proposed by Calvin (1987) and refers to systems within humans or other organisms that are the ultimate products of genetic evolution but which themselves possess the essential mechanisms of an evolutionary process. The concept of a Darwin Machine reconciles the primacy of genetic influence on evolutionary change with the so-called "blank slate" perspectives that emphasize change over the course of individual lifetimes or cultural epochs. The classic example of a Darwin Machine, the human immune system, illustrates this point. Many components of the immune system are products of genetic evolution targeted to specific adaptive functions, such as macrophages, which ingest pathogens. These components largely evolved over millennia. The immune system is also able to respond to environmental changes within the lifetime of an individual through variation and selection for antibodies that target molecular signatures on specific pathogens. An individual's immune response is thus a function of genetic evolution but also a Darwin Machine producing variation and selection within a vastly more immediate time frame.

Echoing Skinner (1974, 1981), Wilson and colleagues (2014) suggest that the learning processes of operant and respondent conditioning represent an additional Darwin Machine shared by many organisms. Through the acquisition of respondent and contingent associations specific to their experience (i.e. an ongoing and evolving act-in-context), organisms can develop behavioral repertoires with no underlying evolutionary change in their genotype.

The presence of learning and symbolic Darwin Machines can account for the evolution of behavioral or symbolic repertoires that function maladaptively at other levels of selection. A gene-centric view of EP would interpret a maladaptive behavior, such as murder, in terms of a "mismatch" between the environment of evolutionary adaptedness (EEA) for the module underlying that behavior (e.g. aggression) and the present-day environment. An alternate interpretation might be that such maladaptive behavior reflects the concurrent operation of learning and symbolic Darwin Machines, which have evolved new contextually situated behavioral processes (Wilson et al., 2014).

In the context of presenting CBS as a distinct extension of evolutionary science, Wilson and colleagues (2014) also provide a novel concept to illustrate the symbolic level of evolution: the *symbotype*. Symbotypes refer to the products and processes of symbolic activities that can be transmitted and recombined in much the same way that Jablonka and Lamb describe symbolic inheritance. In the same way that a genotype is expressed in an organism as a phenotype, or physical trait, a symbotype is expressed in an organism's rule-governed behavior (Hayes, 1989; Hayes et al., 2001), human activities that are regulated by symbolic/verbal processes (see below). Just as genetic evolution involves selection at the level of a phenotypic trait, as opposed to selection of individual genotypes, symbotypic evolution would presumably involve selection at the level of behavior.

As described above, symbotypes may sound similar to "memes," the famous coinage of evolutionary biologist Richard Dawkins to refer to a proposed unit of cultural evolution, such as "ideas, catch-phrases, clothes fashions, ways of making pots or of building arches" (Dawkins, 1976, p. 192). Symbotypes differ from memes in several crucial aspects, however (Wilson et al., 2014). As Dawkins presents them, memes can be said to function in the same "selfish" manner as genes, replicating themselves regardless of their benefit to the human who hosts them. Dawkins's meme concept raises tantalizing questions, such as what formal properties of a meme, such as belief in God, make it relatively more or less successful at propagating itself throughout the cultural-historical meme pool.

Yet the meme's similarity to Dawkins's "selfish gene" is also the source of its inadequacy as a construct for explaining and changing behavior, relative to a contextual behavioral approach and a concept like the symbotype, however novel. For Dawkins and other meme proponents, the propagation of a political ideology might be explained as the successful replication of a specific meme across individuals. The meme analysis would emphasize the formal properties of that ideology and their relative fitness with regard to the surrounding "meme pool." What the meme analysis would overlook or underemphasize, however, are the very processes of primary interest to a science of behavior change: What environmental conditions influence the imitation or replication of a political ideology meme or the expression of its behavioral phenotype?

By contrast, the symbotype concept posits evolution at the cultural-symbolic level without the need for a discrete, self-replicating unit. A symbotype's behavioral expression that brings an individual into contact with reinforcers (social, material, or verbal) is likely to both persist in an individual's symbolic/verbal repertoire and to increase in frequency within a population. For example, in a given sociocultural context, symbotypes associated with prosocial behavior, such as the belief "It is good to share," will likely lead individuals to behave in prosocial ways that select for that symbotype. Applying this analysis to terrorism, the popularity of religious or political extremism in certain sociocultural contexts can be said to reflect the contexts that promote behavior associated with an extremist symbotype (Taylor & Horgan, 2006).

Relational frame theory: a CBS account of complex human behavior

Relational frame theory (RFT; Hayes et al., 2001) is a CBS-informed theory of complex human behavior, postulating that virtually all human behaviors are *symbolically* and *verbally* learned, shaped, and maintained. As stated above, this conceptual position overlaps with conventional behavioral principles explicated by Skinner (Hayes et al., 2012a; Vilardaga, 2009). RFT expands conventional behavioral accounts by highlighting the predominantly verbal and symbolic nature of human conditioning, which is called *arbitrarily applicable derived relational learning*, with the functional and contextual emphasis on predicting-and-influencing the behavior of interest.

Humans are social beings who interact with one another and their environment verbally and symbolically. Verbal and symbolic processes, or symbotypes, are a central part of life, occurring in virtually every facet of human activities (Hayes et al., 2001). According to RFT, human verbal and symbolic behavior is roughly defined as a process of describing, relating, framing, and evaluating an event in terms of other events (Hayes et al., 2001). There seems to be nothing new about this definition. What is innovative about this account is the explication of a contextually situated learning process that can be *arbitrarily applied* and *derived* without direct learning, as well as a conceptualization of the basic symbolic processes of describing, relating, and evaluating using this conceptual framework (Barnes-Holmes et al., 2000). The human symbolic process (e.g. "A is…", "A is better than …") is said to be *arbitrary* in that it goes beyond the restriction of physical property. For example, there is no absolute physical law explaining why English-speaking people call a certain group of mammals a "dog," but Japanese speaking people call it "inu." Naming it "dog" or "inu" is more or less *arbitrarily determined* within sociocultural contexts (i.e. verbal community) where the process of symbolic activity occurs. Similarly, a symbolic behavior is said to be *derived* as humans come up with new symbolic relations without directly learning them. Suppose that one hears that Japanese people are polite and that Aki is Japanese. With these two symbolic networks, many are likely to derive a new relation, "Aki is polite," without difficulty.

Furthermore, symbolically framed events have a certain meaning (psychological function). For example, the term "polite" evokes certain imagery. RFT states that once an event is related to and framed symbolically with other events in a certain way, the framed event acquires new meaning, or nuance, depending on how it is framed with these other events. Suppose the term "polite" evokes a feeling of annoyance for a person. Once Aki is framed as "being polite," that phrase evokes the feeling of annoyance for that individual. A key point here is that this symbolic relating occurs whenever one thinks, understands, speaks, listens, ruminates, wonders, rationalizes, believes, and tries to make sense of something, and so on.

As stated above, a key tenet of RFT is that verbal and symbolic processing has become a dominant part of one's context that regulates other behaviors of that person at both psychological and group levels (Hayes, 1989; Hayes et al., 2001). This regulatory function of symbolic process occurs indiscriminately, whether a behavior (e.g. anything we do or say) is adaptive or not. For example, both the prosocial behavior of caring for the elderly in public transportation and the antisocial act of setting a homemade bomb in a public place are very likely to be regulated verbally. At a group level, many cultural practices are often verbally transmitted from generation to generation (Hayes et al., 2002; Hayes & Toarmino, 1995). In RFT, a behavior that is regulated and maintained verbally/symbolically is called rule-governed behavior (Hayes, 1989).

In order to make sense of their social environment, individuals develop symbolic and relational networks to characterize other individuals and groups in terms of other events (Hayes et al., 2001; Kurzban & Leary, 2001). Each relation is formed on the basis of circumscribed facets, and by necessity, there are a finite number of relations that are potentiated, or attended to, at any one time. As a result, verbal categorizations of an individual are short cuts and not the result of thorough perceptions and understanding of the myriad of aspects that define a human being. The result can be objectification and dehumanization of that individual (Hayes et al., 2002). Often the relations that can come to dominate verbal/symbolic behavior are those based on the salient characteristics of ethnicity, race, or country of origin (Dixon et al., 2003; Hayes et al., 2002). A person who comes in contact with another individual for the first time may respond to that individual based on attributive and evaluative relations derived from the conceptualized group to which the individual is believed to belong.

There are several reasons to emphasize symbolic/verbal processes in service of creating a behavioral science more adequate to the challenges of the human condition. First, in many sociocultural and political contexts, processes of conflict as well as those of conflict resolution at both individual and group levels are verbally and symbolically regulated. Second, what is often called "the root of terrorism," moral conflicts and clashes in ideologies, is also verbal and symbolic (Hayes et al., 1998). As such, terrorism (e.g. a terrorist act, terrorist involvement) can be viewed as an ongoing and evolving process of describing, relating, and evaluating events in terms of other events as well as behaviors that are regulated by this process.

Third, the products of symbolic and verbal processing, such as particular ideologies or stereotypes (e.g. "Terrorists are evil, and they deserve to be punished"), are difficult to eliminate once formed. New attitudes may be created (e.g. "under a particular circumstance, an ordinary person can become a terrorist"), but cannot supplant previously established attitudes (Wilson et al., 2000). Furthermore, efforts to eliminate and suppress strongly held viewpoints, beliefs, and attitudes, are often futile and counterproductive (Wegner, 1994). As mentioned below, the rigidity of ideology is particularly relevant to the process of terrorism at both individual and group levels.

Fourth, symbolic and verbal processing can change the functions of other behavioral processes (Hayes et al., 2001). For example, suppose a person is a dedicated Buddhist in a non-Western society and occasionally takes Western medicine for a physical ailment. After hearing that taking a Western medicine is a sign of toxic Americanization, the person may avoid taking all Western medications as if doing so is committing an immoral act. As noted elsewhere (Hayes et al., 2002; Kurzban & Leary, 2001), this indirect learning is quite efficient and economical in many contexts, but it could be quite debilitating in other contexts.

Fifth, one of the most debilitating features of human symbolic/verbal process is that it can obscure the here-and-now experience (Hayes, 1989; Hayes et al., 2001). This is in part because, through verbal processing, humans respond to a particular event (or person) in terms of its relation to other events. A salient example is stereotyping behavior. The process of stereotyping includes relating a person to a particular social categorization and, as a result, viewing the person as an object in a unidimensional and dehumanizing fashion. The problem of stereotyping or any other symbolic process is that it prevents one from contacting the diverse aspects of that person by focusing instead on a symbolically crafted story of that person. However, given its automatic nature, this symbolic/relational process occurs without the awareness of doing so or the awareness that the product of symbolic framing can be arbitrary and does not necessarily reflect the actual people who are symbolically framed (Hayes et al., 2002). Additionally, the contextual cues that control relating can become increasingly subtle, and a fully formed conceptualization of a person, with the attendant behavioral functions, can be determined by something as small as their last name (Watt et al., 1991), or their choice to grow a beard and wear a turban (Dixon et al., 2009; Dixon et al., 2006).

Finally, symbolic processes may make individuals become relatively insensitive to environmental changes (Hayes, 1989; Hayes et al., 1986). After repeated exposure to multiple exemplars in the media or local culture, stereotypical verbal conceptualizations can become tighter, more internally consistent, and dominate in an increasing number of contexts. This process can be maintained despite changes in direct experiences or contradictory evidence (e.g. a positive experience with a Western person, or changes in Western policies) as correspondence (e.g. stereotype-confirming evidence) in symbolic process is a relatively strong reinforcement for the symbolic process itself (Roche et al., 2002).

Summary

CBS is a distinct extension of evolutionary science that encompasses diverse topics of investigation at different levels of analysis while maintaining a coherent unit of analysis and analytic goal. From a CBS-consistent evolutionary perspective, then, terrorist behavior can reflect the combined influence of the innate and acquired characteristics of genes, operant conditioning, or symbolic behavior—or the interaction of all three. Gene-centric evolutionary accounts of terrorism tend to confine the analysis to discordance between ancestral environments and modern contextual factors. In contrast, CBS invokes the domain general process of evolutionary change, or selection by consequences, to comprehensively theorize and study both the distal factors of innate genetic influence and the proximate factors of cultural, symbolic, and behavioral Darwin machines.

CBS account of terrorism and reactions to terrorism

As stated earlier, the present CBS account views terrorist acts of a perpetrator (e.g. terrorist events and terrorist involvement) as well as the victims' and public's reactions to terrorist acts as ongoing and evolving processes of contextually situated action. It is noteworthy that this definition does not necessarily differentiate terrorism from other forms of behavior. In terms of its topography, terrorism is quite clearly a distinct form of behavior, but in terms of undergirding functional processes, it is undifferentiated. Gene-centric evolutionary accounts have long recognized that a fully functioning adaptive process can propagate dysfunctional outcomes. This occurs, for example, when a dysfunctional phenotypic variation is selected for because of a shared genotype with an adaptive variation. As Wilson and colleagues (2014) have detailed, when viewing evolution as a domain-general process, it becomes apparent that dysfunctional outcomes, such as terrorism, can also be propagated because they are functional for a certain selection criterion. Problems arise when the selection criteria are incongruent with other criteria, such as those of human welfare and cooperation. Because terrorism is the result of an ongoing functioning process, it becomes crucial to identify the functional units involved. In defining terrorism, a CBS approach focuses on identifying the functional units involved, such as those of variation, selection criteria, and the selective environment, with the goal of prediction and influence.

Well-conceptualized accounts of terrorism as psychological process are presented elsewhere (Moghaddam, 2005a, 2005b; Taylor, 2010; Taylor & Horgan, 2001, 2006). We believe that these conceptualizations can be adequately translated into a CBS account of terrorism without losing their psychological and process-focused nuance. Key tenets of these accounts are as follows:

1 Terrorism-relevant behavior (e.g. terrorist events and terrorist involvement) can be understood as an *ongoing* and *evolving* psychological process of an individual, which is shaped by the transaction with his or her environment (Taylor & Horgan, 2006). A given terrorist behavior is the product of previous transactional history, and it will become part of the transactional history for a future terrorist behavior.
2 There are multiple pathways/routes of getting involved in terrorism, and those routes and activities experienced by the individual *evolve* over time (Taylor & Horgan, 2006).
3 The functions that individual members serve in a terrorist organization can be complex and multifaceted (Taylor & Horgan, 2006). For example, some may hold multiple roles simultaneously to sustain the organization, and others may serve different roles as they become senior members of the organization.
4 Terrorism is verbally and symbolically regulated in an individual and political context where ideology-consistent behaviors are reinforced and ideology-inconsistent behaviors are discouraged or often punished (Taylor & Horgan, 2001, 2006).
5 In the context of terrorism, ideology is associated with strong emotional reactions (e.g. anger toward members of an out-group) and often functions as a strong motivating factor for terrorist acts (Moghaddam, 2005b).
6 Terrorist acts involve psychological processes central to interpersonal dynamics: One is social categorization, and the other is psychological distancing (Moghaddam, 2005b).

What CBS can add to these accounts is the possibility to connect different levels of analysis (individual vs. group, psychological vs. transactional) utilizing the same domain-general processes of change. Existing conjunctive frameworks of terrorism often appeal to numerous theories in what can be discrepant areas (e.g. cognitive psychology, behaviorism, social psychology, criminology) in order to address all the relevant factors influencing terrorism (e.g. Roach et al., 2005). Traditional behavioral analyses are often combined with cognitive accounts, despite the fact that these two approaches have different assumptions and analytical goals. The amalgamation is understandable when considering the failure, thus far, of traditional behaviorism to address the cognitive and symbolically mediated aspects of terrorism, such as group dynamics and ideological control. However, by studying symbolic behavior in a functional contextual way with new technologies and research programs, CBS is able to address complex behavior using the general principles of selection by consequences and operant conditioning. In other words, CBS has further explicated the proximal extensions of evolutionary process, of which traditional behavioral learning has always been a part, for the purpose of analyzing individual and group behavior.

Taylor and Horgan (2006) have noted the promise of incorporating a CBS account of symbolic/verbal processes into the models of terrorism as follows:

> A further central research issue emerging from the above relates to how we might understand the effects of ideology and organizational influences on the individual. Explorations of accounts grounded in empirical evidence, such as rule governance and relational frame theory, may offer fruitful avenues for further conceptual development.
>
> (pp. 597–598)

A strong empirical foundation is needed to test the applicability of the CBS perspective to terrorism. While some early laboratory research has been done to test the concepts underlying the CBS perspective in the context of prejudice and terrorism (Dixon et al., 2006), additional work is needed, not only to determine if these early findings can be replicated, but also to expand the existing empirical evidence to begin to develop interventions. The next step is to apply the CBS perspective to real cases of known terrorists and then to implement theoretically consistent interventions (e.g. facilitating direct contact between groups in order to build new verbal relations that underlie the derived processes in acts of terrorism).

Terrorist events and terrorist involvement of the perpetrator

The RFT analysis presented above details how the adaptive and universal process of symbolic behavior (i.e. verbal behavior) can naturally lead to the verbal formulation of other human beings as objects worthy of attack. The question then becomes what process can lead these verbal formulations to dominate over other competing inputs. Terrorists become terrorists through a transactional process of involvement with terrorist groups and activities (Taylor, 2010; Taylor & Horgan, 2001, 2006). In many respects, the RFT interpretation of this process is compatible with the decision tree conceptualization of rational choice theory applied to terrorism (Taylor, 1993) in that the behavior of the individual at any point is determined by the situational factors at hand, which continually change as the individual and context reciprocally interact. This decision tree account is useful in developing intervention plans tailored to particular individual terrorists or groups as the focus of interventions are likely to vary in the extents and functions of terrorist involvement. Extending this account, an RFT interpretation seeks to determine a *verbally/symbolically determined* causal link between a chosen behavior and situational/contextual factors within the contingencies of reinforcement of that behavior (i.e. act-in-context in a historical and situational sense).

In regard to causal links between target behavior and contextual factors, it is necessary to consider the group and social processes of terrorist behavior as symbolically regulated, and symbolic processes are naturally social (Hayes et al., 2001; Hayes & Toarmino, 1995; Skinner, 1974). The concept of group membership and cohesion is highly relevant to intergroup conflicts, prejudice, and stereotype (Eidelson & Eidelson, 2003; Roche et al., 2001). The abstract concept of group membership can be gainfully analyzed using RFT. According to RFT (Roche et al., 2001), the more group cohesion is based on shared characteristics among members, the more salient the conceptualized group becomes, and the greater the subordination of individual identity. Unfortunately, this can create a greater potential for conflict with other groups as the strong sense of group cohesion (e.g. identifying oneself as a member of a particular group) automatically strengthens the sense of differentiation from others who do not belong to the group. For example, evidence demonstrates that the more religious individuals consider themselves, the more they view non-religious groups negatively (Jackson & Hunsberger, 1999).

Relatedly, group cohesion can be viewed as proportional to the strength of the reinforcers for staying in the group and punishers for leaving the group (Cota et al., 1995; Roche et al., 2001). This viewpoint is problematic for the Skinnerian account because group members never directly contact the punishment for leaving a group, and most of the reinforcers, such as mutual security, are abstract (Parrott, 1987). The RFT analysis of rule governance illustrates how a distant, never before experienced consequence of leaving the group can be behaviorally contacted, and how the benefits of mutual security can be relationally derived. For a religious or fundamentalist group, primary reinforcers available outside the group (e.g. sex, food, family contact), as well as punishers within the group (e.g. abstinence, fasting) can threaten group cohesion.

For humans, reinforcing and punishing functions of a consequential stimulus are not in the stimulus, but in how it is symbolically related to other events. A functional class of rules defined as *augmentals* is important to an RFT analysis of group cohesion (Roche et al., 2001). Augmentals are statements that alter the reinforcing or punishing aspects of consequences by verbally and symbolically relating them to other events (Barnes-Holmes et al., 2001; Hayes, 1989). For example, by relating primary reinforcers to concepts like *evil* or *morally weak* terrorist groups can give these consequences punishing functions. In addition, by relating activities like *prayer* and even *violence* to *righteousness* or *god*, reinforcement from distant, abstract consequences will be contacted in the moment.

Verbal rules that indicate behavioral norms are central to any group. Rules reduce stress for the individual by providing guidelines for action in novel situations (Roche & Barnes-Holmes, 2003). There is strong reinforcement for behaving in a manner coherent with group rules and for having self-rules and conceptualizations that are consonant with those of the group. In addition, rules allow groups to both transmit practices and establish control over members without the need for direct and frequent reinforcement. Taylor and Horgan (2001) have detailed how the principles of rule-governed behavior can be used to analyze fundamentalism.

A strong ideological influence is one of the main features of terrorism that differentiate it from other forms of violence (Taylor & Horgan, 2006). In large part due to this ideological influence, the subject of terrorism has resisted attempts at a thoroughgoing functional analysis. It is a strength of the CBS approach, and its insight into rule-governed behavior, that it is able to seamlessly include ideology into the same analysis as direct behavioral inputs and evolutionary process considerations. From an RFT perspective, ideology can be viewed as a set of rules guiding behavior (Taylor & Horgan, 2001), of the same type as the augmentals and explicit rules described previously. Therefore, at the group and cultural level, ideology constitutes a symbotype, as we have defined the term herein, which is selected for by the behaviors of the individuals that it motivates. We have seen how the behaviors of individual terrorist recruits can be analyzed by considering the interplay between direct behavioral inputs and verbally mediated inputs. We have also seen how the dominance of verbal inputs can contribute to extensive group cohesion. It is this group cohesion that may very well be the mechanism that selects for the ideological symbotype in fundamentalist organizations.

A further functional analysis of the particular rules involved may help explain how the fundamentalist comes to be dominated by ideology over competing inputs, and how this ideology can readily lead to violent outcomes. Take the case of Islamic fundamentalist ideology. Similar to other religions, many of the ideological rules relate current directives for action to distant and highly abstract consequences. Research on rule governance has demonstrated that these types of rules are more likely to be insensitive to environmental inputs and to be rigidly followed (Hayes, 1989) as consistency between rules and outward behavior is often reinforced in a given sociocultural context (e.g. verbal community; Hayes et al., 2001; Skinner, 1974). Furthermore, a reliance on abstract worldviews over direct environmental inputs has been identified as a cognitive characteristic that can promote a tendency for violent outcomes (Eidelson & Eidelson, 2003). The "self-contained" nature of fundamentalist Islam could lead to more absolutist thinking because allowances in any area are more likely to threaten the coherence of the network. This could lead to all-or-nothing and us-versus-them mentalities and a greater sense of exclusiveness of moralities between Islam and the West that is characteristic of Islamic terrorist groups.

It is possible to further this analysis by looking at how ideological rules lead to the attitude and behavior change of a terrorist recruit. The relative weight of competing contingencies determines if a person will have a change in attitudes and the accordant behavior change. As noted by Roche and colleagues (2001), this viewpoint is consistent with the *theory of reasoned action* view of attitude change (Ajzen & Fishbein, 1980). According to this theory, whether or not someone will change their attitude and behavior is dependent on the level of functional control of perceived susceptibility to aversive consequences, competence in avoiding negative consequences, and the value placed on behavior change. The Millenarian aspects of Islamic ideology create *augmentals* that give the threat posed by the West a sense of imminence. Perceived injustices are catastrophized and made functionally present. These augmentals, combined with the Islamic rules relating action to certain victory and providing clear directives for behavior, make rule following more likely.

Reactions to terrorism by the target of terrorist attacks and the general public

People express many different reactions to terrorist events. The concepts presented thus far to analyze terrorist behavior are equally applicable to responses to terrorist acts. As noted by Morgan and colleagues (2011) in the context of reviewing Americans' reactions to 9/11, some of these reactions are strong and emotionally charged. These include political intolerance, support for war, discrimination, and hate crimes directed toward the target group or people who are symbolically, not actually, associated with the attackers.

Regarding the post-9/11 anti-Islamic reactions in the U.S., the actions of the American political administration can be viewed as a set of, symbolically clever, rhetorical strategies that take advantage of arbitrarily applicable derived learning to mobilize the nation for wars against Afghanistan and Iraq by framing these two countries with "terrorism." More specifically, these strategies focus on the promotion of *group cohesion* and a strong and coherent abstract conceptualization of the American position (e.g. freedom, democracy, and strength), which is framed as *being incompatible with* terrorism. By reinforcing a conceptualization based on these limited aspects, a relation of opposition was cued between America and anyone who might not share one or more of these values, such as persons in a non-democratic Middle Eastern country. The narrative was highly coherent, and there was little room for ambiguity, which likely promoted all-or-nothing thinking and mutual exclusiveness of American and Islamic moralities (e.g. "us" versus "them"). Once a relation of opposition was established, anything attributed to America would detract from the relational network of Islam symbolically. By focusing exclusively on the evaluations of America as righteous and infallible, a verbal human cannot help but derive negative evaluations of anyone categorized in relations of opposition.

CBS-informed strategies for issues related to terrorism

Evidence of CBS-based preventive and counterterrorism strategies is lacking. However, given a large body of empirical evidence supporting a CBS-consistent framework of symbolically regulated complex human behavior (Biglan, 2009; Biglan et al., 2012; Biglan & Hinds, 2009; Lillis & Levin, 2014; Masuda et al., 2012), it is possible to explicate key tenets for developing effective interventions for issues related to terrorism.

It is important to note that CBS strategies mainly focus on prevention. The rationales for preventive efforts are nicely summarized by Moghaddam (2005b). Metaphorically presenting terrorist acts as the final step on a narrowing staircase, he states that

> psychologists should articulate the limited effectiveness of short-term strategies that have dominated policy in this area for decades: secretive 'counterterrorist' units and measures, a total concern to hunt for the so-called bad apples or needles in a haystack, and a naïve reliance on improved technology and superior military might as the solution to defeating terrorism. The strategy of identifying and eliminating terrorists is extremely costly and counterproductive, because *as long as conditions on the group floor remain the same, every terrorist who is eliminated is quickly replaced by others.* Obviously, long-term and short-term policies can be implemented hand-in-hand, but psychologists have an important role in helping to turn policies toward foundational long-term solutions. (p. 167)

CBS strategies overlap with Skinnerian strategies of behavior change (Skinner, 1971, 1974), which are designed to reduce the likelihood of problematic behaviors by increasing behaviors that are either functionally incompatible with these problematic behaviors or by promoting behaviors that are functionally similar to the problematic behaviors, but socially more adaptive (Miltenberger, 2012). Relative to the immediate effects of punishment strategies applied to problematic behaviors, which are consistent with the current policies against terrorism (e.g. military war against terrorists), the effects of these strategies may be slow but effective in reducing and preventing these problematic behaviors in the long run. Additionally, unlike punishment strategies and other aversive means, these constructive strategies are designed to minimize negative emotional reactions (e.g. hate, anger) by target individuals, which often perpetuates a vicious cycle of interpersonal and intergroup conflicts (Goldiamond, 2002). Once again, CBS extends these Skinnerian strategies by taking the symbolic nature of behavior change into account (Hayes et al., 2007).

The CBS approach is likely most useful for those in academic and public policy settings. Within academia, CBS offers a new perspective from which to understand how terrorism develops, is maintained, and evolves over time (e.g. how past and current physical and symbolic environmental stimuli influence the control of behavior). Policymakers could benefit from creating terrorism prevention programs and interventions informed by the CBS account of terrorism.

CBS-based interventions for modulating the negative impact of human symbolic processes

As noted elsewhere (Biglan, 2009; Biglan et al., 2012; Biglan & Hinds, 2009; Lillis & Levin, 2014; Masuda et al., 2012), the proposed CBS-informed intervention for the negative consequences of human symbolic process, such as prejudice and other forms of social categorization, focuses on (a) the underlying verbal processes of categorization, association, and evaluation rather than the specific topographical content of stigmatizing thoughts; and (b) the promotion of intrinsic and *prosocial actions* alternative to or incompatible with terrorist actions and actions promoting terrorist actions, rather than directly challenging and making efforts to refute ideology or social categorizations (Hayes et al., 2004; Masuda et al., 2009). Interestingly, emerging trends within the literature on interventions for social categorizations and interpersonal conflicts have begun to highlight the effectiveness of promoting these processes. The following are some of the key tenets of CBS informed strategies. Once again, it is important to craft interventions tailored to the target individuals and groups.

Discouraging social pressure and thought suppression

One major attempt to reducing symbolically regulated problematic behaviors is via social influence. For instance, protest (Corrigan & Penn, 1999) and social norms messages (Stangor et al., 2001) can all defy negatively evaluated social categorizations and actions regulated by such categorizations. Unfortunately, the literature suggests that when external motivators (i.e. social pressure) are used, such attempts can result in increases in the impact of social categorization as a behavior regulatory agent (Legault et al., 2011). From a CBS perspective, external pressure is ineffective because it often serves as a suppression strategy (Hausmann & Ryan, 2004). From an RFT perspective, thought suppression fails because the very act of suppression always pairs with the event to be suppressed (e.g. "don't think about IT"). When humans are pressured to refrain from particular ideological thoughts, the very attempt heightens these ideological beliefs.

Being cognizant of contextual and setting factors

A major goal of CBS-based interventions, which is consistent with functional contextualism, is to build and nurture the sociocultural contexts so that individuals in these contexts do not have to engage in interpersonal conflicts

(Biglan, 2009; Biglan et al., 2012). As the literature suggests, ideology itself (e.g. Christian values) does not lead to interpersonal and intergroup conflicts. Rather, it is a symbolically established sociocultural context that amplifies hate and anger from perceived injustice and deprivation and rationalizes the displacement of these strong emotions onto members of the out-group (Eidelson & Eidelson, 2003; Moghaddam, 2005a, 2005b). As such, intervention strategies should assess social and symbolic contingencies that reflect the perceived deprivation and injustice and promote individual and cultural practices that are intrinsically prosocial and reinforcing.

Enhancing internal motivation

Research has shown that increasing personally relevant motivation effectively reduces the negative impact of social categorization and interpersonal and intergroup conflicts regulated by it. For example, increases in internal motivation are related to decreases in stigma and prejudice (Legault et al., 2009). Furthermore, interventions targeting internal motivation have resulted in lower explicit and implicit prejudice (Lee, 2011). In short, it appears that enhancing motivation linked to self-selected, personally relevant prosocial goals and values may be an effective method to reduce the negative impact of social categorization (Masuda et al., 2009).

Increasing awareness of automatic stigma and prejudices

Subtle forms of prejudice are distinguished from more overt prejudice in that individuals deny explicit prejudiced beliefs but demonstrate implicit biases (Todd et al., 2011). It is possible that a lack of awareness or an unwillingness to acknowledge one's prejudices leads to a discrepancy between explicit and implicit beliefs. Thus, raising awareness about this disconnect (Monteith & Mark, 2005) might be a first step in CBS-informed strategies. In fact, a study showed that encouraging awareness of prejudice reduced discriminatory behavior among individuals with low explicit and high implicit prejudice (Son Hing et al., 2002).

Applied to the issues related to terrorism, arranging a sociocultural context so that the diverse aspects of other individuals are acknowledged and experienced by the target individuals or groups is theorized to be a potential solution for global conflicts (Hayes et al., 2012a; Wilson et al., 2014). Because the process of stereotyping is verbal and symbolic (Hayes et al., 2002; Hayes & Toarmino, 1995), making efforts to eliminate particular forms of stereotypes and ideologies is perhaps futile. Instead, CBS-informed strategies, such as acceptance- and mindfulness-based individual and community interventions (Biglan, 2009; Biglan et al., 2012; Biglan et al., 2008; Hayes et al., 2006; Hayes et al., 2012b; Hayes et al., 2011) focus on building alternative ways of coexisting with human symbolic processes of self and others wisely, rather than trying to eliminate them, in service of promoting the well-being of self and others.

Promoting cognitive flexibility, perspective-taking, and empathy

There is a rich literature documenting prejudice reduction success via altering the favoring of perceived in-groups over out-groups by targeting the salience of particular group statuses (Masuda et al., 2009; Masuda et al., 2012; Paluck & Green, 2009). These interventions elaborate perceived group statuses and directly target the emphasis on "us" versus "them." For example, perspective-taking manipulations can increase empathy and reduce explicit and implicit prejudice or in-group favoritism (Galinsky & Moskowitz, 2000). One example of this approach is compassion-focused interventions designed to foster the sense of commonality in suffering (Fredrickson et al., 2008). It appears that the mechanism of change for compassion-focused interventions is increasing self-other overlap and highlighting similarities in important domains (Galinsky et al., 2005).

Increasing contact without conflict

Avoidance is a key aspect of social categorization; in-group members and out-group members are often socially isolated from one another (Tajfel, 1982; Tajfel et al., 1971). While seemingly counterintuitive, it is important for both sides to enter into dialogues for the purpose of understanding each other's contextual settings (Moghaddam, 2005b). A meta-analysis of 515 studies showed that increased contact resulted in reducing social categorization (Pettigrew & Tropp, 2006). Results were particularly strong when contact occurred under certain conditions including equality, cooperation, authority support, and a shared goal. These findings suggest that contact may undermine social categorization by promoting alternative behaviors of increased understanding, perspective-taking, and empathy. In addition, increased contact enables individuals from both groups to view one another based on complex, present-moment interaction rather than on previously held prejudicial beliefs and assumptions.

Conclusion

Terrorism appears to be a recurrent issue that is faced by human beings across the globe. Employing the framework of CBS as a distinct extension of evolutionary theory, the present chapter explicates terrorism as an ongoing and evolving process of contextually and symbolically situated behavior. Because the evidence is scarce, the present CBS perspective is still speculative. Nevertheless, the CBS account of terrorism is theoretically consistent with other evolutionary and psychological perspectives of terrorism and additionally takes into account the powerful influence of the present physical and symbolic environments on behavior. The CBS perspective can also be useful in developing effective interventions because of the focus on prediction and influence of behavior in a particular historical and situational context.

References

Ajzen, I., & Fishbein, M. (1980). *Understanding Attitudes and Predicting Social Behavior*. Englewood Cliffs, NJ: Prentice-Hall.

Barnes-Holmes, D., Barnes-Holmes, Y., & Cullinan, V. (2000). Relational frame theory and Skinner's verbal behavior: A possible synthesis. *Behavior Analyst*, 23(1), 69–84.

Barnes-Holmes, D., O'Hora, D., Roche, B., Hayes, S.C., Bissett, R.T., & Lyddy, F. (2001). Understanding and verbal regulation. In S.C. Hayes, D. Barnes-Holmes & B. Roche (eds), *Relational Frame Theory: A Post-Skinnerian Account of Human Language and Cognition.* (pp. 103–117). New York: Kluwer Academic/Plenum Publishers.

Biglan, A. (2009). Increasing psychological flexibility to influence cultural evolution. *Behavior and Social Issues*, 18(1), 1–10.

Biglan, A., & Hayes, S.C. (1996). Should the behavioral sciences become more pragmatic? The case for functional contextualism in research on human behavior. *Applied & Preventive Psychology*, 5(1), 47–57.

Biglan, A., & Hinds, E. (2009). Evolving prosocial and sustainable neighborhoods and communities. *Annual Review of Clinical Psychology*, 5, 169–196.

Biglan, A., Flay, B.R., Embry, D.D., & Sandler, I.N. (2012). The critical role of nurturing environments for promoting human well-being. *American Psychologist*, 67(4), 257–271.

Biglan, A., Hayes, S.C., & Pistorello, J. (2008). Acceptance and commitment: Implications for prevention science. *Prevention Science*, 9, 139–152.

Buller, D.J. (2005). *Adapting Minds: Evolutionary Psychology and the Persistent Quest for Human Nature*. Cambridge, MA: MIT Press.

Calvin, W.H. (1987). The brain as a Darwin machine. *Nature*, 330(6143), 33–34.

Carey, N. (2012). *The Epigenetics Revolution: How Modern Biology is Rewriting our Understanding of Genetics, Disease, and Inheritance*. New York: Columbia University Press.

Corrigan, P.W., & Penn, D.L. (1999). Lessons from social psychology on discrediting psychiatric stigma. *American Psychologist*, 54(9), 765–776.

Cota, A.A., Evans, C.R., Dion, K.L., Kilik, L., & Longman, R.S. (1995). The structure of group cohesion. *Personality & Social Psychology Bulletin*, 21(6), 572–580.

Dawkins, R., (1976). *The Selfish Gene.* Oxford: Oxford University Press.

Deacon, T. (1997). *The Symbolic Species: The Co-Evolution of Language and the Human Brain*. New York: W.W. Norton & Co.

Dixon, M.R., Branon, A., Nastally, B.L., & Mui, N. (2009). Examining prejudice towards Middle Eastern persons via a transformation of stimulus functions. *Behavior Analyst Today*, 10(2), 295–318.

Dixon, M.R., Dymond, S., Rehfeldt, R.A., Roche, B., & Zlomke, K.R. (2003). Terrorism and relational frame theory. *Behavior & Social Issues*, 12(2), 129–147.

Dixon, M.R., Rehfeldt, A., & Zlomke, K.R. (2006). Exploring the development and dismantling of equivalence classes involving terrorist stimuli. *Psychological Record*, 56(1), 83–103.

Eidelson, R.J., & Eidelson, J.I. (2003). Dangerous ideas: Five beliefs that propel groups toward conflict. *American Psychologist*, 58(3), 182–192.

Fredrickson, B.L., Cohn, M.A., Coffey, K.A., Pek, J., & Finkel, S.M. (2008). Open hearts build lives: Positive emotions, induced through loving-kindness meditation, build consequential personal resources. *Journal of Personality & Social Psychology*, 95(5), 1045–1062.

Galinsky, A.D., & Moskowitz, G.B. (2000). Perspective-taking: Decreasing stereotype expression, stereotype accessibility, and in-group favoritism. *Journal of Personality & Social Psychology*, 78(4), 708–724.

Galinsky, A.D., Ku, G., & Wang, C.S. (2005). Perspective-taking and self-other overlap: Fostering social bonds and facilitating social coordination. *Group Processes & Intergroup Relations*, 8(2), 109–124.

Goldiamond, I. (2002). Toward a constructional approach to social problems: Ethical and constitutional issues raised by applied behavior analysis. *Behavior & Social Issues*, 11(2), 108–197.

Hausmann, L.R. M., & Ryan, C.S. (2004). Effects of external and internal motivation to control prejudice on implicit prejudice: The mediating role of efforts to control prejudiced responses. *Basic & Applied Social Psychology*, 26(2–3), 215–225.

Hayes, S.C. (1989). *Rule-Governed Behavior: Cognition, Contingencies, and Instructional Control*. New York: Plenum Press.

Hayes, S.C., & Brownstein, A.J. (1986). Mentalism, behavior-behavior relations, and a behavior-analytic view of the purposes of science. *Behavior Analyst*, 9(2), 175–190.

Hayes, S.C., & Toarmino, D. (1995). If behavioral principles are generally applicable, why is it necessary to understand cultural diversity? *Behavior Therapist*, 18, 21–23.

Hayes, S.C., Barnes-Holmes, D., & Roche, B. (2001). *Relational Frame Theory: A Post-Skinnerian Account of Human Language and Cognition*. New York: Kluwer Academic/Plenum Publishers.

Hayes, S.C., Barnes-Holmes, D., & Wilson, K.G. (2012a). Contextual behavioral science: Creating a science more adequate to the challenge of the human condition. *Journal of Contextual Behavioral Science*, 1(1–2), 1–16.

Hayes, S.C., Bissett, R., Roget, N., Padilla, M., Kohlenberg, B.S., Fisher, G., Masuda, A., Pistorello, J., Rye, A.K., Berry, K., & Niccolls, R. (2004). The impact of acceptance and commitment training and multicultural training on the stigmatizing attitudes and professional burnout of substance abuse counselors. *Behavior Therapy*, 35(4), 821–835.

Hayes, S.C., Brownstein, A.J., Zettle, R.D., & Rosenfarb, I. (1986). Rule-governed behavior and sensitivity to changing consequences of responding. *Journal of the Experimental Analysis of Behavior*, 45(3), 237–256.

Hayes, S.C., Gifford, E.V., & Hayes, G.J. (1998). Moral behavior and the development of verbal regulation. *Behavior Analyst*, 21(2), 253–279.

Hayes, S.C., Hayes, L.J., & Reese, H.W. (1988). Finding the philosophical core. A review of Stephen C. Pepper's world hypotheses: A study in evidence. *Journal of the Experimental Analysis of Behavior*, 50, 97–111.

Hayes, S.C., Levin, M.E., Plumb-Vilardaga, J., Villatte, J.L., & Pistorello, J. (2013). Acceptance and commitment therapy and contextual behavioral science: Examining the progress of a distinctive model of behavioral and cognitive therapy. *Behavior Therapy*, 44(2), 180–198.

Hayes, S.C., Luoma, J.B., Bond, F.W., Masuda, A., & Lillis, J. (2006). Acceptance and commitment therapy: Model, processes and outcomes. *Behaviour Research & Therapy*, 44(1), 1–25.

Hayes, S.C., Masuda, A., Shenk, C., Yadavaia, J.E., Boulanger, J., Vilardaga, R., Plumb, J., Fletcher, L., Bunting, K., Levin, M.E., Waltz, T., & Hildebrandt, M.J.

(2007). Applied extensions of behavior principles: Applied behavioral concepts and behavioral theories. In D.W. Woods & J.W. Kantor (eds), *Understanding Behavior Disorders: A Contemporary Behavioral Perspective* (pp. 47–80). Oakland, CA: Context Press.

Hayes, S.C., Niccolls, R., Masuda, A., & Rye, A.K. (2002). Prejudice, terrorism and behavior therapy. *Cognitive & Behavioral Practice*, 9(4), 296–301.

Hayes, S.C., Strosahl, K.D., & Wilson, K.G. (2012b). *Acceptance and Commitment Therapy: The Process and Practice of Mindful Change* (2nd edn). New York: Guilford Press.

Hayes, S.C., Villatte, M., Levin, M., & Hildebrandt, M. (2011). Open, aware, and active: Contextual approaches as an emerging trend in the behavioral and cognitive therapies. *Annual Review of Clinical Psychology*, 7, 141–168.

Jablonka, E., & Lamb, M.J. (2005). *Evolution in Four Dimensions: Genetic, Epigenetic, Behavioral, and Symbolic Variation in the History of Life*. Cambridge, MA: MIT Press.

Jackson, L.M., & Hunsberger, B. (1999). An intergroup perspective on religion and prejudice. *Journal for the Scientific Study of Religion*, 38(4), 509–523.

Kawai, M. (1965). Newly acquired precultural behavior of the natural troop of Japanese monkeys on Koshima Islet. *Primates*, 6, 1–30.

Kurzban, R., & Leary, M.R. (2001). Evolutionary origins of stigmatization: The functions of social exclusion. *Psychological Bulletin*, 127(2), 187–208.

Lee, E. (2011). Clinical significance of cross-cultural competencies (CCC) in social work practice. *Journal of Social Work Practice*, 25(2), 185–203.

Legault, L., Green-Demers, I., & Eadie, A.L. (2009). When internalization leads to automatization: The role of self-determination in automatic stereotype suppression and implicit prejudice regulation. *Motivation & Emotion*, 33(1), 10–24.

Legault, L., Gutsell, J.N., & Inzlicht, M. (2011). Ironic effects of antiprejudice messages: How motivational interventions can reduce (but also increase) prejudice. *Psychological Science*, 22(12), 1472–1477.

Lillis, J., & Levin, M.E. (2014). Acceptance and mindfulness for undermining prejudice. In A. Masuda (ed.), *Mindfulness and Acceptance in Multicultural Competency: A Contextual Approach to Sociocultural Diversity in Theory and Practice* (pp. 181–196). Oakland, CA: New Harbinger Publication.

Masuda, A., Hayes, S.C., Lillis, J., Bunting, K., Herbst, S.A., & Fletcher, L.B. (2009). The relation between psychological flexibility and mental health stigma in acceptance and commitment therapy: A preliminary process investigation. *Behavior & Social Issues*, 18(1), 1–16.

Masuda, A., Hill, M.L., Morgan, J., & Cohen, L.L. (2012). A psychological flexibility-based intervention for modulating the impact of stigma and prejudice: A descriptive review of empirical evidence. *Psychology, Society & Education*, 4(2), 211–223.

Miltenberger, R.G. (2012). *Behavior Modification: Principles and Procedures*, 5th edn. Belmont, CA: Wadsworth/Thomson Learning.

Moghaddam, F.M. (2005a). Psychological processes and "the staircase to terrorism." *American Psychologist*, 60(9), 1039–1041.

Moghaddam, F.M. (2005b). The staircase to terrorism: A psychological exploration. *American Psychologist*, 60(2), 161–169.

Moghaddam, F.M. (2009). The new global American dilemma and terrorism. *Political Psychology*, 30(3), 373–380.

Monteith, M.J., & Mark, A.Y. (2005). Changing one's prejudiced ways: Awareness, affect, and self-regulation. *European Review of Social Psychology*, 16, 113–154.

Morgan, G.S., Wisneski, D.C., & Skitka, L.J. (2011). The expulsion from Disneyland: The social psychological impact of 9/11. *American Psychologist*, 66(6), 447–454.

Paluck, E.L., & Green, D.P. (2009). Prejudice reduction: What works? A review and assessment of research and practice. *Annual Review of Psychology*, 60, 339–367.

Parrott, L.J. (1987). Rule-governed behavior: An implicit analysis of reference. In S. Modgil & C. Modgil (eds), *B.F. Skinner: Consensus and Controversy* (pp. 265–276). London: Falmer Press.

Penn, D.C., Holyoak, K.J., & Povinelli, D.J. (2008). Darwin's mistake: Explaining the discontinuity between human and nonhuman minds. *Behavioral & Brain Sciences*, 31(2), 109–130.

Pettigrew, T.F., & Tropp, L.R. (2006). A meta-analytic test of intergroup contact theory. *Journal of Personality & Social Psychology*, 90(5), 751–783.

Roach, J. and Pease, K. (2013). *Evolution and Crime*. Oxford: Routledge.

Roach, J., Ekblom, P., & Flynn, R. (2005). The conjunction of terrorist opportunity: A framework for diagnosing and preventing acts of terrorism. *Security Journal*, 18, 7–25.

Roche, B., & Barnes-Holmes, D. (2003). Behavior analysis and social constructionism: Some points of contact and departure. *Behavior Analyst*, 26(2), 215–231.

Roche, B., Barnes-Holmes, D., Barnes-Holmes, Y., & Hayes, S.C. (2001). Social processes. In S.C. Hayes, D. Barnes-Holmes & B. Roche (eds), *Relational Frame Theory: A Post-Skinnerian Account of Human Language and Cognition* (pp. 197–209). New York: Kluwer Academic/Plenum Publishers.

Roche, B., Barnes-Holmes, Y., Barnes-Holmes, D., Stewart, I., & O' Hora, D. (2002). Relational frame theory: A new paradigm for the analysis of social behavior. *Behavior Analyst*, 25(1), 75–91.

Sidman, M. (2003). Terrorism as behavior. *Behavior & Social Issues*, 12(2), 83–89.

Skinner, B.F. (1971). *Beyond Freedom and Dignity*. New York: Knopf/Random House.

Skinner, B.F. (1974). *About Behaviorism*. Oxford: Alfred A. Knopf.

Skinner, B.F. (1981). Selection by consequences. *Science*, 213(4507), 501–504.

Son Hing, L.S., Li, W., & Zanna, M.P. (2002). Inducing hypocrisy to reduce prejudicial responses among aversive racists. *Journal of Experimental Social Psychology*, 38(1), 71–78.

Stangor, C., Sechrist, G.B., & Jost, J.T. (2001). Changing racial beliefs by providing consensus information. *Personality & Social Psychology Bulletin*, 27(4), 486–496.

Tajfel, H. (1982). Social psychology of intergroup relations. *Annual Review of Psychology*, 33, 1–39.

Tajfel, H., Billig, M.G., Bundy, R.P., & Flament, C. (1971). Social categorization and intergroup behaviour. *European Journal of Social Psychology*, 1(2), 149–178.

Taylor, M. (1993). Rational choice, behavior analysis, and political violence. In R.V. Clarke & M. Felson (eds), *Routine Activity and Rational Choice* (pp. 159–178). Piscataway, NJ: Transaction Publishers.

Taylor, M. (2010). Is terrorism a group phenomenon? *Aggression & Violent Behavior*, 15(2), 121–129.

Taylor, M., & Horgan, J. (2001). The psychological and behavioural bases of Islamic fundamentalism. *Terrorism & Political Violence*, 13(4), 37–71.

Taylor, M., & Horgan, J. (2006). A conceptual framework for addressing psychological process in the development of the terrorist. *Terrorism & Political Violence*, 18(4), 585–601.

Todd, A.R., Bodenhausen, G.V., Richeson, J.A., & Galinsky, A.D. (2011). Perspective taking combats automatic expressions of racial bias. *Journal of Personality & Social Psychology*, 100(6), 1027–1042.

Vilardaga, R. (2009). A relational frame theory account of empathy. *International Journal of Behavioral Consultation & Therapy*, 5(2), 178–184.

Vilardaga, R., Hayes, S.C., Levin, M.E., & Muto, T. (2009). Creating a strategy for progress: A contextual behavioral science approach. *Behavior Analyst*, 32(1), 105–133.

Watt, A., Keenan, M., Barnes, D., & Cairns, E. (1991). Social categorization and stimulus equivalence. *Psychological Record*, 41(1), 33–50.

Wegner, D.M. (1994). Ironic processes of mental control. *Psychological Review*, 101(1), 34–52.

Wilson, D.S., Hayes, S.C., Biglan, A., & Embry, D.D. (2014). Evolving the future: Toward a science of international change. *Behavioral & Brain Science*, 37(4), 395–416.

Wilson, T.D., Lindsey, S., & Schooler, T.Y. (2000). A model of dual attitudes. *Psychological Review*, 107(1), 101–126.

7 Terrorism as altruism

An evolutionary model for understanding terrorist psychology

Rick O'Gorman and Andrew Silke

Introduction

Terrorists are often portrayed as the lowest form of combatant, labelled as murderers, criminals and madmen. Yet, this view is counterbalanced by the fact that those who engage in terrorism do so as a small minority at great risk to themselves, and occasionally even intentionally sacrificing themselves for their war or cause. A suicide-bomber is viewed as psychotic; a regular soldier who leads his troops forward to near-certain death can be heroic. Are these two types of combatant really so different? This chapter presents a fresh model for understanding terrorism and terrorists within the context of altruistic behaviour. The chapter draws on evolutionary approaches to understanding altruism in general in human behaviour, outlining the dynamics that allow altruism to function and flourish. Specific insights and models are then applied to terrorism, providing insight into our understanding of the individual psychology of terrorists as well as the contexts in which terrorist groups can emerge. We will not provide a full exposition of evolutionary psychology (EP), as other chapters in this book will address this. In addition, we do not pretend that all terrorism is altruistic (for any community), nor that altruism is the exclusive answer. Far from it, but we do contend that recognizing the altruistic dimension to terrorism is essential to fully understanding terrorism and, ultimately, moderating it.

The words 'terrorist' and 'altruist' rarely appear in close proximity. Instead, terrorists are usually presented as deranged or cowardly. Occasionally, they are seen as freedom fighters, but the very existence of the alternative term makes clear that the terrorist is not virtuous. Terrorism stands as perhaps the most reviled form of combat, threatened only by its close relative, suicide-bombing, in the revulsion stakes. Contributing to the outcast nature of terrorism is the general trend for terrorism engagement to be very much a minority activity, even in communities and conflicts where there is otherwise widespread support for their activities (Alonso *et al.* 2008). Yet, for scholars of terrorism, the adage that one person's terrorist is another one's freedom fighter is a well-grounded recognition of the vacuous assumptions about terrorists' motivations. Engaging in terrorism is a costly activity, with life and limb on the line, suspension of a normal life – if this is even an option – inevitable and with little obvious gains to be made – the dreams of victorious triumph would seem unlikely to motivate any terrorist and the typical ongoing need to maintain a low profile prevents any immediate gains in community status as a pay-off. Why, then, do those who engage in terrorism do so?

If we move past the negative spin, we are free to look at terrorists and recognize that, as for any other human endeavour, various motivations, proclivities and perspectives will have contributed to people engaging in terrorism. Understanding these motivations is essential to turning down, if not off, the terrorism tap. And while much work has already been undertaken to examine the cues and motivations for terrorism engagement (e.g. Borum 2011; McCauley & Moskalenko 2008; Moghadam 2003; Schmid 2013), the exercise for this present chapter is to examine the worth of applying a framework, EP, that is currently prompting a ground-shift in how general psychology interprets and studies human cognition and behaviour. And one of the central topics where evolutionary thinking has contributed important theory and empirical findings is in prosociality. In light of that, it seems worth examining the answer to the question: what can an evolutionary approach contribute to understanding terrorism as altruism?

Altruism and evolution

The issue of altruism arises very rapidly once an evolutionary framework is adopted for studying human behaviour for the simple reason that the framework, in its simplest form, focuses on the evolution of genetic traits through *individual selection*. Richard Dawkins's popular treatment of the fundamentals of evolutionary theory captured the challenge of altruism full-on with the chosen title of his seminal work on the topic, *The Selfish Gene* (Dawkins 1976). Individual selection is the process of competition between individuals within the same population for reproductive success. Those who do so successfully in relation to rivals will be responsible for transmitting a greater proportion of genes into the next generation. Fundamentally a simple yet elegant process, natural selection as so conceived requires only differential reproductive success in a population of organisms due to differing heritable traits to drive adaptation to the local environment. That is, there must be variation in traits, that variation must affect reproductive success and it must be heritable. Such a formulation suggests that selfishness should trump any altruism.

Of course, both in *The Selfish Gene* and elsewhere, Dawkins clarifies how altruism can still result from selfish genes, although, for many, the message was lost. Nonetheless, as far back as Darwin himself, the challenge of explaining altruism evolutionarily was readily apparent. While his own development of his theory of evolution by natural selection presented individual selection as the primary means through which the process of evolution occurs, he also acknowledged obvious shortcomings in the theory to address prima facie cases of altruism, such as in honeybees and human societies. He proposed *group selection* as a mechanism to explain these phenomena and the two mechanisms coexisted in a relatively unformalized relationship until the 1960s. Group selection proposes that the interactions within a group can contribute to reproductive success of group members if such interactions provide an advantage over competitor groups. Cooperative groups (or, if you prefer, groups of cooperators) therefore have a theoretical advantage, and in practice we would predict some balance between individual and group selection pressures dependent upon the relative strengths of said pressures.

Group selection fell from favour in the 1960s after a stinging critique (Williams 1966) and the development of a new framework, *inclusive fitness theory*, for examining the fitness consequences of social interactions (Hamilton 1964). In particular, a view arose that groups of altruists are always vulnerable to invasion by non-altruists, who would outcompete the altruists in any group, driving altruism ultimately to extinction. Inclusive fitness focuses on the genetic success of any allele (a version of a gene, where a gene codes for a trait and an allele codes for a version of that trait) in enhancing its genetic success, which thus includes not just direct success through the allele's carrier (the organism) but also any success where the allele prompts the carrier to help other carriers of the same allele. Ironically, selfish genes can produce cooperative, even altruistic traits, something recognized in Dawkins's *The Selfish Gene*. Inclusive fitness became commonly referred to as *kin selection* after the suggestion that the process of inclusive fitness would only be felt among close relatives (Maynard Smith 1964) and this then constrained thought about altruistic behaviour for most until the recent decade or so. Kinship is an obvious channel through which such altruism can work, with an above-average probability of kin sharing a particular allele.

More recently, however, group selection has been restored to good favour through refined mathematical analyses that show that a multilevel selection framework (MLS; Sober & Wilson 1998), incorporating individual- and group-level selection, is equivalent to an inclusive fitness framework (Lehmann *et al.* 2007; Wilson & Wilson 2007). This recognition was important to countering the critique of altruist groups being unable to resist invasive non-altruists. MLS places explicit emphasis on *population structure*, in that individuals rarely randomly interact but more likely interact with subsets of the population and those restricted sets of interactions impact differentially on group members' fitness. Insofar as individuals who are altruists interact with others who are altruists, irrespective of how they find each other, then altruism can evolve if the process is sufficiently robust to being undermined by non-altruists' advantage. This is reminiscent of the earlier group selection framework, although modern incarnations have more nuanced models of the relationship between groups and reproduction.

This background is important to appreciate the complexities that surround an application of altruism to human behaviour in any domain, including terrorism. It does so because it points us to thinking about the evolved psychology that can be expected if altruism is a legitimate phenomenon, and not an illusion. The most important implication is that, while altruism *could* exist simply due to a group structure to human society, it is unlikely to do so because the extinction of groups as humans evolved would have needed to be substantial (alternatively, highly restricted migration would facilitate evolution of altruism but that also is very unlikely). However, altruism can exist due to the group structure in human society provided some additional mechanisms are in place that buttress altruism against exploitation. Where this potentially intersects with terrorism lies in the issue of exploitation.

The recent literature on human social behaviour, and particularly human group behaviour, has grown dramatically, stimulated in part by the flourishing debate around altruism. Much of this work has focused on the scaffolding that allows cooperation to function in human societies, and particularly given that cooperative behaviour often occurs in apparently anonymous situations, or interactions with strangers. We acquire goods where one party pays before receipt of goods, or vice versa. We donate money to strangers having limited proof of their genuineness. People are hired on limited proof of who they are and what they have done previously. Taxi-drivers take people places before being paid. Companies often provide a complaining customer with a replacement product without verifying whether the previous item was actually broken. The opportunities for exploitation are rife, yet, while exploitation does happen, it is perhaps noteworthy for how *little* it happens. How can societies function in the face of their vulnerability to exploitation? The answer may lie in the mechanisms that we have evolved, some possibly group-selected, to deal with protecting our altruism more generally.

Consider studies that show that when participants in an economics experiment are asked to make contributions to a common pot (a 'public good') that yields a benefit to all players at a cost to a contributing individual, they often initially do so at a moderate level, beyond what seems 'rational'. As they learn the ropes of the game, and particularly as they see the decisions of other players, however, they gradually make lower and lower contributions. Is this a microcosm of the 'tragedy of the commons', a defence against exploitation? Indeed, but a defence played out in a very odd format. These are games played (usually) via computer, in anonymous groups where no one is sure of whom they are playing with, with no means to deviate from the preset structure of either contributing a share of points to the public pot, or withholding. In the face of seeing some contribute less, what other response seems reasonable than to withdraw?

In actual society, however, this is not how things operate. More importantly, in the likely societies that humans and our ancestral forms created over our evolutionary time period, the above is not how things would have worked. Instead, our ancestors would have been part of a community of individuals who regularly interacted, and likely had a sense of 'their own community' or at least their own group. They would have recognized group members, they would have known their ways, and they would have for at least our more recent past had the ability to gossip and spread information about behaviour to others. Groups would have been able to coordinate activity to regulate the behaviour of troublemakers, seeking to constrain their harmful ways or expel or even kill them (Boehm 1999; Boehm 2000; Boehm 2012). Boehm has extensively researched how hunter-gatherers regulate behaviour within groups and has found that there is an escalating series of steps that communities tend to follow, beginning with teasing and light banter about inappropriate behaviour, escalating to confrontation, ostracism (temporary or permanent) and, more rarely, assassination (for more serious transgressions). It is not hard to see this reflected in our own modern social ways, even at the level of complex urban populations, where newspapers and twitter serve as channels of information flow (read: gossip), and allow coordination of activity (think of the Arab Spring). Fear of gossip itself is often enough to regulate negative behaviour (Ellickson 1991; Kniffin & Wilson 2010). More formally, there is a judicial system which incarcerates wrongdoers but not so long ago such individuals were often cast out ('outlaws'; an outcome still followed often for non-citizens). Finally, some countries even today still retain capital punishment for extreme crimes.

Thus, human societies at all levels have mechanisms to deal with those who violate expected behaviour. In addition, societies generally have a shared sense of appropriate behaviour, and a conceptualization of right and wrong behaviour: morality. Much of this can be seen as scaffolding to support cooperation and altruistic endeavour in human societies, and appears to be supported by evolved psychological dispositions that in turn support such cultural mechanisms. A variety of research programmes show that, psychologically, people respond to various cues and situations in line with what we would expect theoretically if we have evolved to facilitate cooperation and regulate cheating. These include sensitivity to vigilance of us by others, gossiping when behaviour is inappropriate, and punitive responses to antisocial behaviour, particularly selfish behaviour. These psychological responses not only underpin altruistic behaviour, but provide the emotionally driven motives to respond to perceived transgressions, likely a key motivator in terrorist activity (O'Gorman 2011).

Evidence that our prosocial behaviour is readily impacted by relatively crude cues to the social dimension of our behaviour comes from work on the impact of reputational concern on contributions in public goods games. Researchers have found that the presence of eyes adjacent to where participants were being presented with opportunities to either contribute prosocially or withhold resulted in greater contributions to the (experimental) social good (Haley & Fessler 2005; Sparks & Barclay 2013). Public goods studies serve as the arena for understanding our propensities to punish, alongside our tendencies to cooperate. Fehr and Gächter (2002) found that if participants could punish other players for their low contributions, then contributions do not collapse over time (as discussed earlier) but remain at more substantial levels. Fehr and Gächter, along with a raft of related studies (e.g. Herrmann *et al.* 2008; Gintis 2008; Eldakar *et al.* 2006; O'Gorman *et al.* 2009; Henrich *et al.* 2006), show that cooperative behaviour is viable, even if in an anonymous situation, if there are mechanisms that can regulate selfish behaviour. More important for our present thesis, they showed that people would actually incur a cost to punish another player: Punishing another was not free. As O'Gorman *et al.* (2009) show, this even occurs when only one player in a group is designated for a round as a punisher, thus shouldering the entire cost.

While researchers debate whether this can be legitimately called 'altruistic' – because we cannot be sure that players are not mistaken about the public goods games' conditions, or because they have a vested interest in punishing (Pedersen *et al.* 2013) – it shows that people will pay a cost (both relative and absolute) to punish. What this stream of research has not particularly addressed, though, is whether there are individual differences in willingness to engage in punishing behaviour. Certainly there is variance in levels of punishing that occur, though whether this is behavioural noise or is related to individual dispositions is not known. There does appear to be evidence that some participants operate in what has been termed as spiteful punishing, punishing high contributors (Herrmann *et al.* 2008). What has been shown is that individuals do vary in their willingness to be altruistic. For example, Van Lange *et al.* (1997) developed the social values orientation scale as a measure of people's dispositions toward being individualistic (maximizing individual gain), prosocial (maximizing collective gain) or competitive (getting the bigger share, even if losing out on a larger amount). They show that these different strategies are distributed through the population with prosocials dominating, but with non-trivial numbers of individualists and competitive types. Kurzban & Houser (2001) found a similar pattern of participants whose behaviours in an economic game could be decomposed into three categories, which they termed strong free riders, conditional cooperators of reciprocators, and strong cooperators, though the proportions differed somewhat from Van Lange *et al.*

Together, these mechanisms show that humans are equipped to respond to transgressions and violations of morality at a personal cost. But it may seem one thing to want to pay a few pennies to punish another player, a different thing to want to detonate a bomb with the intention of killing and maiming. Yet the idea here is that the lab captures as a microcosm the reality of the world writ large. A small transgression yields a small retribution. With larger transgressions we may expect larger responses. Calibrating responses to transgressions, evidence suggests, is the role of emotions (Damasio 1994; Haidt & Kesebir 2010; McCullough *et al.* 2013). One of the key developments in understanding human behaviour has been the recognition, driven by a variety of studies, showing that emotions and what might be termed unconscious thoughts shape how we respond to various situations. In particular, these responses occur in response to fundamental aspects of daily life in the area of morality and normative behaviour. Key work in this area is summarized by Damasio (1994), showing the importance of emotions for making socially appropriate judgements. Damasio demonstrates his thesis through an exploration of various forms of damage to the frontal lobe of the brain, arguing that, without emotional input, individuals do not act in accordance with normative behaviour. Critically, this shows that emotions shape many of our activities and decisions. Expanding on this basis, Haidt (Haidt & Kesebir 2010; Haidt 2008; Haidt 2007) has demonstrated that emotions and intuitions are central to how people make moral judgements. In turn, the implication is that these emotions are shaped by human evolution to prompt behaviours and decisions that yield evolutionarily adaptive outcomes. Insofar as people are entrained by their emotions and intuitions, a strong emotional response can be expected to beget a strong action, at least from some individuals. We argue those will be the prosocials, the strong cooperators, the altruists, choosing to act on behalf of their community.

It is important to revisit at this stage in the argument that the evolution of human social behaviour would have centred on the fact that we lived in small communities of familiar individuals, many of them kin. As such, issues of justice and morality would have revolved around transgressions by members of the community, a neighbouring community, or strangers. The abstract nature of political states is not something that humans think upon very effectively, just as we struggle to work with percentages rather than frequencies (Galesic *et al.* 2009; Hoffrage *et al.* 2000). The notion that the actions of a transgressor in the political arena may be the result of complex internal dynamics is lost on many. From an evolutionary perspective, we would expect that humans thus react today to transgressions as though operating in a more intimate world. Moreover, individuals may be cued by their own pain at the transgressions, or by the pain of those they consider close to them. They may be shaped in how they think about this rationally by their culture (O'Gorman 2011), but ultimately we expect that their emotions and intuitions drive their decisions. This may be most notable when deciding whether and how to respond to the transgressions, with emotions running strong.

When the situation has moved past teasing, gossip, or even some level of ostracism, or such responses would not work, individuals are predicted to respond with violence on at least some occasions. Not every dumped lover kills their ex-partner's new beau, but enough do that we know it is a possible outcome in such situations. The majority of homicides for any country show that those with an emotional component (argument, anger, revenge) dominate the numbers (Daly & Wilson 1988; Dooley 2001). For terrorism, revenge is a particularly salient motivator, given the typical delay between any ascribed cause for terrorism engagement and acts of terrorism. Various studies in countries such as Ireland, Australia, and Hong Kong suggest that about 10 per cent of murders are due to premeditated revenge (where there is evidence of planning); this expands to up to 20 per cent of homicides if more impulsive acts of revenge are included (McCullough 2008). Indeed, McCullough (2008) suggests 20 per cent may be on the conservative side, as many murders are motivated by sexual jealousy or sexual infidelity, some of which also have a revenge component to them. For some cultures, those which have a *culture of honor* (Nisbett & Cohen 1996), revenge may be a particularly salient response to insults and transgressions (O'Gorman 2011).

One shortcoming in the literature on costly punishment is whether age or sex play a role. In O'Gorman *et al.* (2009), a study that explicitly examined for sex differences, none were found. The structure of public goods experiments may liberate women to punish in a way that real-life affords much less, and experimental demand may prompt action in a way that other situations might not. However, other literature that looks at punishing sometimes find that women resort less to physical violence than men (Eldakar *et al.* 2006), but this is not consistently so (O'Gorman *et al.* 2005). Archer (2004) in a meta-analysis of sex differences in aggression across all social settings reports that there is little evidence of sex differences in anger in social conflicts, but men are more likely to injure and to engage in physical aggression. In addition, men, and particularly younger and single men, are much more likely to engage in physically risky behaviour, including aggression, violence and homicides (Daly & Wilson 1988; Daly & Wilson 1994). This is due to risky behaviours in general allowing males to show off their potential mate quality to females, combined with males having the less certain reproductive strategy (females are generally the choosy sex among mammals, having higher costs for poor mating choices). However, while risk-taking behaviour may be a factor for some males to engage in terrorism, it will not necessarily have a relationship to moralistically driven actions.

And so, turning to the terrorism literature, do we see these mechanisms at work? A critical starting point when considering terrorist psychology and motivation is the realization that the vast majority of psychological research on terrorists has concluded that they are not abnormal or suffer from higher rates of psychopathology. Indeed, many studies have found that terrorists are actually psychologically much healthier and far more stable than other violent criminals (e.g. Silke 2008). Taylor and Qualye (1994) provide a frank overall assessment of terrorist psychology which is worth bearing in mind:

> With rare exceptions and contrary to popular misconceptions … terrorists are neither madmen nor blind bigots. They have considerable insight into their own actions, and often show a striking awareness of how others view them. In the main, they have come to terms with the violence they commit, and are able to justify it in terms of their own perception of the world, and their role in its maintenance. For example, few object to the use of the term terrorist to describe themselves, although euphemisms such as volunteers or members are generally preferred descriptions. Relatively few individuals offer sophisticated political justifications of the violence they may admit to or imply being involved in, yet all show a strength of what can only be described as belief in the rightness of their actions.
>
> (Taylor & Qualye 1994, p. 103)

Victoroff (2005) notes that 'it seems plausible that many terrorists act in a prosocial manner, both believing themselves to be serving society and judged by their in-group to be acting in its interest'. In considering key differences between terrorists and criminals, LaFree and Dugan (2004) highlight that one essential and common difference is that 'those partaking in terrorism are more likely to have a self-perception of altruism'. Certainly surveys of terrorist and criminal prisoners, for example, find that the terrorists express a very different view of the motivations for their offending compared to the typical criminal prisoner (e.g. Crawford 1999).

Identity tends to play a major role in terrorist motivation and this also directly linked to how we can think about altruism in a terrorist context. The more strongly an individual identifies with another person (or group of people), the more strongly they will react emotionally to events in that person/group's life. They will feel positive emotions when things go well for the person they empathize with (Smith *et al.* 1989), and negative emotions when things go badly (Hoffman 1991). These negative emotions include sadness, but also importantly can include anger (Vitaglione & Barnett 2003).

Altruistic tendencies can be increased by stressing similarities with others. The stronger a person can identify with others the more they care about what happens to those others (Levy *et al.* 2002). In contrast, efforts which stress the differences weaken such bonds and interest and concern declines. A further important factor in limiting altruistic tendencies is that in order to act or think altruistically, one first needs 'the ability to assess and influence others' welfare' (Farsides 2007). If an individual is burdened with extreme demands on their own time, energy and resources, then they are much less likely to be able to show the awareness that altruism requires (Evans *et al.* 2005).

Thus the capacity to exercise altruistic tendencies here links in with many of the theories regarding poverty and deprivation and terrorism. It is widely recognized that most terrorists do not come from the most deprived backgrounds of their constituent communities and that on the contrary they are more likely to come from what constitutes the middle and upper classes of their communities (bearing in mind that the middle class in a refugee camp will be very different to the middle class in a British city) (Maleckova 2005). Surveys have also found that support for terrorism tends to be stronger among middle-class and upper-class respondents than among the lower class. For example a survey of 1,357 Palestinian adults in the West Bank and Gaza found that support for terrorism against Israeli civilians was more common among professionals (43.3 per cent) than among labourers (34.6 per cent). Similarly, there was more support among those with secondary education (39.4 per cent) than among illiterate respondents (32.3 per cent) (Krueger & Maleckova 2002). Interestingly, further research has found that in the Middle East, respondents who owned a computer or mobile phone were more likely to express support for terrorism than respondents who did not own these items (Fair & Shepherd 2006). This last result may be related to the relative deprivation factor and/or to an increased awareness of others with a shared identity.

Altruism then is likely to have an impact on support for terrorism when it is considered within the context of identity. Individuals who feel their identity is closer to the militant group, and who score higher on altruistic measures, are arguably the ones who will express and feel the strongest support for the group including the group's use of extreme measures. Potentially, they will also be more likely to act on these sentiments.

What is certainly widely accepted in the literature is that terrorists usually view and portray themselves as acting in an altruistic fashion. Though their numbers are very few in terms of the wider communities they are drawn from, the organization and individuals typically emerge from an enabling environment where they share a wider sense of injustice and grievance (e.g. Alonso *et al.* 2008). The terrorist movement itself usually presents itself as a self-declared vanguard representing the interests of the aggrieved. Thus, while there are very few actual terrorists, they claim a far wider representation and that they are fighting on behalf of the Umma, the proletariat, the nation, or whatever other constituency is advocated within their specific ideology. It is in such terms then that the violence is typically explained and justified. A good example of this is the rationale provided by Eric Rudolph who was responsible for bombing the Atlanta Olympics in 1996 as well as attacks against several abortion clinics in the US:

> Because I believe that abortion is murder, I also believe that force is justified in an attempt to stop it … There is no more fundamental duty for a moral citizen than to protect the innocent from assault. This [is] inherent in the values of all higher civilizations. You have the right, the responsibility and the duty to come to the defence of the innocent when the innocent are under assault … [I]f you … recognize abortion is murder and that unborn children should be protected and you still insist that force is unjustified to stop abortion, then you can be none other than cowards standing idly by in the face of the worst massacre in human history.

This theme of fighting on behalf of others and in reaction to the suffering of others appears to be almost a constant in terrorist ideology and recurs frequently in accounts of the personal motivation of individual terrorists. Consider the following from a left-wing Italian terrorist:

> our lives too could be sacrificed in order to reach an ideal; a high price for any ideal, but this seemed to be the price the situation required … It was a life so oriented towards a presumed *sacrifice-for-others* as to include the sacrifice of some and of course of oneself.
>
> (de Cataldo Neuburger & Valentini 1996, p. 161, emphasis added)

Such themes clearly echo within the context of modern Jihadi extremism. Consider Mohammad Sidique Khan, the leader of the suicide bombers responsible for the 7 July 2005 attacks in London, who in a video filmed before the attack said:

> I and thousands like me are forsaking everything for what we believe. Our driving motivation doesn't come from tangible commodities that this world has to offer. Our religion is Islam – obedience to the one true God, Allah, and following the footsteps of the final prophet and messenger Muhammad ... This is how our ethical stances are dictated. Your democratically elected governments continuously perpetuate atrocities against my people all over the world. And your support of them makes you directly responsible, just as I am directly responsible for protecting and avenging my Muslim brothers and sisters. Until we feel security, you will be our targets. And until you stop the bombing, gassing, imprisonment and torture of my people we will not stop this fight. We are at war and I am a soldier. Now you too will taste the reality of this situation.

That said there is still clear acceptance that the reasons why individuals become involved in terrorism are varied and do not boil down to just one factor, whether that is some form of altruism or another factor. Overall, terrorists are a very heterogeneous group and the range of people who become involved is vast. They can vary hugely in terms of education, family background, age, gender, intelligence, economic class, etc. Consequently the manner in which they became a terrorist can also vary, and factors that played a pivotal role in one person's decision to engage in terrorism can play only a very minor role for others, or indeed may have played no part at all.

Becoming a terrorist is for most people a gradual process and is not usually something that happens quickly or easily. Ultimately, it is the combined impact of a number of factors that push and pull the individual into becoming a terrorist, and these factors will vary depending on the culture, the social context, the terrorist group and the person involved.

Perceptions of grievance and a desire for revenge can be powerful motivations in any situation. Indeed, evolutionary psychologists sometimes explain this in terms of a response to a threat to perceived social status; value of social status is something that has evolved in humans and other primates because of its strong association with sexual selection. Competition for social status can lead to intense, and often violent, behaviours, usually in adult males (Gottschalk & Ellis 2009). Psychologists have also shown that the individual seeking revenge demonstrate higher levels of goal fulfilment when they see their perceived offender suffer, and that the offender's understanding of why the revenge was sought is even more important (Gollwitzer & Denzler 2009).

Certainly a desire for revenge has been found to be a key factor in the radicalization process for many, if not most, extremists. Radicalization has been explained in terms of a perceived threat to the in-group (McCauley & Moskalenko 2008) – and here again the importance of group identity is highlighted – and so grievance and revenge motivations are important drivers of individual decisions to become involved in militant activism as well as motivating those already involved into action. Catalyst events (i.e. violent acts which are perceived to be unjust) provide a strong sense of outrage and a powerful psychological desire for revenge and retribution (Silke 2003). Significantly, these catalyst events do not need to be experienced first-hand to have this effect. For many individuals witnessing such events vicariously on television, the Internet or in propaganda, etc., can have an equally powerful impact and can provide a strong motivation to become involved. Many terrorists report that they first joined the organization after witnessing events on television. They did not come from the area where the events occurred – or indeed even know the people who lived there – but at some level they identified with the victims. In this way it can be seen that two powerful psychological processes – identity with a particular group and a desire for revenge when it is perceived that this group, or the status of this group, is threatened or has been treated unjustly – combine to help compel the individual to join a terrorist group in order to redress the balance. Both elements tie in to thinking on how altruism may play a role. Consider the following account from Sean O'Callaghan (1998, p. 22) a former member of the Provisional IRA. O'Callaghan lived in the Republic of Ireland and had never been to Northern Ireland until after he joined the IRA.

> I was sitting watching television along with childhood friends ... when the news clearly showed Royal Ulster Constabulary (RUC) officers brutally attacking Civil Rights marchers in Derry. We saw RUC officers kick, punch and baton completely defenceless and peaceful marchers. We were totally shocked by the naked hatred and violence of some of the police ... That event had a huge effect on me. All of my sympathy was with the marchers and I formed the opinion there and then that the RUC were a totally bigoted police force on a par with the Nazis ... My two friends and I ... were all to join the Provisional IRA.

Conclusion

We do not suggest that there are not other psychological processes that are relevant to terrorism, and particularly to engagement with terrorism. Fundamentally, people are equipped to respond to transgressions with calibrated responses, with more harmful transgressions prompting stronger emotional response, which in turn can be expected for some to translate into violent action, or certainly support and facilitation of such action. Certain cultures may exacerbate such responses, and individuals will vary in their proclivity for seeking to punish those who have wronged them, as they perceive it. In situations where terrorism is a viable option, then turning to a terrorist structure is one pathway to revenge. Once engaged in a terrorist structure, of course, other mechanisms and processes can shape continuing engagement. For some, the revenge desire may continue to burn strong, for others the organization may need to stoke the flames, while for others, membership of the organization and subordination to its goals may be enough to maintain their engagement.

References

Alonso, R., Bjørgo, T., Della Porta, D., Coolsaet, H., Khosrokhavar, F., Lohker, R., Ranstorp, M., Reinares, F., Schmid, A., Silke, A., Taarnby, M. & de Vries, G., 2008. *Radicalisation Processes Leading to Acts of Terrorism. A Concise Report Prepared by the European Commission's Expert Group on Violent Radicalisation.* Available at: www.clingendael.nl/sites/default/files/20080500_cscp_report_vries.pdf [Accessed December 15, 2013].

Archer, J., 2004. Sex differences in aggression in real-world settings: A meta-analytic review. *Review of General Psychology*, 8(4), pp. 291–322.

Boehm, C., 1999. *Hierarchy in the Forest: The Evolution of Egalitarian Behavior*, Cambridge, MA: Harvard University Press.

Boehm, C., 2000. Conflict and the evolution of social control. *Journal of Consciousness Studies*, 7, 1(2), pp. 79–101.

Boehm, C., 2012. Ancestral hierarchy and conflict. *Science*, 336(6083), pp. 844–847.

Borum, R., 2011. Understanding terrorist psychology. In A. Silke, ed., *The Psychology of Counter-Terrorism*, pp. 19–33. London: Routledge.

Crawford, C., 1999. *Defenders or Criminals: Loyalist Prisoners and Criminalization*, Belfast: Blackstaff Press.

Daly, M. & Wilson, M., 1988. *Homicide*, New York: A. de Gruyter.

Daly, M. & Wilson, M., 1994. Evolutionary psychology of male violence. In J. Archer, ed., *Male Violence*, London: Routledge.

Damasio, A.R., 1994. *Descartes' Error: Emotion, Reason, and the Human Brain*, New York: Putnam.

Dawkins, R., 1976. *The Selfish Gene*, Oxford: Oxford University Press.

de Cataldo Neuburger, L. and Valentini, T., 1996. *Women and Terrorism*, London: Macmillan.

Dooley, E., 2001. *Homicide in Ireland 1992–1996*, Government of Ireland. Available at: www.crimecouncil.gov.ie/documents/DooleyE.HomicideinIreland1992–1996.pdf [Accessed December 9, 2013].

Eldakar, O.T., Wilson, D.S. & O'Gorman, R., 2006. Emotions and actions associated with altruistic helping and punishment. *Evolutionary Psychology*, 4, pp. 274–286.

Ellickson, R.C., 1991. *Order Without Law: How Neighbors Settle Disputes*, Cambridge, MA: Harvard University Press.

Evans, G.W., Gonnella, C., Marcynyszyn, L.A., Gentile, L. & Salpekar, N., 2005. The role of chaos in poverty and children's socioemotional adjustment. *Psychological Science*, 16, pp. 560–565.

Fair, C. & Shepherd, B., 2006. Who supports terrorism? Evidence from fourteen Muslim countries. *Studies in Conflict and Terrorism*, 29(1), pp. 51–74.

Farsides, T., 2007. The psychology of altruism. *Psychologist*, 20(8), pp. 474–477.

Fehr, E. & Gächter, S., 2002. Altruistic punishment in humans. *Nature*, 415(6868), pp. 137–140.

Galesic, M., Gigerenzer, G. & Straubinger, N., 2009. Natural frequencies help older adults and people with low numeracy to evaluate medical screening tests. *Medical Decision Making*, 29(3), pp. 368–371.

Gintis, H., 2008. Punishment and cooperation. *Science*, 319(5868), pp. 1345–1346.

Gollwitzer, M. & Denzler, M., 2009. What makes revenge sweet: Seeing the offender suffer or delivering a message? *Journal of Experimental Psychology*, 45(4), pp. 840–844.

Gottschalk, M. & Ellis, L., 2009. Evolutionary and genetic explanations of violent crime. In C.J. Ferguson, ed., *Violent Crime: Clinical and Social Implications*, California: Sage Publications.

Haidt, J., 2007. The new synthesis in moral psychology. *Science*, 316(5827), pp. 998–1002.

Haidt, J., 2008. Morality. *Perspectives on Psychological Science*, 3(1), pp. 65–72.

Haidt, J. & Kesebir, S., 2010. Morality. In S.T. Fiske, D.T. Gilbert & G. Lindzey, eds, *Handbook of Social Psychology*, Hoboken, NJ: John Wiley & Sons, Inc. Available at: http://onlinelibrary.wiley.com/doi/10.1002/9780470561119.socpsy002022/abstract [Accessed February 25, 2013].

Haley, K.J. & Fessler, D.M.T., 2005. Nobody's watching? Subtle cues affect generosity in an anonymous economic game. *Evolution and Human Behavior*, 26(3), pp. 245–256.

Hamilton, W.D., 1964. The genetical evolution of social behaviour. I. *Journal of Theoretical Biology*, 7(1), pp. 1–16.

Henrich, J., McElreath, R., Barr, A., Ensminger, J., Barrett, C., Bolyanatz, A., Cardenas, J.C., Gurven, M., Gwako, E., Henrich, N., 2006. Costly punishment across human societies. *Science*, 312(5781), pp. 1767–1770.

Herrmann, B., Thöni, C. & Gächter, S., 2008. Antisocial punishment across societies. *Science*, 319(5868), pp. 1362–1367.

Hoffman, M.L., 1991. Is empathy altruistic? *Psychological Inquiry*, 2, pp. 131–133.

Hoffrage, U., Lindsey, S., Hertwig, R., Gigerenzer, G., 2000. Communicating statistical information. *Science*, 290(5500), pp. 2261–2262.

Kniffin, K.M. & Wilson, D.S., 2010. Evolutionary perspectives on workplace gossip: Why and how gossip can serve groups. *Group & Organization Management*, 35(2), pp. 150–176.

Krueger, A.B. & Maleckova, J., 2002. *Education, Poverty, Political Violence and Terrorism: Is There a Causal Connection?* (No. w9074), Cambridge, MA: National Bureau of Economic Research.

Kurzban, R. & Houser, D., 2001. Individual differences in cooperation in a circular public goods game. *European Journal of Personality*, 15(S1), pp. S37–S52.

LaFree, G. & Dugan, L., 2004. How does studying terrorism compare to studying crime? In M. DeFlem, ed., *Terrorism and Counter-Terrorism: Criminological Perspectives*, pp. 54–56. New York: Elsevier.

Lehmann, L., Keller, L., West, S. & Roze, D., 2007. Group selection and kin selection: Two concepts but one process. *Proceedings of the National Academy of Sciences*, 104(16), p. 6736.

Levy, S.R., Freitas, A.L. & Salovey, P., 2002. Construing action abstractly and blurring social distinctions. *Journal of Personality and Social Psychology*, 83, pp. 1224–1238.

Maleckova, J., 2005. Impoverished terrorists: Stereotype or reality? In T. Bjorgo, ed., *Root Causes of Terrorism*, Oxford: Routledge.

Maynard Smith, J., 1964. Group selection and kin selection. *Nature*, 201(4924), pp. 1145–1147.

McCauley, C. & Moskalenko, S., 2008. Mechanisms of political radicalisation: Pathways towards terrorism. *Terrorism and Political Violence*, 20(3), pp. 415–433.

McCullough, M.E., 2008. *Beyond Revenge: The Evolution of the Forgiveness Instinct*, 1st edn, San Francisco, CA: Jossey-Bass.

McCullough, M.E., Kurzban, R. & Tabak, B.A., 2013. Cognitive systems for revenge and forgiveness. *Behavioral and Brain Sciences*, 36(1), pp. 1–15.

Moghadam, A., 2003. Palestinian suicide terrorism in the second intifada: Motivations and organizational aspects. *Studies in Conflict and Terrorism*, 26(2), pp. 65–92.

Nisbett, R.E. & Cohen, D., 1996. *Culture of Honor: The Psychology of Violence in the South*, Boulder, CO: Westview Press.

O'Callaghan, S., 1998. *The Informer*, London: Bantam.

O'Gorman, R., 2011. The evolutionary logic of terrorism: Understanding why terrorism is an inevitable human strategy in conflict. In A. Silke, ed., *The Psychology of Counter-Terrorism*. London: Routledge.

O'Gorman, R., Henrich, J. & van Vugt, M., 2009. Constraining free riding in public goods games: Designated solitary punishers can sustain human cooperation. *Proceedings of the Royal Society B: Biological Sciences*, 276(1655), pp. 323–329.

O'Gorman, R., Wilson, D.S. & Miller, R.R., 2005. Altruistic punishing and helping differ in sensitivity to relatedness, friendship, and future interactions. *Evolution and Human Behavior*, 26(5), pp. 375–387.

Pedersen, E.J., Kurzban, R. & McCullough, M.E., 2013. Do humans really punish altruistically? A closer look. *Proceedings of the Royal Society B: Biological Sciences*, 280(1758). Available at: http://rspb.royalsocietypublishing.org/content/280/1758/20122723 [Accessed March 6, 2013].

Schmid, A.P., 2013. *Radicalisation, De-radicalisation, Counter-radicalisation: A Conceptual Discussion and Literature Review*. ICCT Research Paper, 97.

Silke, A., 2003. Becoming a terrorist. In A. Silke, ed., *Terrorists, Victims and Society: Psychological Perspectives on Terrorism and its Consequences*, Chichester: Wiley.

Silke, A., 2008. Holy warriors: Exploring the psychological processes of jihadi radicalisation. *European Journal of Criminology*, 5(1), pp. 99–123.

Smith, K.D., Keating, J.P. & Stotland, E., 1989. Altruism reconsidered: The effect of denying feedback on a victim's status to empathic witnesses. *Journal of Personality and Social Psychology*, 57, pp. 641–650.

Sober, E. & Wilson, D.S., 1998. *Unto Others: The Evolution and Psychology of Unselfish Behavior*, Cambridge, MA: Harvard University Press.

Sparks, A. & Barclay, P., 2013. Eye images increase generosity, but not for long: The limited effect of a false cue. *Evolution and Human Behavior*, 34(5), pp. 317–322.

Taylor, M. and Quayle, E., 1994. *Terrorist Lives*, London: Brassey's.

Van Lange, P.A.M., De Bruin, E.M.N., Otten, W. & Joireman, J.A., 1997. Development of prosocial, individualistic, and competitive orientations: Theory and preliminary evidence. *Journal of Personality and Social Psychology*, 73(4), pp. 733–746.

Victoroff, J., 2005. The mind of the terrorist: A review and critique of psychological approaches. *Journal of Conflict Resolution*, 49, pp. 3–42.

Vitaglione, G.D. & Barnett, M.A., 2003. Assessing a new dimension of empathy: Empathic anger as a predictor of helping and punishing desires. *Motivation and Emotion*, 27, pp. 301–325.

Williams, G.C., 1966. *Adaptation and Natural Selection: A Critique of Some Current Evolutionary Thought*, Princeton, NJ: Princeton University Press.

Wilson, D.S. & Wilson, E.O., 2007. Rethinking the theoretical foundation of sociobiology. *Quarterly Review of Biology*, 82(4), pp. 327–348.

8 Terrorism's footprint of fear

Jason Roach, Ken Pease and Charlotte Sanson

Introduction

Terrorism is a term with connotations. It connotes four implicit invitations to citizens.

1 To ascribe political or quasi-political purpose to acts or threats of violence
2 To evoke distinctive emotional responses
3 To regard such acts as justifying levels of retaliation and vigilance which are inappropriate in other circumstances.
4 To regard themselves as potential targets.

Generally, when terms have extensive connotative baggage, it is wise to denude them. In the context of this paper, the only attribute we feel might be retained from the terrorism label is its implication that in such attacks, *classes* of people are deemed more or less equally 'legitimate' targets such that each citizen *regards herself* as a legitimate target. In the terrorist's ideal scenario, insofar as it is thought through, the evocation of public fear of victimization advances their cause. It leads to pressure on governments to settle or serves to destabilize the target administration by making daily life more problematic and by devoting resources to combatting terrorism's threat that cannot be sustained indefinitely. The evolutionary context to this book leads us to consider anti-predator behaviour by prey animals alongside public fear of victimization generated by acts of terrorism.

The modal tactic in applying evolutionary thinking to human behaviour involves making observations of other species, and identifying parallels with the human condition which are then subject to empirical test, to avoid the charge that such explanations are nothing more than 'Just So' stories (Gould, 1980). In crime science, the most developed application of this approach has concerned analysis of the spatial and temporal distribution of crime events (Johnson *et al.*, 2009). The image of offender as optimal forager has gained some traction in the literature (Jones and Fielding, 2012) because it makes sense of the two phenomena of crime spates and patterns of offender travel, and hence has rich implications for optimizing police patrol deployment (McLaughlin *et al.*, 2006; Johnson *et al.*, 2009; Koper, 1995). For volume crime, it seems, risk transmits itself over astonishingly short distances, as does the perception of risk. A description of Neanderthal hunting practices (Bar-Yosef, 2004) could have come from a twenty-first century description of journeys to crime, 'Middle and Upper Palaeolithic hunting and gathering was largely determined by what was available seasonally in the local environment' (p. 333).

A second relevant area of work has concerned the conscious application of defensive tactics evolved in non-human organisms to extend the repertoire of crime reductive technology (Ekblom, 1999; Sagarin and Taylor, 2008). For example, Smokecloke and similar products respond to criminal intrusion by emitting dense (non-toxic) smoke into an area under attack. This disorients attackers and thwarts the intended theft or robbery. It is typically used in commercial premises. Smokecloke was self-evidently a squid's defence. Squid (like other non-human organisms) tend not to claim intellectual property rights, so borrowed crime-reductive technologies represent a rich seam of defensive tactics against crime, one yet to be fully mined. Perhaps of particular interest and as yet unexplored is the use of deception in the service of crime reduction, given its prevalence as a defence in other species (Caro, 2005), and the use of collective action as in nest protection by mobbing birds (Arnold, 2000), although the practice of rough music, the beating of pots and pans outside the homes of ne'er do wells, has unexplored parallels with cooperation against shared threats in other species (Alford, 1959).

In general, then, evolutionary thinking has permeated the understanding of crime in terms of offender movement and defensive technology, rather than victim response in terms of behaviour or affect. In this context, the literature on crime fear would be the obvious place to look for an infusion of evolutionary thinking, but that body of work has generally not been couched in evolutionary terms except in relation to gender differences (Fetchenhauer and Buunk, 2005) and the difficulties associated with fear reduction (Sidebottom and Tilley, 2008). Gender differences in crime fear have a plausible evolutionary underpinning, in that female survival, at least through the potentially child-bearing years, is more important for the purposes of inclusive fitness maximization (Campbell, 1999). Resistance to fear reduction is explained by predation adaptation shaped by natural selection (Sidebottom and Tilley, 2008) with, for example, fear of victimization playing a major part in explaining why older people tend not to frequent nightclubs.

Vicarious victimization is important in engendering crime fear (Skogan and Maxfield, 1981). A terrorist attack in which observers see people just like them being killed, maimed or displaced *may* elicit such fear. Recent work on mirror neurons provides a possible mechanism underpinning possible fear contagion (Lacoboni, 2009). In this chapter we speculate about the spatial limits of the propagation of anti-predator sentiment and action through a civilian community. Under what circumstances and how well do terrorism-induced responses propagate over time and space? Do media representations of terror attacks in other lands fire our mirror neurons? Do they evoke defensive actions? If they do, what kind of defensive actions are involved? The answers to such questions may possibly already be found in the bowels of security service buildings and unanalysed records of counts of suspect package reports and similar indices of concern, but we know of little of this data that is both trustworthy and readily accessible. To begin to remedy this deficiency, let us first look at the broader literature which may help to see what we might profitably look for.

Prey animal responses to predation risk

There is a substantial and fascinating literature on the responses of non-human prey species to predation (Caro, 2005). It is argued here that there is heuristic value in applying this literature to responses to acts of terror, which have many features in common to predator ambush. Terrorism and animal predation have in common the fact that prey numbers are always greater than predator numbers, the attack is by ambush, and any member of a prey species is a feasible target, albeit with varying levels of worth. Each kill becomes known to nearby members of the prey species. Capture and consumption of a neighbouring wildebeest, for example, may serve as a memento mori for other wildebeest in the area. Alternatively, it may offer some relief that one's local predator is not currently hungry, and is probably sleeping off his recent wildebeest feast. How do the remaining wildebeest think and act? (Anthropomorphism runs riot at this point.) What are the possible implications for terror attacks? A terrorist attack happens. What do local people infer from this? Is it that there is an active terrorist cell in the area capable of attacking at will? Or is it that a terror attack is difficult to mount and consumes resources so that there is likely to be a period of relative safety? Misguided as this may be, one of the writers who lived in Northern Ireland during the Troubles found it difficult not to think in the latter way. To avoid ambiguity, it is perhaps necessary to distinguish between the temporary feeling of relative safety speculated to exist by the above reasoning, and habituation, which is the longer term reduction in response to terror which attends repeated incidents. In Northern Ireland from personal experience, people became remarkably phlegmatic about a succession of bombings and assassinations. This is habituation. What is posited here is a temporary change following an atrocity which could lead to counter-intuitive behaviour, a point developed below.

So there are some possible parallels between animal predation and terror attacks. These may be superficial. If they are not, responses to acts of terror may be shown to be inappropriate to modern circumstances. The predation sequence from the prey's perspective consists of identification, avoidance and fight or flight, the aim being to truncate the process as early as possible. Best of all is to be in a predator-free environment. Failing that, it is better to identify predators who are present than to fail to do so. Having identified a potential predator, it is better to avoid it where possible. Where avoidance is impossible, fight or flight is better than offering oneself up for consumption. When the predator is a terrorist and the prey civilians, the process is more complicated but may nonetheless have recognizable features in common.

Predator detection

Lions kill in person. They are always present at the kill. They do not disguise themselves. By contrast, the Boston Marathon bomb was hidden in a bag and Richard Reid's shoes held the explosive. Zebras can recognize the animals which pose a threat of harm. Potential victims of terrorist attack usually cannot. If lions could conceal themselves in bags or shoes, probably more zebras would die. Although we acknowledge that some animals can disguise themselves, such as the Pygmy Seahorse which can camouflage itself in sea fans,[1] the range of objects and organisms which may evoke apprehension is immensely wider in the human than in the animal predation context. Should Richard Reid's shoes make us shoe-averse? Should backpacks frighten us? Should the location of past attacks make us wary? That way lies fear of everything (Rogers *et al.*, 2007).

A raft of studies show how animals generalize from the distinctive characteristics of predators. For example, bonnet macaques make less diminishing alarm calls and flight responses to an upright model of a spotted leopard than to an upside-down model and to an upright melanistic leopard (black panther) model than to an upside-down model (Coss and Ramakrishnan, 2000). More generally presence of eyes or eye-like structures often trigger a response, and increasing realism of the model is usually important (Caro, 2005). Speculatively generalizing predator alerts to things that look a bit like predators makes sense up to the point at which foraging activities are so constrained that the prey animal goes hungry.

Along what dimensions (if any) does citizen response to terror cues generalize? This is a crucial question for policy against terrorist attacks. Some generalizations are directed by authorities, with transport hubs echoing to warnings about any unattended baggage and unspecified 'suspicious' objects. Determining what makes an object suspicious is an enterprise in its own right. A pernicious effect may be generalization on the grounds of ethnicity, culture, dress or location. How many readers who see themselves as tolerant and not at all racist, worry when they see a lady in a burqa in the queue to board an aircraft, and feel guilty about that reaction? The most elementary generalization is by distance. A zebra does not fear a distant lion. Does an attack in Manchester make me worried if I live 30 miles away in Sheffield? Does an attack in one part of Manchester worry me if I live in a different part of Manchester? Does the same distance decay relationship (if there is one) apply to transport hubs, or does a different distance metric apply there? If one measures distance in time needed to travel between places, Manchester Airport is closer to Barcelona than Sheffield. So do anti-terror responses consequent upon a Manchester Airport explosion propagate equally to Sheffield and Barcelona? With regards fear of crime, ongoing research suggests that proximity to crime influences levels of fear significantly, particularly in relation to violent crime and burglary (Sanson, Roach and Pease, in production).

To reprise, other species' generalize from predators to predator-like objects, we should anticipate similar gradients of generalization in human responses to terrorism, and that these will be complex because of the proxies for predator presence, some invited by authority (untended baggage is dangerous) some more spontaneously but regrettably culturally orientated (e.g. people in formal Islamic dress are considered suspect by those not so attired). The complexity of human generalizations has been recognized at least since the identification of Humphrey's arpeggio paradox (Humphrey, 1927), where the conditioning of musical notes to behaviours disappears when the notes are part of a sequence. Although a contour map of the perceived threat of terrorism would be hugely complicated, one for perceptions of more general risk is less so.

Slovic, Finucane, Peters, and MacGregor (2004) claim that risk is understood and dealt with on three levels (p. 311):

1 *Risk as feelings* (our initial, intuitive, instinctive reactions to a perceived danger);
2 *Risk as analysis* (more logical and reasoned thinking about a perceived threat); and
3 *Risk as politics* (which arises when ancient instincts clash with modern scientific developments and analyses, such as genetic cloning).

In this chapter we are concerned more with the 'risk as feelings' perception of terrorist threats, because individuals base their risk judgements on the feelings created in response to the risk, suggesting that most are formed rapidly and automatically (Slovic *et al.*, 2004), most likely in response to media reports and images of acts of terrorism. This will have the strongest influence on levels of fear and public perceptions of victimization, and is most likely to reflect predator-prey relationships.

The qualitative differences and difficulties notwithstanding, the contention here is that understanding predator-prey relationships generally provides a vocabulary and a cognitive frame within which to seek an understanding of public responses to acts of terrorism. We hope to identify some hypotheses about responses to predation in prey species and include a very modest empirical test of one such hypothesis. We presumptuously delineate anticipated changes in citizen behaviour contingent upon acts of terrorism; the where, what and when of responses to an attack labelled terrorist.

Some things we know about predator-prey relationships

This short section outlines some of the established facts of predator-prey relationships.

1 The greatest effect predators have upon their prey is not through slaughter, but intimidation. If the foraging range of prey animals is restricted, nutrition and consequent breeding success is compromised. These effects trickle through entire ecosystems as land is left ungrazed and unfertilized by prey animals (Caro, 2005). In what might be seen as an interesting parallel, the public perception of risk has been shown to have important implications for physical health. For example, in the aftermath of the September 11 attacks, many US citizens changed their travel behaviour from flying to driving, resulting in a sharp increase in the number of road traffic accidents (Gigerenzer, 2006; Gray and Ropeik, 2002). The central trade-off in anti-predator tactics is that between foraging and avoidance tactics. (Creel *et al.*, 2014). Which shops and waterholes are avoided? How far from the familiar places are prey animals prepared to go, and how attractive must the more distant places be deemed to be before venturing there? What attributes of places come to bespeak danger and preclude foraging?
2 Common responses to predation are increased vigilance, retreat to habitats deemed safer (Kotler *et al.*, 1991; Sih, 1997) and increasing group size (Creel *et al.*, 2014). It is this tactic, seeking safety in numbers, which is most intriguing when seeking human parallels.

Responses to predation are shaped by interactions of predator species, prey species and setting. The two basic tactics of predation are ambush and coursing (Caro, 2014). Self-evidently, coursing involves vastly more energy expenditure than ambush. Terrain and prey capacities determine the optimal anti-predation response. Different species have different favoured responses in similar places under similar threat. *Insofar as a parallel holds, it seems reasonable to suppose that citizen responses to terrorist acts will be shaped by context and avoidance tactics available.*

Only hinted at above is the notion of the range over which terror terrorises. A naive comparison across species would suggest that human fear of predators would operate over short distances only. Hunting by humans took advantage of individual stamina (evidenced in endurance running) and group cooperation (Bramble and Leiberman, 2004). As prey, they could escape so long as ambushing predators could be kept at a sufficient distance for stamina to prevail. If we inherit in some sense our threat map from our distant forebears, there should be short distance limits over which terror terrorizes.

Drawing the strands together and reprising observations made earlier in the chapter, what this discussion suggests is that the aspects of behaviour we might wish to concentrate upon in exploring parallels between terrorism and predation are maintaining distance, enhancing vigilance, seeking refuge and changing preferred group size. Each of these demands research attention in its own right, but distance is perhaps the most intriguing because of the counter-intuitive prediction that terror, with exceptions, increases the tendency to congregate in groups when the circumstances of predation characteristic of terror acts mentioned earlier (absence of predator in person, range of objects which represent risk) make risk estimation particularly difficult.

Readers in Western Europe or North America are here invited to engage in a thought experiment. Consider your reaction to atrocities committed by the terrorist group Boko Haram. A bomb attack in Lagos on 13 July 2014 was claimed by that group.[2] If the reader's response is similar to ours, there was sympathy for the victims but no change in the sense of personal safety. In a meta-analysis of psychological impairment in the wake of disaster (Bubonis and Bickman, 1991), two results of relevance to the present chapter emerged. Distance of respondents from a disaster's core locale was not studied, but the outlier showing the largest effect was described as having victims living exclusively in the worst affected village. Perusal of the article strongly suggests that distance from the disaster's epicentre may have been crucial in determining effect size, and the distances making a difference were short. Of greater interest because less speculative is the observation that disasters with an element of human agency led to much *less* psychopathology in victims than natural disasters. Terrorism has human agency par excellence, hence presumably reducing the degree to which the sense of personal safety is compromised. The writers of the meta-analysis seemed unprepared for the mitigating effect of human agency

> one of the most interesting findings concerned the relationship between disaster responsibility (natural vs human) and impairment effect size. Natural disasters showed significantly higher effect size estimates than those that were caused by humans.
>
> (p. 395)

> this finding appears to contradict much of the educated speculation in the field.
>
> (p. 396)

The writers settled on an explanation in terms of the stress-reductive effects of being able to attribute blame, as a means of mitigating learned helplessness (Abramson *et al.*, 1978). But the implications of this are profound. Human agency ranges from misfortune to motivated action, and terrorism falls at the motivated action pole of that continuum. The paradox is that its placement there may limit the range and intensity of its effects. John Mueller and Mark Stewart refer to the 'terrorism delusion', where they calculate the actuarially determined risk of death from terrorism in the USA to be less than one in

35 million (Mueller and Stewart, 2012). In brief, such evidence as the writers have found does suggest that terrorism's footprint of fear may be surprisingly small.

Coming closer to home for the writers living in the North of England, what were our reactions after the London bombings of 7 July 2005, some 200 miles away? Four bombs were detonated (three on packed commuter subway trains and one on a bus), 52 people killed and some 700 injured. Sympathy and horror were part of our response certainly, but it did not feel as though it had relevance to our own safety. Why? We might not be 'blessed' with an underground subway system in our neck of the woods, but we do have buses.

There are two strands in our thinking here. The first is that a terrorist act evokes lifestyle changes only within a short distance of where it happened. The second is that increased congregation in crowded places may be the (counter-intuitive) response in the small area affected. Ideally we would have had data on the effects of the London bombings on people at varying distances from London. Lacking such data, we gambled on the congregation effect applying, to see whether that had a spatio-temporal footprint.

We can explore this in a tangential way. The British Crime Survey (now rebadged as the Crime Survey for England and Wales) contains a question about how many times in the preceding month the respondent visited clubs. Based on the above discussion, the tentative prediction is that attending clubs *increased* in the month of a terrorist attack but only in the area of the attack itself.

Figure 8.1 shows the average number of times clubs were visited in the month before completion of interviews by respondents to the British Crime

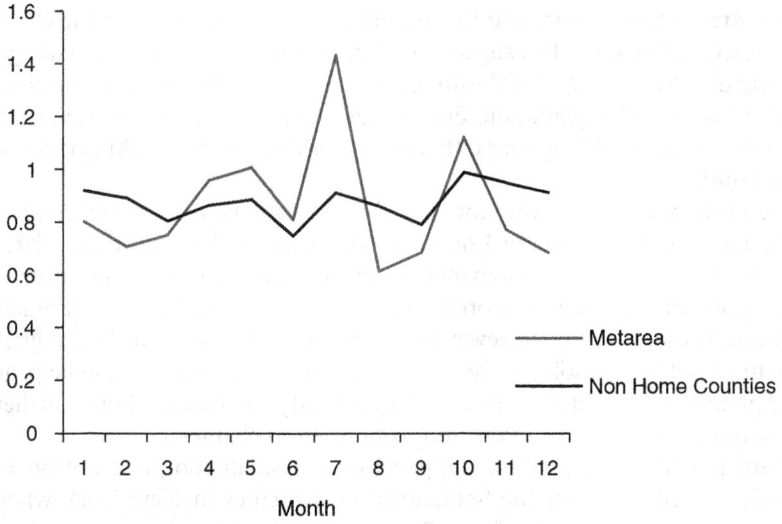

Figure 8.1 Trends in club going in 2005 relative to preceding years

Survey. The ordinate is mean number of visits to clubs in the preceding month expressed as a ratio to the mean number of visits in corresponding sweeps over the corresponding month in years 2002–2004. The abscissa notes the month of completion of the BCS interview. It will be seen that there is a spike in the number of club visits in the month of the bombing relative to previous years, contrasting trends in the Metropolitan Police area where the bombings occurred and areas outside the Home Counties (i.e. the counties contiguous with London). It will be seen that there is no equivalent spike in the 'provincial' trend. The results are at least consistent with a short run and spatially limited change in behaviour specific to the area of the attack.

The bombings occurred on 7 July so the spike would be evident in the July figures, the bulk of the month being reflected in that figure.[3]

The increase in club-going in the wake of the bombings is counter-intuitive unless one takes a line from the predation literature, suggesting that one tactic to predation is gathering in greater numbers. There is also the possibility of the 'sated predator' hypothesis outlined above. However, the focus of this chapter is the footprint of responses to terrorist events, and it is relevant to observe that there is no suggestion that (insofar as it is captured in the data) there was a change in lifestyle outside London.

The trends shown in Figure 8.1 are of course a conflation of the number of people who go clubbing at all, and the number of times those who go clubbing, go clubbing. Is it possible to tease out whether the 2005 spike was a consequence of a change in the number of people who went clubbing or greater frequency of clubbing of those who were already clubbers? Figures 8.2 and 8.3 tell the story. It will be seen that the effect is much more a consequence of a higher proportion of people visiting clubs than the same proportion of people going more often.

Of more central relevance to the present chapter is the fact that the effect was limited to London. The suggestion that people who didn't normally go clubbing did so in the wake of the attack is at least consistent with a 'huddling together for safety' explanation, even though that makes more sense at the waterhole, or for mobbing birds, than in a world when any backpack could hide a bomb.

One probable, but perhaps more tenuous, evolutionary-based explanation for the increase in clubbing in London in the wake of the bombings, relates to the 'discounting time' phenomenon whereby, faced with uncertain futures, young people in particular are more likely to take 'risks' in order to secure mates (Daly and Wilson, 2005). However, suffice to say of course, that the analyses above must not be oversold. More precise timings than a month would help, as would greater resolution as to area, and more lifestyle indicators. Some further suggestions are made in the discussion section of this chapter.

There is additional possible support for the small footprint notion in research carried out after the September 11 atrocities in New York when airliners were flown into the Twin Towers. Some extraordinary work was done in the wake of the September 11 attack on the World Trade Centre.

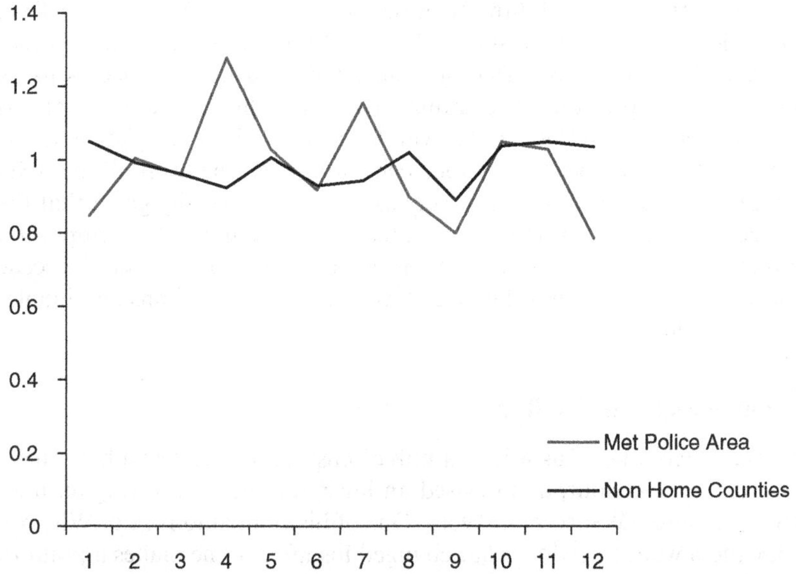

Figure 8.2 Number of club visits in previous month: 2005 relative to mean of three previous years

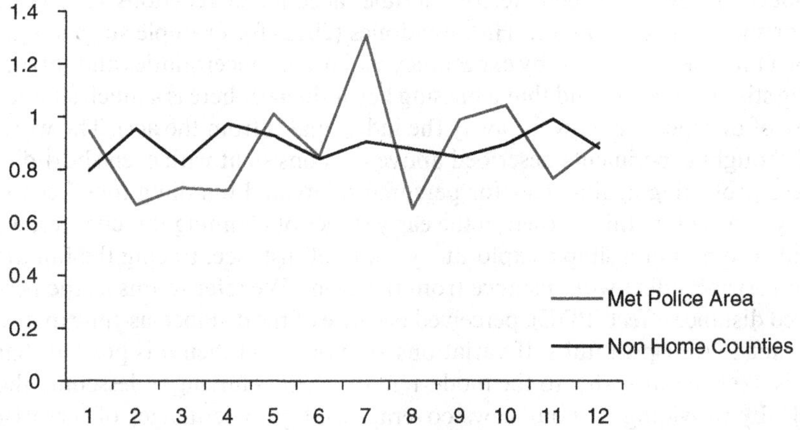

Figure 8.3 Prevalence of club going in previous month: 2005 vs mean of three previous years

Telephone interviews were conducted with New York residents, establishing provisional diagnoses of post-traumatic stress disorder (PTSD) and depression. Respondents were classified into those living south of Canal Street (within one mile of the World Trade Centre) and those living north of

Canal Street but south of 110th Street (i.e. from one to six miles of the Twin Towers). Respondents living south of Canal Street were nearly three times as likely to be labelled as suffering from PTSD and nearly twice as likely to suffer from depression. The trauma implicated in the PTSD diagnosis was the September 11 attack. Other variables are no doubt at play, and one would wish to know about avoidance behaviours, but the drop-off in PTSD diagnoses over so few miles seem truly astonishing especially given that the media coverage was presumably the same across all areas. The temptation is to think that 'range' of prey concerns decrease as sharply when the scene of known predation is a hijacked plane as when it involves lions and jungles (Galea *et al.*, 2002).

So whom does terror terrify?

Many years ago, one of us was in a pub discussing how to test a hypothesis about human behaviour, and devised an ingenious method relying on non-reactive measures (Webb *et al.*, 1966). One of his companions said 'Why not just ask them what they do?' That changed his life, and he makes a point of asking people what they do, feel and think before inferring that from indirect measures. There will be occasions when one would wish to check self-serving accounts, but asking is always important.

The variables which have hitherto been linked to risk perception have excluded distance. In their 'terror module' account of reactions to acts of terrorism, Tritt, Inzlicht and Harmon-Jones (2012) for example suggest that such a module is activated by expectancy violations, uncertainties and threatening stimuli. We contend that a missing key influencer here is a much simpler sense of distance (i.e. how far away the individual is from the act). The work and thought experiments described above are consistent with even short distances protecting against fear for personal safety and huddling together for safety. To explore this further, in the early stages of planning this chapter, we decided to mount a simple exploratory study of distance, tracing the fall-off in terrorism's effect with distance from the event. We refer to this as the perceived distance effect (PDE), perceived because of the distance-as-time metric relevant to transport hubs. If variations are not found then it is posited that this is likely because due to the modern mass-media blurring or lessening the PDE, by providing 24-hour news coverage and graphic images of terrorist events which serves to make the world seem smaller and horrific events seem nearer. This is also explored.

With hindsight, if we were designing the study now, we would have chosen shorter distances as values of the key variable 'distance'. We had at that point not yet read the most dramatic evidence of drop-off with distance noted above (Galea *et al.*, 2002) and, just as crucially, had insufficiently valued our own experiences in England and Northern Ireland during the 'Troubles', when Provisional IRA and the Irish National Liberation Army were waging their campaigns. Distress for the victims was real, but the effect on one's daily life concerned how to get to work avoiding the congestion that would ensue. The vast literature on offenders' travel to crime distances emphasizes how short the modal distance is. The work on near-repeat crimes of burglary for example deals only in distances of some hundreds of metres (Bowers *et al.*, 2004). In short, if we were starting again, we would choose much shorter distances for the study. Hindsight is wonderful. The next section describes what was in fact done.

In order to test if varying distance from a terrorist event produces a regional effect on levels of safety generated, a pilot questionnaire was developed to measure individual levels of safety across four fictitious terrorism scenarios, all involving bomb attacks or threats.[4] Only the distance between the attack and where the respondent lived varied overtly across the scenarios (i.e. the independent variable). However, it was thought that the scenarios (although all depicting fictitious bomb attacks and threats) had to differ moderately in context to add a sense of realism, to minimize the likelihood of respondents answering all questions the same irrespective of the scenario, and most importantly to avoid respondent boredom/fatigue. The differences in context are minimal when compared with the differences in distance.

Respondents were presented with four different bombing or bomb threat scenarios described below. Two questionnaires with counterbalanced orders were used to minimize any order effects.

1 You see on the news that a bomb has been detonated in a shopping centre in a city in the north of England. A local group claim responsibility for the attack.
2 You see on the news that there has been a bomb attack at a busy market place in a city in Syria. A local group claim responsibility for the attack.
3 You see on the news that a suspicious package has been found at a busy airport terminal in France and is being investigated. A local group claim responsibility for the planned attack.
4 You see on the news that a bomb has been detonated on a train close to a city in the south of England. A local group claim responsibility for the attack.

After each scenario respondents were asked the same three questions, all of which required a Likert Scale answer from 0 'unaffected by the event' through to 5 'not at all safe'.

1 How safe would you feel in your home town?
2 How safe would you feel from the threat of another attack?
3 How safe would you feel visiting or travelling to the same context as the scenario?

Finally, respondents were thanked for their participation and in line with the British Psychological Society ethical guidelines, contact details were provided for respondents should they wish to withdraw their participation at any stage or request feedback on the completed study. Support services contact numbers were provided in case anybody felt they had been affected by the issues raised.

The respondent sample consisted of 96 people attending a public lecture at a university: 33 per cent were male and 67 per cent female. Around 88 per cent classified their ethnicity as 'white' (11 per cent were 'other') and the mean age was 27.6 years (range = 18–76 years, sd = 12.6 years). The median age was 21 years. Some 81 per cent of participants considered their nationality to be 'British' (11 per cent stated 'non-British' and 3 per cent 'non-European'). Around 63 per cent of participants stated that Huddersfield was their term-time address and 70 per cent said that they had never lived outside of the UK (12 per cent said they had with a further 18 per cent saying that it had been outside of Europe).

The results of interest here are the self-expressed feeling of safety when the terror event occurred at varying distances. Respondents felt less safe in their hometown after a bomb attack in the same region relative to an event in Syria, France or in a different region of the same country ($p<.001$, Wilcoxon matched-pairs signed ranks test). The differences between expressed home-town safety consequent on events at different distances were all statistically reliable (i.e. the effects of a bomb in another part of the same country were greater than those in a neighbouring country, which was greater than an explosion in a distant country e.g. Syria). All differences were significant at the alpha level $p=.05$ by the Wilcoxon Test. It should be noted that even after the closest terror event (same region) two-thirds of people still anticipated feeling reasonably safe or better.

As noted above, parallel questions were asked about the threat of another attack and safety felt in a similar location to that in which the different fictitious events occurred (e.g. shopping centre, airport, public transport or marketplace). As had been found in questions asking about the fear of repeat attacks, exactly the same was found for 'hometown' safety (i.e. $p<.01$ or less in all cases). Again, even with the closest distance from an attack (i.e. same region) half of the respondents reported feeling reasonably safe or better.

The pattern for the 'like context' question was even more interesting. Distant events involving transportation evoked concern for personal safety, but levels of concern in the aviation and public transport examples were not reliably different ($p=.767$, Wilcoxon).

Does the distance effect differ by personal characteristics? Taking the two same country events, is the difference between the two contexts in rating safety in one's home town different? A *difference* score was calculated between home town safety after a 'local' bomb and one in a different region of the same country. There was no reliable difference in the score by gender, age or ethnicity.

Is the distance effect affected by having lived previously in another country? In order to explore whether having lived outside of the UK had influenced respondent's answers to the bomb scenario questions, an Independent Samples Mann-Whitney U- Test was conducted for the 'UK only' and 'UK and other' respondent categories. No statistically significant difference was found between the two groups' answers, apart from those for question 1, scenario 1 prefaced as follows:

> You see on the news that a bomb has been detonated in a shopping centre in a city in the North of England. A local group claim responsibility for the attack. How safe would you feel in your hometown?

The Mann-Whitney test statistic (= 684, N1=68, N2=28, p= 0.024) suggested that those who had lived outside of the UK felt safer in this scenario than those who had only ever lived in the UK. Indeed, two respondents from this group answered that they would be totally unaffected in this scenario. This finding we consider worthy of further exploration in the future alongside 'ethnicity', but is not dealt with here.

A related-samples Friedman's two–way analysis of variance by ranks test showed that the difference in the median answers for all question 1s ('How safe would you feel in your home town?') was statistically significant across all four scenarios. The same result was found across all four scenarios for the second question ('How safe would you feel from the threat of another attack?') and third ('How safe would you feel shopping/travelling, etc.?'). The results are shown in Table 8.1. This supported our hypothesis that respondents would answer the three 'feelings of safety' questions differently for each scenario because of the differences in distance away from the attacks, with the independent variable being the distance between the location of the terrorist bomb scenario and where the participants currently lived.

In order to conclude that respondent answers were indeed different according to the distance away from the bomb attack in each of the scenarios, the possible effect of having lived outside of the UK (or not) again had to be discounted. A related-samples Friedman's two–way analysis of variance by ranks test was conducted on the answers given by those respondents who had lived outside of the UK to all questions for all four scenarios. The results are shown in Table 8.2.

Table 8.1 Related-samples Friedman's two-way analysis of variance by ranks for all questions in all scenarios

Question	*N*	*Test stat*	*DF*	*P. values*
Q1	94	132.507	3	.001
Q2	93	148.369	3	.001
Q3	94	107.369	3	.001

Table 8.2 Related-samples Friedman's two-way analysis of variance by ranks for those respondents who had lived outside of the UK for over six months

Question	*N*	*Test stat*	*DF*	*P values*
Q1	27	32.571	3	.001
Q2	27	32.282	3	.001
Q3	27	21.957	3	.001

As can be seen, the answers given by respondents who had lived outside of the UK were equally different across all three scenarios, as was the case for those who had only lived in the UK. Distance in respect to where a respondent originated did not appear to have an influence on how safe they thought they would feel in any of the terrorist bomb scenarios.

Before discussion of the significance of the findings it is prudent to recap what was found here. Self-expressed feelings of safety varied when the terrorism event occurred at different distances. Respondents reported that they would feel less safe in their hometown after a bomb in the same region, relative to a similar event in Syria, France or a different region in England. The hypothesis: *the further away the terrorist event the safer respondents would report that they would feel*, was supported, irrespective of where the respondent came from.

Chapter summary and reprise

In brief, distance matters. This chapter began with observations about predator-prey relationships as they have evolved in other species. Gathering in greater numbers was one anti-predator response. If this is also a human response to terrorist attack, it is probably counterproductive, since bombs can be hidden (i.e. as far as our experience of terrorism is concerned, there generally is no undisguised predator presence). Over what distance should anti-predator responses be evident? A priori it may be quite small, given endurance running as the attribute of Homo which made for successful hunting. A lengthy discussion of Pleistocene gender roles and their implications for this hypothesis could be undertaken at this point, but let us pass on.

Taking a leap which was likely to yield nothing useful, we looked at club-going in the wake of the 7 July bombings in London in 2005. The long shot was that club-going would increase relative to normal seasonal trends and that the increase would be limited to the police area in which the attacks of July 2006 occurred. Astonishingly, this is exactly what was evident. A special licence is required to look at spatially disaggregated data and this has been applied for, to see if (as we now anticipate) the area of effect is even more localized than the analysis at force level suggests.

The simple exploratory study reported reinforces the importance of distance decay of effect, with the interesting exception of public transport facility-based events. The suggestion here is linked to the notion of locus of control. Giving oneself up to public transport is to relinquish control, and anxiety comes with loss of control as demonstrated by the work of H. Levenson and his development of the *Locus of Control Scales* (1973). The exploratory study asks hypothetical questions of course and the development of a fuller understanding of distance decay around acts of terrorism will rely more on accessing non-reactive measures.

So what should be done next, and why? This chapter argues that the emphasis should be on non-reactive measures rather than questions about how people think that they would feel. One of us first saw the images of the London bombings in the back of a Milan taxi, and had concern for colleagues who worked at University College nearby. It never occurred to him that this might affect the safety of his friends and family elsewhere. It is asking for insight beyond the norm to have anticipated this reaction.

In developing the argument further, first, the tentative conclusions reached here should be tested in diverse ways. For example, the distribution over time and place of 'suspicious package' incidents after a terror event should be examined, with the expectation that such events will be temporally brief and concentrated tightly in the area of the attack. Incidents on transport reported to the British Transport Police would be an exception as attacks on forms of transport appear to have a wider footprint, as demonstrated by the change in US citizens' travel behaviour after the September 11 attacks. Similar work should be done around other events, the Madrid train bombings of 11 March 2004 being the obvious European candidate for study. Medical records of the incidence of PTSD and panic attacks at varying distances might also be usefully studied. If town centre and transport hub CCTV footage is available for periods around events, they should be scrutinized for changes in congregation in public places. In the brief analysis of events in London around 7/7 discussed here, one of many shortcomings is that going to clubs is a minority occupation. Even property prices may track aversion to sites which have hosted terror events.

The effect of the media and the use of social networking sites on perceived distances from and fear generated by terrorist events also needs, in our opinion, exploring further. Has the availability of 24-hour media coverage and associated potent imagery, begun to blur human estimations of distance from safety? In essence, has the media made the terrorist's job of terrorizing easier? Although we did not really explore this area with our pilot study (as we only used basic fictitious scenarios), our findings suggest it unlikely that an act of terrorism will produce an even distribution of fear and changes in behaviour irrespective of where it occurs, suggesting that for the terrorist, the effects of their acts are limited both spatially and temporally to a relatively small footprint of fear. But work establishing the influence of generalization and the nature of generalization gradients is needed to sufficiently test this.

Is this make-work for social scientists or does it matter? In the extreme case, insofar as humans appear to congregate more after a terror attack, they make themselves vulnerable to greater carnage in follow-up events. If the footprint of threat is as circumscribed as we suspect, terrorists need to leave a lot of bombs in a lot of places to terrorize a population. If the effect is as transient as we suspect, the impact is correspondingly limited. Alongside studies of distance and time decay, as we have emphasized, generalization gradients are important to determine the attributes of settings which are seen as suspicious. The particular issues around transport hubs provide the obvious first target for research. But overall, we suggest that deeper scrutiny of predator-prey relationships will certainly yield novel hypotheses to test, and perhaps practical benefits.

Notes

1 www.dailymail.co.uk/news/article-2216091/Can-spot-predator-Masters-disguise-blend-background-survive-kill-killed-world.html#ixzz3EE1SlcKh, accessed 22 September 2014.
2 http://saharareporters.com/2014/07/13/boko-haram-leader-claims-responsibility-lagos-bombing, accessed 14 July 2014.
3 The reader may be puzzled by the absence of figures for the Home Counties, i.e. those force areas with a common boundary with the Metropolitan police area. This showed a modest spike but reflected an exceptionally high rate of club-going captured in the June figures. Figures including the Home Counties are available on request.
4 A full copy of the questionnaire is available from j.roach@hud.ac.uk.

References

Abramson, L., Seligman, M.E.P. and Teasdale, J. (1978). Learned helplessness in humans: Critique and reformulation. *Journal of Abnormal Psychology*, 87, 32–48.

Alford, V. (1959). Rough music or charivari. *Folklore*, 70, 505–518.

Arnold, K. (2000). Group mobbing behaviour and nest defence in a cooperatively breeding Australian bird. *Ethology*, 106, 385–393.

Bar-Yosef, O. (2004). Eat what is there: Hunting and gathering in the world of Neanderthals and their neighbours. *International Journal of Osteoarcheology*, 14, 333–340.

Bowers, K., Johnson, S. and Pease, K. (2004). Prospective hot-spotting: The future of crime mapping? *British Journal of Criminology*, 44, 1–18.

Bramble, D. and Leiberman, D. (2004). Endurance running and the evolution of Homo. *Nayire*, 432, 345–352.

Bubonis, A. and Bickman, L. (1991). Psychological impairment in the wake of disaster: The disaster-psychopathology relationship. *Psychological Bulletin*, 384–399.

Campbell, A. (1999). Staying alive: Evolution, culture, and women's intrasexual aggression. *Behaviour and Brain Sciences*, 22, 203–214.

Caro, T. (2005). *Antipredator Defenses in Animals and Birds*. Chicago, IL: University of Chicago Press.

Coss, R. and Ramakrishnan, U. (2000). Perceptual aspects of leopard recognition by wild bonnet macaques. *Behaviour*, 137, 315–335.

Creel, S., Schuette, P. and Christianson, D. (2014). Effects of predation risk on group size, vigilance and foraging behaviour in an African ungulate community. *Behavioural Ecology*, 25, 773–784.

Daly, M. and Wilson, M. (2005) Carpe diem: Adaptation and devaluing the future. *Quarterly Review of Biology*, 80 (1), 55–60.

Ekblom, P. (1999). Can we make crime prevention adaptive by learning from other evolutionary struggles? *Studies on Crime and Crime Prevention*, 8, 27–51.

Fetchenhauer, D. and Buunk, B. (2005). How to explain gender differences in fear of crime: Towards an evolutionary approach. *Sexualities, Evolution and Gender*, 7, 95–113.

Galea, S., Ahern, J., Resnick, H., Kilpatrick, D., Bucuvalas, M., Gold, J. and Vlahov, D. (2002). Psychological sequelae of the September 11 terrorist attacks on New York City. *New England Journal of Medicine*, 346, 982–987.

Gigerenzer, G. (2006). Out of the frying pan into the fire: Behavioural reactions to terrorist attacks. *Risk Analysis*, 26 (2), 347–351.

Gould, S.J. (1980). Introduction. In Kurtén, B. (ed.), *Dance of the Tiger: A Novel of the Ice Age*. New York: Random House.

Gray, G.M. and Ropeik, D.P. (2002). Dealing with the dangers of fear: The role of risk communication. *Health Affairs*, 21 (6), 106–114.

Humphrey, G. (1927). The effect of sequences of indifferent stimuli on a reaction of the conditioned response type. *Journal of Abnormal and Social Psychology*, 22, 194–212.

Iacoboni, M. (2009). *Mirroring People*. New York: Picador.

Johnson, S., Bowers, K., Birks, D. and Pease, K. (2009). Predictive mapping of crime by ProMap: Accuracy, units of analysis, and the environmental backcloth. In Weisburd, D. (ed.), *Putting Crime in its Place*. New York: Springer.

Johnson, S., Summers, L. and Pease, K. (2009). Offender as forager? A direct test of the boost account of victimization. *Journal of Quantitative Criminology*, 25, 181–200.

Jones, V. and Fielding, M. (2012). 'Disrupting the optimal forager': Predictive risk mapping and domestic burglary reduction in Trafford, Greater Manchester. *International Journal of Police Science and Management*, 14, 30–41.

Koper, C. (1995). Just enough police presence: Reducing crime and disorderly behaviour by optimising patrol time in crime hot spots. *Justice Quarterly*, 12, 649–672.

Kotler, B., Brown, J. and Hasson, O. (1991). Factors affecting gerbil foraging behaviour and rates of owl predation. *Ecology*, 72, 2249–2260.

McLaughlin, L., Johnson, S., Bowers, K., Birks, D. and Pease, K. (2006). Police perceptions of the long- and short-term spatial distribution of residential burglary. *International Journal of Police Science and Management*, 9, 99–111.

Mueller, J. and Stewart, M.G. (2012). The terrorism delusion: America's overwrought response to September 11th. *International Security*, 37 (1), 81–110.

Rogers, M.B., Amlot, R., Rubin, G.J., Wessely, S. and Krieger, K. (2007). Mediating the social and psychological impacts of terrorist attacks: The role of risk perception and risk communication. *International Review of Psychiatry*, 19 (3), 279–288.

Sagarin, R. and Taylor, T. (2008). *Natural Security*. Los Angeles: University of California Press.

Sanson, C., Roach, J. and Pease, K. (2015). How does proximity to crime influence people's perception of safety (in production).

Sidebottom, A. and Tilley, N. (2008). Evolutionary psychology and fear of crime. *Policing*, 2 (2), 167–174.

Sih, A. (1997). To hide or not to hide? Refuge use in a fluctuating environment. *Trends in Ecology and Evolution*, 12, 375–376.

Skogan, W. and Maxfield, M. (1981). *Coping with Crime: Individual and Neighborhood Reactions*. Washington DC: Bureau of Justice Statistics.

Slovic, P., Finucane, M.L., Peters, E. and MacGregor, D.G. (2004). Risk as analysis and risk as feelings: Some thoughts about affect, reason, risk and rationality. *Risk Analysis*, 24 (2), 311–322.

Tritt, S.M., Inzlicht, M. and Harmon-Jones, E. (2012) Toward a biological understanding of mortality salience (and other threat compensation processes). *Social Cognition*, 30 (6), 715–733.

Webb, E., Campbell, D.T., Schwartz, R. and Sechrest, L. (1966). *Unobtrusive Measures: Nonreactive Research in the Social Sciences*. New York: Rand McNally.

Index

Page numbers in **bold** indicate tables and in *italics* indicate figures.